THE FUTILE PURSUIT OF POWER

THE FUTILE PURSUIT OF POWER

WHY MUSSOLINI EXECUTED HIS SON-IN-LAW

ANDREW SANGSTER

Whittles Publishing

Published by

Whittles Publishing Ltd,
Dunbeath,
Caithness, KW6 6EG,
Scotland, UK

www.whittlespublishing.com

© 2023 Andrew Sangster
ISBN 978-184995-533-1

Printed in the UK by Micropress Printers Ltd.

CONTENTS

ACKNOWLEDGEMENTS

I would like to acknowledge the help given to me by my Italian historian colleague, Dr Pier Paolo Battistelli, both for his insights and for finding the necessary information for this work to proceed. I am very grateful to my wife Carol for her patience and support when I have disappeared for hours to write, and for her checking the text for bloomers.

Foreword

Ciano's role in the history of World War II is important – much more so than his own character – and Andrew Sangster succeeds brilliantly in understanding this issue. Ciano was not a prominent figure in history, having been relegated to the backstage by Mussolini, but he has now moved into the limelight because of his diaries, which are, as shown in this book, potentially controversial but not previously analysed as they should have been.

This new account makes Ciano's personal history more important in the understanding of why he wrote his diaries but also in assessing their reliability. This book focuses on a crucial Italian debate. On the one hand we have Ciano, a ruthless career-maker with few merits and many faults; on the other we have his diaries, which historians, almost without exception, have considered a first-class source for Italy's history relating to World War II.

Understanding Galeazzo Ciano's history is a key to knowing Italy, his character being as multifaceted as that of his country. The account of his relationship with his wife Edda, Mussolini's daughter, is revealing. No matter how many infidelities and differences there might have been, the two remained loyal to one another until the end, and in the case of Edda long after the end of Ciano's life; their relationship was a matter of substance, rather than simple form and circumstance.

This study does what history studies should do – that is, explore the essence at the central core of events. In it there is passion, which is part of human nature, yet that is balanced with the knowledge that reason will ultimately prevail.

Dr Pier-Paolo Battistelli

Preface

Italy has the reputation of being politically divided, with its residents associating themselves more with their cities or provinces than with the national image. None of this accounts for what happened in the period 1935–45, ten years of mayhem which left Italy invaded by both the Allies and Germans, its citizens fighting against both sides and one another in a bitter civil war. In popular Anglo-Saxon histories little time is given to the inside story of Italy, and this book is an attempt to open the door for a glimpse of what happened. It will reveal the way certain issues in Italy were dealt with, and the tragic consequences.

During this period Italy was dominated by the fascist leader Benito Mussolini, but it was also suffering from the influence of the monarchy and the Vatican. Mussolini hated both, and he also had to fight personal family problems while adopting Hitler as his patron. Mussolini had already been making his mark on the national scene when Hitler was still street-brawling, but he finished as Hitler's puppet, humiliated, and killed by his own people.

Galeazzo Ciano, Mussolini's son-in-law and his foreign minister, provided many insights through his writings. Ciano does not appear an appropriate person for the powers he held, described by one of Mussolini's biographers as 'vain, pompous, frivolous, hedonistic, a snob and devoid of any fixed belief'.[1] This book describes Ciano's Machiavellian diplomatic intrigues with his rise and fall from power, gaining an insight into these years through his critical meetings with heads of state, and the political machinations which preceded the war.

Ciano's diaries must be treated with caution, and his wife Edda's memoirs with a degree of scepticism. Anglo-American histories, when drawn towards Italy, often make disparaging statements, but, like him or hate him, Ciano was interesting, and his life reveals some wider historical perspectives offering some incisive insights.

Introduction

Galeazzo Ciano, 2nd Count of
Cortellazzo and Buccari
(NAC, photographer unknown)

Following World War I, the Treaty of Versailles failed to secure a stable Europe. Far from it, in fact; the reprisals by the victors produced an era of instability, creating irredentist* nationalistic claims which generated conflict. Germany was humiliated, Italy felt the rewards were inadequate, France appeared harsh and Britain softer, and the Americans, unsettled by the treaty, rejected the League of Nations.

---

*   demanding the return of previously held territories

Europe started to mutate into three ideological blocs. The grip of Bolshevism developed into Stalin's dictatorship, and after the March on Rome in 1922 Italy turned fascist under Mussolini. Then in 1933 Hitler came to power in Germany. The democracies differed, as some were unstable; in France there were so many governments it was known cynically as Musical Chairs. There were some in the democracies who admired the strong leadership of the dictators, and many Western intellectuals believed that communism was a solution for social injustice. The three ideological blocs all varied.

In this study of Ciano, Italy is the central focus. Germany had been Italy's traditional ally from Italy's unification in 1866. Since Austria-Hungary also controlled some ethnically Italian areas, Italy's 1915 switch of alliances to the Allies was understandable, given that Italy's rewards at the end of the Great War were known as the 'mutilated victory', with France and Britain not inclined to concessions; this perceived slight was probably part of Mussolini's alienation towards the Western powers.

Following the end of the war in 1945 Italy suffered from historical indigestion, as many felt that had Mussolini avoided the Hitler alliance he might have died in his bed, like the Spanish Franco. Many regarded this alliance as the fatal error, and this study of Ciano reflects that contentious issue; it all led to the Italian myth that the Italian people had no responsibilities for the war, and that they were victims of Mussolini. A myth with possible foundations, reflected in Churchill's broadcast on 23 December 1940, in which he said, 'Italians, I will tell you the truth. It is all because of one man.'[2]

Mussolini was necessary for Italy's self-acquittal myth, but many historians have proved reluctant to blame him. It could be understood that he had led Italy to ruin, yet no comparison with Hitler was possible. Mussolini's decision to enter the war was explained by his fear of German domination or dictated by his perception that war was to make Italy great again, and him a world leader – an erratic behaviour which has bewildered historians. Ciano described this as Mussolini's 'see-sawing' state of mind, and Mussolini's decision to join Germany is important in this study of Ciano's life, with his observations of events and of Mussolini.

CIANO'S CHARACTER

It is generally understood that many Italians were against the 1939–45 war, with many realising that the outcome would be highly problematic for them. Sumner Welles, an American envoy sent by Roosevelt to investigate Europe, met Ciano and believed he belonged in both camps.[3] Malcolm Muggeridge believed that had Ciano been raised in Germany he would have been a Nazi, in Russia a Communist, and in Britain or France a Conservative Democrat.[4] Mussolini was a dictator who surrounded himself with minions, of which Ciano was one. Ciano's rise to fame was meteoric, as was his fall from power, and his diary provides insights into his own character and, through his perceptions of Mussolini and others, what was happening internationally.

Ciano remains an enigmatic character with, as Welles noted, some good qualities but with serious defects: he had personal charm and a sense of dignity, but was undoubtedly financially corrupt. Welles wrote 'I am inclined to the belief that Count Ciano possessed many of the qualities of the men of the Italian Renaissance'; he may have been involved in 'assassinations', and was 'a creature of his times', which were amongst the worst moments of this century.[5] Ciano exposed his own folly and the inane behaviour of Mussolini. The nature of Ciano's and Mussolini's characters reveal that while Ciano eventually started to gain an understanding of the dangers, Mussolini had no realistic grasp of them.

Mussolini, and to a certain extent Ciano, wanted to appear as global figures, but Mussolini's obsession with Nazi power led his country into chaotic disaster. Mussolini was impressed by the military strength of the Nazi regime, but the German power equally concerned him, and it eventually dawned on Ciano, before Mussolini, that the road they had taken was perilous.

From the personal aspects of Ciano's life, he was raised as a spoilt child in the upper classes of Italian society, developing into a playboy with a dubious reputation as a profligate womaniser. He could be charming when required, and while he was subservient in Mussolini's presence he was haughty with others. He was a loving father to his three children – but a line, if true, from his son Fabrizio's book might raise a few eyebrows; Fabrizio 'remembered his more self-consciously upper-bourgeois father summoning him to stand to attention and then slapping his face, just to be going on with'.[6] Ciano and Edda lived in an open marriage, both indulging in continuous affairs and having a tumultuous relationship, which was the subject of continuous gossip as they shared the futile pursuit of power alongside Mussolini. Edda claimed that she never minded love affairs but she would ensure that all children she bore would be Ciano's, and in the end days she proved to be loyal to her husband even though it meant parting company from her father. Paul Schmidt, Hitler's interpreter, described her as 'the tall elegant daughter of the Italian dictator who raised political questions with Hitler and did not hesitate to express views opposite to his own vehemently and with great ability', such as demanding to know why someone with a Jewish grandmother should be punished, and complaining about 'the treatment of Italian POWs'.[7]

Undoubtedly many people, including Ciano himself, believed he would succeed Mussolini. He had aligned himself with fascism, but whether he was an extremist is questionable. Although he has been depicted as a 'fascist fanatic, this man who trotted off to his golf course for his daily dose of gossip and good times', he seems to have been more the typical bourgeois playboy (or, in modern parlance, yuppy), whose adamantinely fascist phrases were scarcely to be taken seriously.'[8] Ciano was obsessed with golf, some critics claiming he played this game because it was socially acceptable. As far as religion is concerned, Mussolini was an atheist, but Ciano, critical of Mussolini's anti-Church attitudes, attended services and before his execution received the sacraments. Edda believed it had been '[Ciano's] father who succeeded in inculcating Christianity into his son'.[9]

Ciano's change of political attitude emerged with Germany's occupation of Poland, when he foresaw its wider consequences. In March 1941 Joseph Goebbels in despair wrote 'the chief culprit in this respect is Ciano. I tell the Führer a few facts about Ciano, which disturb him deeply. Ciano is a social climber who has lost all respect in Italy. He is also stupid, without manners, tactless and insolent. The Führer is sharply critical of nepotism.'[10] This biography will explore his behaviour, views and attitudes during those critical years, and you may make your own assessment.

MUSSOLINI

In 2020, on a popular BBC radio programme called 'Great Lives' a Professor Margaret MacMillan, a Canadian historian and professor of history, proposed Mussolini, not offering him as someone to be admired, but warning that he should 'not be dismissed as a buffoon'.[11] In his early years Mussolini had been admired by Churchill and Chamberlain, regarded as a moderate who restored Italy after its mutilated victory of 1918. Opinions of Mussolini differ vastly both in Italy and beyond.

Mussolini was born in Romagna, in central Italy, known for its anarchists and others who did not appreciate the *status quo*. He was often referred to as 'il Duce', literally 'the Duke' but which basically meant 'the Boss.' Stalin, Hitler, and later Franco exercised more political control than Mussolini, who was no saint – he reputedly had some opposition 'disappear', and he had many repugnant aspects to his character – but in any examination of Mussolini it is important that he is not overly coloured by Anglo-Saxon prejudice.

Mussolini's family life was well known and 'his extended family never overlooked the advantages of being related to Benito Mussolini'.[12] In the first decade of the 20th century he had started out as a socialist (self-exiled in Switzerland for a time) and a journalist, and it is claimed that he could hold a conversation in three languages. After the Great War he turned to the right wing; he was not the only socialist to change political leanings because of war.

From his youth Mussolini had a disordered sex life, enjoyed drinking and often indulged in violent duels, but he was good at public speaking, thereby attracting public attention. He rose, with some slight glitches, to power very quickly following the famous March on Rome in 1922. Throughout his life he had an endless string of mistresses, with women writing in to his office so that it could organise them in terms of his taste and timing. He had a variety of lovers, including Margerita Sarfatti (his biographer, who was left-wing, and Jewish), and his long-term mistress Claretta Petacci, who eventually died alongside him.* Petacci and her family were to cause Mussolini serious political problems, but like his wife Rachele, Claretta became part of the Mussolini furniture.

He had married his childhood love, Rachele Guidi, in September 1916 in a civil ceremony, but he had had a child with Ida Irene Dalser, with whom he had had some form of acknowledged ceremony, making his subsequent marital status legally dubious. There are differing accounts of his early family status, and many more about his mistresses. Ida Dalser bore him a son called Benito Albino, and Rachele Guidi bore Edda (Ciano's future wife) and a second child, Vittorio.

His lifelong wife Rachele was a strong-minded fanatical fascist who despised Ciano because of his 'parvenu ways'. But Rachele was not spotless, and was possibly involved in profiteering.[13] Rachele herself wrote that 'Benito and she were not yet regularly married; hence the stupid insinuation that Angelica Balabanoff was the mother of Edda.'[14] Rachele was an angry woman, and Edda wrote 'my mother could be harsh and brutal with her children.'[15] Mussolini may have had mistresses, but his wife was a permanent, if difficult, fixture. His daughter Edda wrote that Mussolini felt that a wife 'should be prepared to accept her husband's infidelities gracefully', a policy she too seemed to follow.[16]

Mussolini had some assassination attempts on his life, the first planned by a Tito Zanibóni and Luigi Capello in November 1925, and then in 1926, when an upper-class Irish woman called Violet Gibson fired a shot which slightly damaged his nose. She was considered mad and sent back to Britain. There are varying accounts of these incidents, some claiming that Mussolini was embarrassed by his bandaged nose, others that he was pleased to demonstrate how close he had been to death. It is entirely possible that both accounts are true. A third attempt was on 11 September when the anarchist Gino Lucetti threw a bomb, wounding bystanders; but Mussolini was unharmed and, like Hitler, believed that providence guarded him. His personality cult flourished: Churchill's wife Clementine thought he was wonderful; Mahatma Gandhi was an early admirer; and many democracies believed they could work with him.

---

* Claretta was two years younger than Edda, and her relationship with Mussolini had started as early as 1933.

Among Mussolini's fixations was his obsession with demographics; he often commented on the problems he perceived with the British population in terms of gender balance and the number of its potential fighting men, and the numerical decrease in the French population. He was not, however, an expert in economic matters, which would cause problems later on. His support of Franco cost Italy dearly in economic terms, and he had a romantic view of war but lacked military insight. His hope of empire and nationalistic aspirations left a gulf between fantasy and reality.

What cannot be overlooked in this brief introduction to Mussolini was the 'Hitler ramification'. Had it not been for the Nazi connection Mussolini might have gone down in history as a 'figure of some lightness and some darkness' – not as one of the best, but as a man who governed without too many unforgiveable sins.[17] The historian Ian Kershaw noted that Hitler used the term 'Führer' in relation to Mussolini from the time of his March on Rome in 1922, and he admired Mussolini. This early veneration of Mussolini was, however, not returned, but German military power and the need for Italian status was eventually to drive him into the Nazi embrace. The racist inclination of the Nazis prompted many of them to see Italians not as Aryans but as a Mediterranean people, feckless and fickle, who in the Great War had betrayed the Triple Alliance and behaved like vultures, grasping the South Tyrol. Field Marshal Albert Kesselring suggested that the southern temperament was not belligerent, believing the Italians did not make 'natural soldiers', and observing that in the changing of the guard they appeared to have no enthusiasm for their profession.[18] The distrust was mutual; many Italians in the 1930s were disgusted by German racism, some suggesting it might improve once they became established.

In today's Germany Hitler is to most an embarrassment or worse. In Russia when Khrushchev took power the name 'Stalin' was concealed in the amnesia files, and in Spain there have been heated debates over the disinterring of Franco's body from his tomb. In Italy, however, there is less rancour against Mussolini; in the small Italian town of Predappio his remains have been laid to rest, and have become a tourist site and an attraction for fascists. When I was in Sardinia once, I spotted his name on a tall building. He is a somewhat enigmatic figure on the world stage, much disliked and vilified, often with good cause – but never as hated as Stalin or Hitler.

For this exploration Mussolini was not only Ciano's father-in-law but his political boss, and much of Ciano's life was entangled with Mussolini, for better or worse. At times Mussolini was seemingly admired, if not loved, by Ciano – and at other times feared – but the growing cynicism of Ciano's perceptions of the Duce eventually led to his son's book *Quando il nonno fece fucilare papa* (*When Grandpa had Daddy shot*). Although Ciano's life is the focus of this study, it provides many curious insights into Mussolini's character.

THE DIARY

Ciano's diaries were calendar notebooks used by the Italian Red Cross, often making his writing cramped. To experts it appears that occasionally he may have experimented with redactions, but they appear as a systematic record. Later he wrote that his reflections might be 'sufficient not only to protect me from all political vengeance and persecution but will rehabilitate me even in the eyes of my adversaries.'[19]

Diaries have over the centuries been written for a variety of reasons, and some can be trusted more than others. Diaries, like memoirs, can be changed, redacted or used as an apologia, creating issues for historians. Some diaries are fake, such as the Hitler Diaries forged by a Konrad Kujau and sold for millions, authenticated for a brief time by Hugh Trevor-Roper. Mussolini too became the centre of fake diaries purchased by a gullible British press. In reading historical diaries it is essential to recall the nature of the person writing and the time of their composition. Field Marshal Lord Alanbrooke's diary is evidently genuine, not least because he mentions personal matters and he is downright rude about the national hero Churchill along with other leading figures. He also made it clear where he added later comments to the original text.

There has been considerable debate as to the reliability of Ciano's diaries, but their authenticity has had a variety of supporters, ranging from Welles, who had seen them being written, to the Spanish diplomat Ramón Serrano Suñer, who had been socially acquainted with Ciano. As a diary they are considered truthful, even 'incontrovertible' by many historians of fascism, including Renzo De Felice. One celebrated Italian historian of international relations, Mario Toscano, wrote in 1948 in the *Rivista Storica Italiana* that 'apart from a few remarks, one must recognize in the diary of Ciano one of the most important sources for the history of Fascist foreign policy.'

There have always been doubts as to the historical veracity of the pages, even dating to Allen Dulles's personal observations when Edda sold them; she had used the diaries to try and blackmail her father and the Nazis to save Ciano's life, and later as a means of making money. In them there are historical errors, questionable political facts and serious omissions. Others see them as Ciano's attempt to create the myth of 'good fascism' and create a legend around himself, a form of self-absolution, which Joachim Ribbentrop stated in the Nuremberg trials, calling them Ciano's 'alibi diary'.

There is no doubt considerable truth in some of these thought-provoking criticisms. It has been mooted that Ciano would have had little time to make major changes, which is also questionable given his time kicking his heels at the Vatican. There remains the distinct possibility that Ciano removed or changed some pages, but given the time parameters of his life this would probably not have been a total revision

It must also be noted that he probably wrote with selective prudence, especially when touching upon Mussolini. In the early days, a degree of caution may have dominated his thinking on the grounds he probably assumed he would succeed Mussolini, but then came another shade of vigilance when he realised Mussolini was turning against him. Ciano never made it a secret he kept a diary – Mussolini knew about it – and there was probably an underlying concern in Ciano's mind that Mussolini would demand to read his work.

Ciano's diaries revealed his sense of vanity and his self-importance, but exposed his inner thinking. He wrote because of his sense of self-grandeur, suggesting he was the master player conducting the war in Spain, and the man who eventually tried to save Italy. Many people have kept diaries when they realised that they were watching history unfold: John (Jock) Colville, Churchill's secretary, was one example. It is tempting to think that Ciano believed he was not so much watching as making history, even when he was playing golf. In 1937 there are heavy-handed hints that by sending orders about cutting the water supplies to Santander and ordering bombing raids from Palma, he was in control of the Spanish war, at least while it seemed to be going well. In his diary there is an exaggerated sense of his self-importance, often built up by underplaying the role of Mussolini and others, twisting some accounts, and writing with a sense of authority which in places was unjustified.

Although Ciano was intelligent he often drew the wrong conclusions, making arrogant statements, misunderstanding people and situations. His diary on careful reading indicates his loves and hatreds, but there are only a few references to Edda; and his hatred of Ribbentrop comes through with the same venom as that towards Goebbels when commenting on the German foreign minister. There are hints that Ciano was not a dedicated fascist, just a clever opportunist, but whatever the views on Ciano and the reliability of the diary, there is no question that these documents are historically important, if treated with caution.

His diaries are like the proverbial curate's egg, good in parts. His views on some of the major figures of the day have in places been justified, his interpretation of events less so, but undeniably the diaries are historically important. Mussolini's biographer Bosworth made an incisive comment when he wrote 'certainly his [Ciano's] celebrated diary remains the best single source on Mussolini's Italy and much else, not least because it is studded with conscious wit and less conscious insight.'[20] There are also the often-quoted diplomatic papers, which were Ciano's natural supplement to his diary, but what remains of them suggests no doubt that 'there is no text included in Ciano's *Diplomatic Papers* which is not found among the Lisbon Papers', and historians the world over owe a debt of gratitude for the insights that these documents, along with much of the extant diary, have preserved.[21]

A whole, and dramatic, book could be written on the pursuit of Ciano's diaries and papers, some buried then dug up to be stolen and finally retrieved, some spread amongst relatives, some hidden in a clinic boiler room at Ramiola where Edda spent recuperation time, and copies buried by a friendly SS major in her rose garden – all this followed by the pursuit by the Gestapo and the torture of Edda's lover, Emilio Pucci, the Marchese di Barsento.* However, the diaries are the 'most interesting and important Italian memoir material regarding World War Two' and the moments leading to Italy's entry into that war, not least because they reveal the influences of major figures in and outside Italy and help paint a portrait of Ciano and the ever-present Mussolini.[22]

---

* It was indeed he who was to become, after World War II, the celebrated fashion designer; more about him nearer the end of this account.

1

THE YOUNG CIANO

*Ciano's father, Costanzo Ciano, with the
Collar of the Annunciation
(Italy: public domain)*

CIANO'S EARLY LIFE

Ciano's father Costanzo had started his career as a naval officer, and was associated with the wireless communication school at La Spezia, where he knew Marconi, the acclaimed inventor. After action in the Great War Costanzo was awarded four silver medals, which were enhanced by Mussolini's award of a gold one, and the king of Italy, Victor Emmanuel III,* raised him to Count of Cortellazzo, which title

---

*   On the throne since 1900; he would abdicate in May 1946.

Galeazzo inherited. Immediately after the Great War Costanzo headed a shipping company and took his family to Genoa. While there, he unsuccessfully stood for a right-wing party for parliament, then in 1921 he joined the Fascist Party, and in the spring election was one of the 33 fascists to win a seat in parliament, moving to Rome as a professional politician.

When Mussolini came to power in 1922 Costanzo was made under-secretary of the navy and commissioner of the merchant marine, and elevated as a member of the Fascist Grand Council.* Initially he was minister for posts and telegraphs, and later minister for communications. In an unpublished document of 1926 Mussolini made Costanzo his successor in the event of his unexpected death. There was a 'trusted intimacy' between Mussolini and Costanzo which was 'perhaps significant in forwarding the career of his son', Galeazzo Ciano.[23] There seems little question that Costanzo was corrupt even by Italian standards; he benefited from pay-offs in business deals, and after World War II there were some belated investigations into this corruption.

Ciano was born on 18 March 1903 in the Tuscan port of Livorno, and baptised as Gian Galeazzo; his sister Maria followed three years later. Ciano was devoted to Maria, to whom he remained emotionally attached. She eventually married a Count Massimo Magistrati, in November 1930. She suffered from anorexia, however, and, defying her father's wishes for her to eat, died from tuberculosis aged 33, weighing less than 83 pounds (38 kilos).

Ciano was brought up not smoking, drinking or gambling but suffered from ear, nose and throat problems. Even as a teenager he developed the image of the playboy. When at school, his wife Edda later wrote, he had a quick temper, claiming he was expelled for throwing an inkwell at a teacher.[24] He enrolled at Rome University studying law, a subject he never followed professionally. He developed a friendship with a Jewish girl, a curious aspect in the light of the growing anti-Semitism; it was a relationship which worried both sets of parents. Ciano later seems to have had a distaste for Jews, but it was apparently a social, not biological, bigotry.

As he became politically aware, Ciano built up the false story that he had taken part in the March on Rome in 1922, and backdated his membership of the Fascist Party; in her memoirs Edda took this as a fact.[25] There are confusing accounts, some stating that 'young Ciano was even accorded, retroactively, this fascist honour'.[26] He falsely claimed that in May 1921 he had been a member of the Florentine squad known as the *Disperata*, strutting around in their black-

---

* The Fascist Grand Council had the power to dispose of the leader, but only Mussolini had the power to convene meetings and set the agenda. Between 1937 and 1943 Mussolini summoned it only 23 times, mainly for him to harangue members.

shirted regalia. While ostensibly studying law, he worked as a journalist, and as the fascists came to power, he became the deputy theatre critic for the *Nuovo Paese*, a pro-fascist paper.[27] He also decided he would become a playwright – he found it pleasurable to move in the café society of such people – but abandoned this hope when his efforts failed. (In this he mirrored Goebbels in Germany, who had tried to be a playwright – and, mirroring Ciano, Goebbels pretended he had joined the Nazi party earlier than he really had.)

Following graduation Ciano's father persuaded him to apply for the diplomatic corps. There were some 35 posts available with 600 applicants, and Ciano came 27th, indicating some ability (unless some form of corruption had been activated).* His French was weak, but it improved, and he developed sound English and Spanish. He was appointed as vice-consul to Rio de Janeiro, but while there he created problems with an angry man who accused him of being a predator in pursuit of his daughter; and then, having put his foot in it at an official reception, he was transferred to Buenos Aires as a second secretary, an appointment he disliked. He was happy to leave, having been embroiled with a married lady, and in May 1927 was sent to Peking. It was rumoured that while there he had an affair with Wallis Simpson, the future wife of the Duke of Windsor. It was mere gossip, but it has been claimed that there was a document called the China dossier which underlined Wallis's sexual proclivities; whether this file existed, and if it did was destroyed or remains hidden, cannot be answered.[28] Mussolini's biographer Bosworth described him as a 'yuppy of the day'. Later Ciano's wife Edda referred to his sexual behaviour as if it were an achievement, writing that he 'made many female conquests, one of whom was the celebrated actress Paola Borboni.'[29] As always, it is difficult to distinguish myth from reality, and gossip from fact.

EDDA

After nearly two years in Peking Ciano was recalled, some suggesting that Mussolini had been concerned about his daughter Edda, with his brother Arnaldo deciding that Ciano would be an appropriate match. His public appearance, which he like many young men undoubtedly cultivated, was that of a suave debonair man of society. How far Arnaldo was the marital organiser is not known, but in February 1930 Ciano proposed to Edda in a cinema in Rome, and a colleague apparently told him that 'you have found an insurance policy for life' (which turned out to be true for a time, but not for life).[30] Edda's account differs, claiming that their families were unaware of their romance. Ciano married Edda on 24 April 1930 in a lavish society wedding at San Giuseppe in Rome. Edda

---

* In 1928 Mussolini and Dino Grandi encouraged senior diplomats to take early retirement, to make room for younger ones more inclined to fascism.

would later claim 'I knew from the moment of our first encounter that with Galeazzo everything would be beautiful, clean, and pure, because we were both serious about each other.'[31] This was part of her post-war effort to whitewash Ciano, justifying their past. The king and queen of Italy gave Edda an expensive brooch as a wedding present (which she would later utilise to bribe her escape from Italy across the Swiss border).

Edda
(Rijksmuseum)

They appeared the idyllic couple and became part of the elite social circles because of their status. She was pretty, and he looked dashing especially in uniform, but it has been noted that this impression was marred by his 'high-pitched nasal voice, a flat-footed somewhat comic walk, and an attempt to ape Mussolini's gestures of chin thrust out and chest pushed forward.'[32] Nevertheless, people tended to like him, regarding him as an attractive personality, albeit that many recognised him as career-motivated with no fixed moral compass.

Edda had been born on 1 September 1910, and unlike the young Ciano enjoyed drinking and smoking, causing concern to her parents, who were frequently apprehensive about her boyfriends. She had fallen in love with a Jewish boy, horrifying Mussolini, who sent his brother Arnaldo to inform the parents there could be no marriage, only to be rebuffed by them as they too objected on religious grounds. Edda had a variety of boyfriends, including one called Mangelli, who blundered by asking Mussolini about a dowry.

It is claimed that Mussolini loved her most but worried about her habits, as she was among the first Italian women to wear slacks and drive cars. He never appreciated her love of makeup, and was concerned because she was attractive.

MARRIED LIFE

Ciano's and Edda's married life was always of interest when it became public knowledge that they shared an open marriage, in which both knew the other was indulging in extramarital love affairs. There was an occasion when Edda later wrote 'when he carried on a flirtation, he generally had the good taste to choose his partner from among my most attractive and likeable friends.'[33]

After their honeymoon Ciano went back to Peking as envoy extraordinaire and minister plenipotentiary; prior to this he had been attached to the Vatican

Embassy, where the Italian ambassador claimed that Ciano was a gossip, vain, and generally a waste of time. This was undoubtedly accurate, and it appears that the young Ciano was being supported by Mussolini. China in those days was a glitzy place for Europeans, with parties, gambling, and opium. Edda became embroiled in gambling, and had to be rescued from her debts by Ciano. On 1 October 1931 their first child, Fabrizio, was born, whom Edda nicknamed the 'little Chink'. The couple were fond of nicknames, and Edda knew Ciano as 'Gallo' (rooster). Later their daughter Raimonda would be called 'the mistake,' and their son Marzio the 'child of reason'. Edda wallowed in her status in China, and when there was fighting on the outskirts of Shanghai during the Sino-Japanese conflict she and Ciano remained there; she was thrilled with the headline 'the First Lady of Shanghai refuses to leave the city'.[34] Her ego was as rampant as Ciano's, and she wrote 'in a word, I was at one and the same time the Chinese Empress Tz'u Hsi, Catherine II of Russia, Catherine de Medici, Richelieu, Fouché, Queen Victoria, Mata Hari and so forth'.[35] She admitted it was a boost for her ego when *Time* magazine used her picture on the cover, informing the readers she had her first Coca-Cola in China.

They returned from China in 1933 with Edda pregnant with their daughter Raimonda, and briefly settled with Ciano's parents, but Edda did not appreciate Ciano's mother, Carolina, and the feeling was mutual. Mussolini, of course, doted on Edda even if Carolina did not; in 1933 he wrote to Edda 'as in your adolescence when times were tough, so today, you were and are the special favourite of my soul'.[36]

Ciano and Edda found their own upmarket residence in Rome, with a German governess living on the floor below, and later they purchased a villa in Capri; money was not an issue. Ciano asked Mussolini for work; Mussolini responded by sending him to an international monetary conference in London in 1933. Later Ciano would claim his love of the Latins when compared to the Germans, but he seemed to have a sneaking regard for the British, probably based on this London experience, Edda later writing 'Ciano enjoyed going to London and he much admired the English for their self-possession, their humour and their elegance'.[37]

On Ciano's return to Italy Mussolini appointed him head of the press office, enhanced in 1934 to under-secretariat for press and propaganda, which then became a ministry. At the age of 32 Ciano was Europe's youngest minister, a meteoric rise, because of family connections. Mussolini regarded himself as the senior statesman but was concerned about Hitler's long-term plans, not least because after the Great War the Austrian South Tyrol had been ceded to Italy and renamed Alto Adige; Mussolini realised that Hitler had nationalistic irredentist policies which might well expand southwards. Where Ciano stood on the question of Hitler remains enigmatic; as a young man in the ascendency, he probably followed his benefactor's views, not least because he was now part of the family, and also because like Mussolini he wanted the world to know that Italy was of growing importance.

1935 ETHIOPIA (ABYSSINIA)*

Mussolini had nationalistic plans looking for an empire in North Africa, which he anticipated would resolve some of Italy's ongoing financial problems, and he had prepared for this by sending soldiers and civilians to Ethiopia to build up the necessary resources. This desire for a rejuvenated Roman Empire, with the concomitant military preparations, had an impact on Ciano, especially on hearing that Mussolini's son Vittorio was, along with Arnaldo's son, undergoing pilot training. As part of the family, Ciano decided it would be expedient for him to follow the same route. According to some accounts he was a mediocre pilot, but he graduated as a captain and took command of the 15th Bomber Squadron, naming it *La Disperata* after the Florentine fascist group of which he had pretended to be a member. It seems inconceivable now that because of family he, having passed through elementary flying training, was given a major command.

Ethiopia was economically costly. Although Mussolini was regarded as a genius in such matters, which was far from the truth, relying as he did on ineffective technocrats, Ethiopia would cause financial problems for Italy, already economically poor. Businessmen such as Albert Pirelli and fascists such as Agostino Lanzillo observed that Italy's 'gold reserves were dribbling away'.[38] It has been suggested that Mussolini went to war in Ethiopia to detract attention from home economic problems, but the underlying reason was more his often expressed concept of Roman grandeur based on military power.[39] The Ethiopian campaign would earn Mussolini international derision backed by sanctions, creating the danger of making Italy a pariah state.

On 2 October 1935 war was declared with the ringing of church bells. It was a brutal onslaught, using bombing and gas against tribesmen. It was a war when untold thousands died, many in suspicious circumstances. Marshals such as Pietro Badoglio and Rodolfo Graziani ordered war crimes to be carried out, with Mussolini simply nodding encouragement in the background. The use of gas did not win the war, but a modern state fighting tribesmen did. The war and subsequent occupation were ruthless, and led to outbreaks of revolt against Italian domination. Later, in July 1936, Mussolini appointed Graziani as viceroy of Ethiopia and instructed him to adopt 'a systematic policy of terrorism and

---

* Ethiopia was formerly known by exonym Abyssinia, and the names were often interchanged over the years.

extermination against rebels and any in the population who favoured them.[40] The Ethiopian conquest was short, but it was a manifestation of what became known as crimes against humanity if not genocide.

During this brief war Ciano, Mussolini's son Vittorio, and Arnaldo's son Bruno all took part in the initial bombing attack on the town of Adowa. Ciano's plane was damaged, and he became disillusioned with the war. It generated international condemnation of Italy and was followed by sanctions and national isolationism. Mussolini accused Britain and France of being hypocrites, their empires having been taken by military strength, and it has been suggested he looked to Germany for a sympathetic ear. Many of the clergy supported the war, but Pope Pius XI, often regarded as one of the more modern pontiffs, condemned it as an 'unjust war of conquest'. The irony was that Mussolini was never able to visit his new domain and became the conqueror of 'the most fleeting empire in history'.[41]

Ciano, who was suffering from another nasal infection, had returned to Rome, where Mussolini was aware that his son-in-law was gathering a reputation for the 'evening life'. Ciano then returned to Ethiopia; he flew his bomber too close to the city airport and was fired at, returning home with a plane riddled by bullet holes. Looked at objectively, this was a foolhardy action even in a one-sided conflict – but Ciano was awarded two silver medals. He was further rewarded by Mussolini, who promoted him to a seat on the Grand Council. Despite the gathering social rumours about Ciano, Mussolini was impressed by him in May 1936 following his speech to the Chamber of Deputies, when he demanded that anti-fascist publications should be eliminated, unquestionably following Mussolini's directions.

As propaganda minister Ciano launched an attack through the press against the international condemnation of the campaign. His activity drew the attention of Anthony Eden, the British foreign secretary from 1935 to 1938, who later wrote 'the fact that Count Ciano was the Minister of Propaganda encouraged this activity, his object being to add to his own authority. Confident in the support of Mussolini, his father-in-law, he was eager to show his independence of the wiser counsels of the Italian Foreign Office'.[42] Eden's words were perceptive, as the ambitious Ciano was indeed using his power to increase his reputation.

2

1936 – RISE TO POWER

Ciano and Edda greeted in Hungary, 1936
(Izsák Pölösekei, Romsics—Urban)

FOREIGN MINISTER APPOINTMENT

When Mussolini sent his foreign minister, Dino Grandi, to Britain as ambassador, Mussolini undertook the foreign minister role, and Ciano and Edda were ambitious, hearing the rumour that Ciano was to take on this position. This curious appointment, made on 11 June 1936, of a young family member raised questions, but in Germany for some inexplicable reason it was interpreted as Rome drawing closer to Berlin. Not all the Italians were happy with a family promotion; the old fascist guard were critical, and it is known that Mussolini was content for that sector to lose some influence, because its members were too powerful for a dictator. Mussolini was suspicious of the traditional powers of the monarchy and the Vatican, and he needed his own men doing whatever he demanded, making Ciano the best choice.

Ciano was inexperienced, a member of the family, and one whom Mussolini believed would be obedient. Before Ciano's appointment Mussolini had experienced continuous battles with the career professionals of the foreign office, but Ciano conducted business through the 'ministerial cabinet', and the old guard had to cope with his selected favourites. Ciano marked a change of style on the diplomatic front, described as having a sparkling temperament which contrasted with the 'flighty Eden, the lugubrious Halifax, the shifty Bonnet and the dire Ribbentrop and Molotov', his personality a contrast to the norm of those who normally held this office.[43] In her memoirs Edda attempted to demolish the rumour that the appointment was nepotism, which at the time, and indeed now, feels like an abject apologia.[44]

The foreign press had a field day on hearing of the appointment, producing headlines concerning Ciano's propensity to imitate Mussolini, suggesting he had appointed his puppet. Edda explained this behaviour on the grounds that Ciano frequented the company of her father.[45] Professional diplomats – notably Welles, known for his analytical mind – were quick to note Ciano's subservience to his master.

THE LEAGUE OF NATIONS

There seems little doubt that Ciano's new role increased his arrogance; in the foreign office at the Palazzo Chigi people were impeccably correct with him, and it was probably his sense of self-importance which prompted his diary-keeping, which he continued until his downfall. The obvious power vested

Inside Palazzo Chigi
(PROPOLI-187)

in this inexperienced youth brought, however, a degree of ridicule upon the Italian image. Haile Selassie, who had been forced into exile following the occupation of Ethiopia, was preparing to give a speech at the League of Nations, during which he intended to attack the Italian aggression and their use of gas. During his speech Italian journalists whistled deafeningly, and it has been suggested that it was Mussolini who had instructed them to do this, but Ciano certainly increased this stupidity by providing them with sport whistles, further blemishing the Italian image. The journalists were arrested by the police. On 9 June Ciano received the Swiss ambassador, and following Mussolini's advice he used his new authority, noting that 'I addressed him in a very sharp tone', warning the Swiss ambassador that if the journalists were not released immediately there could be recriminations against Swiss reporters.[46] In these diplomatic exchanges there was a hint that Ciano was announcing himself as the new bully boy on the block.

Italy then faced sanctions, but these were never fully applied, indicating the weakness of the League and encouraging Mussolini to later withdraw Italy on the grounds that fascist Italy did not need it. It has been argued that Britain and France were too obstinate in this matter, as this isolated Italy and had the effect of drawing Rome and Berlin closer together.[47] Dominating the international scene were issues including access to the Black Sea (the Montreux Conference), the fear of Bolshevism, the rise of German power, and Spain's emerging civil war.

Ciano's condescending attitude appeared when the Turkish ambassador met Ciano regarding the Montreux Conference, with Ciano writing 'I gave him no ground for hope'.[48] At the Montreux Convention, signed on 20 July, 1936, it was agreed that Turkey should have control over the Bosphorus and the Dardanelles. It was a source of aggravation to the Soviet Union, and an annoyance for Mussolini, because he believed the Mediterranean was *Mare Nostrum*,[*] including its access and exit points.

THE SPANISH CIVIL WAR

The Italian Foreign Office was consumed with the question of the Spanish Civil War. Initially Mussolini had opposed Ciano's wish to respond to Franco's request for air transport to convey his troops from North Africa to Spain, but he acquiesced because of his fear of communism infiltrating the Mediterranean, a fear shared by the Western democracies. Mussolini was also disturbed that the left-wing Léon Blum in France was supporting the Spanish republicans. This was the start of Italy playing a major role in the Spanish Civil War. General Mario Roatta warned Mussolini that 'Spain is like a quicksand. If you stick in a hand,

---

[*]   *Our Sea*, the Roman name for the Mediterranean.

everything will follow. If things go badly, they will blame us. It they go well they'll forget us.'[49] This insight was to prove all too true.

The Balearic Islands were occupied by Italy, and the Italian Arconovaldo Bonaccorsi, who was in charge, became infamous for his brutality. The French and British ambassadors appeared in Ciano's office, trying to reach an agreement of non-intervention in Spain; this was the beginning of a long diplomatic conflict. Anthony Eden, who was vitriolic about dictators, took the immediate line of demanding an international arms embargo on Spain. Over the next few years it would become a situation of nefarious dealings and smokescreens. It was, as Eden noted, drawing a clear distinction between 'direct and indirect interference'.[50] Mussolini, as a fascist, was in total support of Franco, and Blackshirts, described as volunteers, were consistently 'ordered' to Spain, their presence glossed over by diplomatic talk to which everyone was alert.* When Eden asked the British Ambassador Sir Eric Drummond to speak to Ciano about the Balearic Islands he was irritated on hearing that Ciano had dealt with the enquiry in a 'light-hearted fashion', and tried to assure the British 'that no negotiations would be held with General Franco which would change the *status quo* in the Mediterranean'.[51] It was clear to the more discerning that Mussolini's support for Franco was part of his own political dreams, which included the resurrected *Mare Nostrum*.

The British and French were equally curious about the German–Italian relationship, as these two countries seemed to be drawing closer together. On 29 June 1936 the French ambassador challenged Ciano directly on any military or political agreements between Nazi Germany and Italy. Ciano denied this with some justification at this time, but he was aware that the Germans were being especially gracious. The German ambassador, the anti-Nazi Ulrich von Hassell, turned up in Ciano's office on 18 June claiming, undoubtedly under instructions, that the Germans had been impressed by the victory in East Africa. A month later von Hassell was back, informing Ciano that Germany was closing its legation in Addis Ababa and replacing it with a consulate, thereby elevating the importance of the area. Naturally Ciano was pleased.

GERMANY CALLS

Edda had been in Berlin, visiting Ciano's sister whose husband was serving in the Italian embassy, and had realised the Germans had paid her considerable attention because of Ciano's elevation. Goebbels, a well-known womaniser, was indulging in his latest obsession, boats on the Wannsee Lake; he took Edda to his new home

---

* The Italian troops were known as the *Corpo Truppo Volontario* (CTV) and were bolstered by massive resources; this title was deceptive.

and introduced her to Hitler, and the three of them went on a boat trip. For years she remained ardently pro-Nazi. In her memoirs she elevated her importance, claiming she was the main link between the Duce and the Führer (which was nonsense; Mussolini loved her as his daughter, while Hitler appreciated pretty women).[57] She considered Goebbels the greatest propaganda chief of all time, and later defended Göring challenging the (justified) accusation that he plundered art works.[53] She loved the social circuit, the drinking and the male attention, and it was these social aspects of life that formed her opinions.

On 24 August Hitler's decree extending military service by another two years raised concerns across Europe. Ciano had heard of Hitler's meeting with Miklós Horthy from Hungary and Villani, the Hungarian minister in Rome, in which it had been agreed that communism was the danger, but he gathered that Hitler had become heated over the issue of Czechoslovakia. It was becoming known that he was considering reclaiming territories removed from Germany by the Treaty of Versailles, based on reuniting German peoples, and demanding the return of the confiscated German colonies as well.

Ciano had taken over the foreign office when the ideological divisions in Europe were widening, and diplomatic dances developed as each country sought alliances in a Europe which was beginning to feel precarious. In Britain the main concern had been the Bolshevik threat, but as in France there was growing apprehension about dictators, so the British had decided to court Mussolini, whom they considered less of a threat.

Mussolini had always been suspicious of Hitler as his military power developed, but he was now seeking a closer relationship with Germany, primarily because he had been affronted by the reaction of the Western democracies over Ethiopia. This was an indicator of an Axis agreement taking embryonic shape. However, Mussolini remained concerned about the German intentions relating to their mutual neighbour, Austria. The incipient power of the Germans and their military lurked in Mussolini's mind, and Ciano followed his master's voice.

In September 1936 Mussolini met the German Hans Frank, who had been minister of justice and was at this stage minister without portfolio. It was a meeting of self-assuring observations, as the Germans tried to entice Mussolini into their sphere of influence. Frank explained that Germany would support Franco on political principles, and as part of this seduction informed Mussolini that the Germans regarded the Mediterranean as his zone. It was a wide-reaching discussion, with Mussolini claiming he was watching English activities in the Mediterranean because of his fear that they would encircle Italy. The meeting gives the impression that the toybox contents were being given an airing, even sharing attitudes on the question of religion, with Mussolini explaining that the

Jewish faith was different because it involved race; both Frank and Mussolini were trying to please one another, with Ciano present as Mussolini's lapdog.[54]

The British ambassador returned after his leave, confirming that Britain wanted good relations with Italy and that the Abyssinian issue was closed, adding that he wished the Italians would stop the anti-British propaganda emanating to Egypt. It was a diplomatic dance of influence, of balance and counterbalance, at a time when Ciano was new to the post, pleasing Mussolini – but it was his playboy reputation which constantly caught the public interest.

CIANO IN GERMANY

Mussolini's central concern was the growing relationship with Hitler, and it was this that was behind Ciano's first official visit to Germany, in October 1936. Ciano, unlike Edda, was not overwhelmed by the Germans at a social level, finding them boring; he was unimpressed by the Nazi leaders, he developed a lifelong distaste for Ribbentrop, found Goebbels unpleasant, and described Göring as a vulgar ox – but being Ciano, he enjoyed their attention. On 21 October he recorded a conversation he had held with his host, Constantin von Neurath, at that time foreign minister.* Ciano informed Neurath that the Italians were not anti-British but were aware of their activities in the Mediterranean. Neurath informed Ciano that Germany would recognise Franco once he had taken Madrid. They agreed on three common positions regarding Spain: the first, a joint military effort supporting Franco; the second, the recognition of Franco once he had occupied Madrid; and finally an investigation of a joint action to prevent the consolidation of a Catalan state, an issue which reverberates to this day. Hitler was less enthusiastic about Spain than was Mussolini, but he significantly 'dominated the process from the start', giving the world a lesson which would one day become all too familiar.[55]

A few days later, on 24 October, Ciano met Hitler at Berchtesgaden, enquiring about relations with Britain; Ciano repeated the theme he had discussed with Neurath, and gave Hitler papers indicating the hostility in London towards Nazi Germany. These documents related to a circular by Eden and a telegram from the then British ambassador to Berlin (Phipps, 1933–37) which described Germany's new leaders as 'a bunch of adventurers'. Ciano explained that Mussolini was sending some 50 planes to Spain and two submarines, further pleasing the Führer by claiming that although Mussolini wanted peace he was nevertheless preparing for war. They agreed that the two major problems were Bolshevism and Britain's encirclement of Italy. At this stage of events Ciano appeared a fervent advocate

---

* Neurath was tried at Nuremberg as a major war criminal based on his compliance with the Nazi regime; he was sentenced to 15 years but was released in 1954 and died two years later.

of closer ties with Germany, even though Mussolini had his doubts about Hitler; the 'inexperienced Ciano, who despite his pose of world weariness, was easily star-struck'.[56]

Ciano was pleased with his own performance, noting that 'the Führer showed himself particularly cordial towards me', and was always asking about Mussolini.[57] This friendly meeting had the required effect, and Hitler started explaining to Ciano that some form of alliance between Germany and Italy was essential for progress. This was igniting the fuse which would lead to disaster for Italy.

Back home in Italy the diplomatic dance continued, with Ciano meeting the British ambassador on 6 November to sign trade deals. The British, aware of his recent German visit, sought to reassure him that they were looking towards conciliation and better relationships, in which Ciano detected a 'degree of urgency'. He was correct in this assumption, because although the British remained critical of the Ethiopian occupation, they were desperate, with the emergence of Nazism, to keep Italy on side.

CIANO IN VIENNA THEN BUDAPEST

During November Ciano and Edda paid an official visit to Austria, where they were not met with the same enthusiasm expressed towards them in Germany. Edda appeared more sensitive to the situation, but even Ciano detected the atmosphere, observing that the Italian national anthem was never played, and although Chancellor Kurt Schuschnigg was polite, others were less cordial. It was supposed to be an official meeting with Austria, Italy and Hungary, but Austria's concerns about Hitler's possible intentions dominated the proceedings. When Schuschnigg met Ciano at a personal interview, he questioned him about Hitler's views, complaining that the Nazis interfered too much in Austrian politics. The unpleasant tension Schuschnigg was suffering from would be used by Ciano in another silly manoeuvre in May the following year, when he instructed a journalist to suggest that Schuschnigg had agreed to allow Nazis into his government. It is easy to gain the impression that Ciano was treating his position like a boy playing chess for fun, seeing what would happen with a particular move.

Ciano then visited Budapest, where he noted that 'there is no lack of polite offers from London aimed at making Yugoslavia join in the game England wishes to play in the Balkan area'.[58] He also heard the rumour that Göring was saying that the time was coming when Czechoslovakia would soon cease to exist. He found the Hungarian and German relationships good, which was probably a misreading, but he was gratified that he received a better reception than in Austria.

As Ciano travelled between Vienna and Budapest he was pursued by a professional journalist, George Ward Price, working as the foreign correspondent for the *Daily Mail*, who evidently encouraged Ciano to speak about international relationships. In a private letter from Budapest on 16 November 1936 the journalist wrote: 'I have seen a good deal of Ciano during his stay in Vienna here, and I have had some long talks with him alone. In these he has been explicit enough about Anglo–Italian relations to make me think it may be worthwhile passing on his views to you'. The letter was passed on to Eden.[59] The journalist concluded with 'on reflection, my little run round central Europe has made me more optimistic about next year being free from war—barring complications arising out of Spain.'[60] Eden was widely known for despising the fascist system and Italy's invasion of Abyssinia, but the frank way Ciano spoke to a foreign journalist is curious; perhaps it arose either out of charming friendship, or more possibly in the hope that his statement would reach official desks (which it did).

Ciano and Mussolini inspect East Africa troops, Brindisi 1936.
(PD Italy, Author unknown)

SUMMATION OF 1936

The impression is that Ciano's ego was almost out of control, causing him to behave like an all-important member of a medieval court. Although instructing journalists to blow whistles at the League of Nations and planning an attack on Schuschnigg through his press amounted to silly pranks, these had ramifications which not only degraded his office but inflated his dubious reputation. Many of his colleagues seeking his approval convinced him that he was widely appreciated when in fact he and Edda had many critics. He believed he was almost the top man in Italy and would one day replace Mussolini – but after an illness, Mussolini made it clear to his son-in-law that this would not necessarily be the case. Even so, although Ciano and Edda's social proclivities and appetites were well-known on the gossip circuits, they were rarely publicly aired because of the Mussolini connection. Those who worked with Ciano in the Foreign Office had to tread with care, as he was hot-tempered, and it was dangerous to cross him unless one was prepared to be exiled to some far distant embassy. At one stage it was claimed that Ciano was 'the effective boss of Italy'.[61] His reputation grew, and at one stage he was suspected of arranging assassinations, which may well have been true. His final international engagement was with the Japanese, wanting to seek closer relationships for Italy with Germany and Japan. The year 1936 was a time for seeking would-be partners, but it was clear that the fascist-type states were drawing closer together, and so the dancing would continue.

3

1937 – DIPLOMATIC DANCING

Dino Grandi and John Simon, British
Foreign Secretary 'Tap-dancing'
(Bibliothèque nationale de France)

THE NATURE OF DIPLOMACY

This chapter is entitled 'Diplomatic Dancing' because various countries, anticipating stormy years ahead, tried to negotiate their way into alliances or create spheres of influence. It became integral to Ciano's life as he followed Mussolini's instructions while gradually developing his own perceptions. Italy's national interests and geopolitical position dictated that Mussolini manoeuvred between the great powers, employing his 'customary opportunism' to play one off against the other in order to extract maximum advantage.[62] The British tried to detach Mussolini from German influence, and the diplomatic machinations which passed through Ciano's office and golf club always led to questions about Mussolini's intentions. The enquiries varied – sometimes ideological, or looking to be a peace-broker, or realpolitik, or mere propaganda – and were a focus for continuous debate.

Italians and foreign observers could never be certain where Ciano stood in some matters, because like Mussolini he vacillated on a weekly basis. He sometimes claimed to be pro-British, then anti-British, and he was the same towards his northern neighbours – pro-German, later anti-German – much of this dependant on the latest incident or the vibrations reverberating from Mussolini's office. When anti-Semitism raised its ugly head in Italy Ciano tended to toe the Mussolini line, but most observers did not regard him, as mentioned earlier, as racist beyond social bigotry. As with so many aspects of Ciano, there is a constant sense of ambivalence marking his professional life. Where Mussolini and Ciano stood in matters of foreign policy was equally bewildering for most countries. Some historians have seen the drawing together of Italy and Germany as natural under the circumstances of the day, while others regarded Mussolini as willing to challenge the traditional European balance of power. The truth is confusing, as neither Mussolini nor Ciano appeared to have had definitive policies, and it is easy to gain the impression that they were feeling their way as events unfolded. It soon became apparent, in contrast, that Germany had fixed strategies and would be the controller of events in the next few years.

On 6 January the British ambassador questioned Ciano as to the nature of the so-called volunteers in Spain, and a week later he was back on the same subject, dropping hints that the numbers of volunteers disembarking in Spain were immense. Ciano claimed they were working with the Germans to reach an agreement, but he asserted to the British visitor that no one could stop volunteers, and that 'our line of conduct has always been correct and loyal'. There is the usual hint in his papers that Ciano very much enjoyed the position of power he held. The gentlemen's agreement about not interfering in Spain was clearly being ignored, and trust was minimal.

Göring in Rome

Göring had arrived in Rome on 13 January for a visit which, it being Göring, was a mixture of tourism and art collecting, but was also, like the British visits, a test of the waters. Ciano kept a detailed record of the conversations between Mussolini and his German guest. In a curious aside the German interpreter described

Mussolini sitting behind his desk with himself and Göring sitting before him, and 'Ciano, to whom his father-in-law paid little attention, found himself a seat next to us'.[63] This may have struck the German as strange, but Mussolini always displayed his superiority. Mussolini proudly talked of the growing Italian fleet, with Göring enthusiastically pointing out that if aligned with the German and Japanese fleets they would be formidable. This was part of Göring's strategy to bring the Italians into a closer relationship, and this would not have eluded Mussolini or Ciano, as Göring was incapable of being subtle.

They discussed the democratic system, this self-important cabal gloating in their belief that countries with strong dictators were more effective than democracies, where an election could change a country's leadership overnight. (This happened, of course, to Churchill in 1945 but only Göring survived long enough to witness that the Atlee government continued with the war policy.)

Göring challenged Mussolini as to why the Italians had not left the League of Nations, with Mussolini explaining that they had *de facto*, but proudly announcing that they were doing more damage by staying within it. The two enjoyed a moment talking about the British, whom Göring believed to be controlled by Jews and Freemasons, adding that despite the British fears over communism they had a growing communist party on their own doorstep. Göring then raised the delicate subject of Austria, hypocritically claiming that the Austrian government was brutal, claiming there were rumours of the Austrians restoring the Hapsburg monarchy, adding that the Austrians were anti-Italian. The meeting concluded with the ebullient Göring saying that the Führer would welcome a visit by Mussolini. Göring, in his usual way, believed he had been a diplomatic success, as he dropped less than subtle hints that Germany could assist Italy economically.

In democratic countries the role of the foreign minister was to offer guidance and advice, even if it meant a clash with the political leaders. This was however, not the case in dictatorships; both Ribbentrop and Ciano were subservient to their leaders. As Ciano took his notes of the meeting, he was the mere observer of events and knew his role.

THE BALKANS

During February and March the diplomatic dancing continued, with secret negotiations with Yugoslavia and placatory interviews with Turkey, all overshadowed with the Austrian–German tensions. The Turkish Ambassador Rustu Aras called to see Ciano, declaring what Ciano described as a 'clumsy declaration of friendship for Italy and admiration for Mussolini. I refrain from describing the series of acrobatics he performed'.[64] It was obvious from the interview that Turkey wanted peace (a position it would uphold against all forms of pressure until the end of World War II). There was a distinct impression that Ciano behaved like a potentate.

Ciano was involved in the Yugoslavian talks, which were generally secret, a characteristic of these pre-war years, revolving around borders in the diplomatic dance of identifying possible partners or identifying those who might cause problems. Ciano and the Yugoslavian prime minister, Milan Stoyadinovitch, met and discussed the future, the Yugoslavian being acutely aware of the rise of Nazi Germany. He confided in Ciano that the Little Entente was useless and the French connection more so.* Hoping for a more secure future, Stoyadinovitch had signed an agreement with the Italians on 25 March.† Ciano and Stoyadinovitch talked about the Anschluss, about France under Blum moving further left and communism being a dangerous infection, and it was acknowledged that Albania was a vexatious problem. Ciano carefully explained he wanted to visit its king, Ahmed Zog, to which Stoyadinovitch made no objection.‡

Mussolini and Ciano had avaricious eyes on the Balkans, and these meetings helped test the waters and explore other nations' opinions. Ciano obviously gained some pleasure in Stoyadinovitch's views on England, quoting them in full: 'I wonder if England is able to help us ... in view of the fact that she has so often found herself at daggers drawn with you. Poker is an Anglo-Saxon game, and we all know that bluff is very often used'.[65]

AUSTRIA

Dominating the diplomatic stage was the Austrian question, with a growing sense of alarm over Hitler's intentions. Göring, who was an impatient annexationist, persistently informed the Austrians that they needed German economic help, only helping to raise their suspicions. On 22 April Mussolini held a conference with Chancellor Schuschnigg in Venice, with Ciano present. The Austrian chancellor said that he was looking for peaceful relationships with Germany and was reliant on the Rome protocols, with the agreement of 11 July 1936 signed in Vienna. Austria and Germany had appeared to have buried their traditional hatchet over

---

* The Little Entente was an alliance formed in 1920–21 by Czechoslovakia, Romania and the Kingdoms of the Serbs, Croats and Slovenes for defence against Hungarian revanchism, and signed by France. It did not survive beyond 1938.

† Milan Stoyadinovitch (Stojadinović) served as prime minister of Yugoslavia during 1935–39. During the 1938 election he presented himself in the fascist role. There were problems after he barely won the election, and by 1939 Prince Paul realised Stoyadinovitch was a threat to his own power. Paul enlisted British help and Stoyadinovitch was sent into exile to the British Crown Colony of Mauritius; Churchill always regarded him as a potential Quisling.

‡ King Zog had started his rise to power as prime minister, then president and finally an uncrowned king. He eventually fled to various countries, eventually to England when France was invaded, but after the war was invited to Egypt by King Farouk, finally settling in France in 1955, dying in 1961.

Nazi attempts to dominate the country, and Schuschnigg and Franz von Papen had drafted this peace-forming treaty in the hope that it would remodel the European political map. The Rome Protocols were the result of three international agreements reached in Rome on 17 March 1936 between Austria, Hungary and Italy, signed by the Austrian prime minister, Engelbert Dollfuss, the Hungarian Gyula Gömbös and Mussolini. Dollfuss paid the price a few months later when he was killed in a failed Nazi takeover bid.* Schuschnigg had based his hopes on these agreements, but he would discover, like Chamberlain, that as Hitler's megalomaniac pursuit of power intensified, such agreements meant nothing.

During May 1937 Ciano sat with Mussolini, meeting Neurath again, who was unquestionably checking what had been said in the meeting with Schuschnigg. Mussolini told Neurath that he had suggested to Schuschnigg that he should have some nationalistic members in the government, and this was not helped by Ciano suggesting to journalists, as mentioned earlier, to portray Schuschnigg as agreeing.

In England, King George VI was crowned in May, and Italy's political leadership was not represented. This was on the grounds that the Negus (ruler of Abyssinia) had been invited; but Grandi was there, representing the king of Italy. Mussolini was more interested in relations with Germany than with Britain, and that same month Ciano, following his father-in-law's instruction, addressed the Chamber of Deputies, stressing the importance of the Italian–German friendship. However, Mussolini remained ambiguous, because although he had an admiration for the growing German military strength he also feared the Germans, and pondered the implications of having German troops on the borders of Alto Adige.

BRITISH OVERTURES

During June and July 1937 the diplomatic concerns were focused on Hitler's intentions, and the British were rearming, observing the development of the Berlin–Rome relationship and the war in Spain. The diplomatic dance of testing relationships continued, and evident tensions between Italy and Britain were growing but were played down with diplomatic politeness, although Italian journalists were recalled from London and the British press were barred from Italy after some of their newspapers had referred to the fascists as 'gangsters'. At the beginning of June the Turkish ambassador called upon Ciano with the message that the English were hoping for a return to normal relationships with Italy, with

---

* As matter of curiosity, Mussolini and Rachele were looking after the Dollfuss family when he was killed, and Mussolini had to break the news, which he found appalling. He ordered the Italian military to the borders and referred to the Nazis as a bunch of criminals who would bring ruin on civilisation, and he called Hitler a murderer.

a hint that he had been asked to convey this message. The German Ambassador von Hassell told Ciano that Neurath had been invited to London, which Ciano considered to be a mistake, stating 'I received the news with great coldness.'[66] He had the impression that Hassell was pleased, however, which was probably correct, as Hassell was vehemently opposed to any conflict between Germany and Britain. Ciano was more concerned that such a move ought to involve Rome because of the Italians' growing relationship with Germany. Ciano's diary indicates he was claiming 'we are in the big boys' club now' and must not be ignored; but the situation would not improve, and Neurath never made it to London.

The British Ambassador Drummond returned to Rome, thanking Ciano for his gift to Drummond's daughter on her recent marriage, Ciano was cynical about this; according to him the British diplomat was trying to befriend the Italians, with the concern that 'dabbling journalists' were almost enjoying the tensions. Another major press interest was that the Spanish nationalists had lost the battle of Guadalajara, a major and widely publicised republican victory fought mainly by Italian troops, a matter of deep sensitivity to Mussolini. Some of the press had blamed Franco for the nationalist defeat, and a few had accepted that the republicans were stronger, but it was generally portrayed as an Italian military failure. As the Italian military historian Pier Paolo Battistelli wrote, 'the notorious failure at Guadalajara was the first Italian defeat, which soon created an international echo casting doubts on Italian fighting skills after years of rule by Mussolini'.[67] Mussolini had taken this as a personal affront; furious, he ordered that Italian soldiers should always fight alongside other nationalities to avoid a repetition of such a national embarrassment, and demanded that no Italian troops could return to Spain until this failure had been avenged. Mussolini also felt bitter that Franco had faced some left-wing Italians in battle. Many of the Spanish were critical of the Italians, and the Spanish general Queipo de Llano claimed the 'Germans behave with dignity and avoid showing off. The Italians are quarrelsome and despotic bullies'.[68]

The German ambassador returned to discuss the 'London idea', namely that the major powers should reach an agreement to withdraw a certain number of volunteers from the Spanish conflict. Ciano was not interested, but it was clear that the various embassies were watching who visited Ciano's office and who was dancing with whom. The British *chargé d'affaires*, Maurice Ingram, suddenly turned up there in early August, suggesting the British were seeking Ciano's advice based on his knowledge of his time in China; the British were wondering whether Italy would join an international action to seek peace. Ciano, flattered at the request, explained it was not their business, but must have realised that this was a 'charm offensive' by the British.

Two weeks later Ingram was back with Ciano, stressing that his visit was not a formal approach by his government, but raising the question of the ships in the Mediterranean, including some British ones, which had been the subject of attack by what appeared to be Italian planes and submarines. Ciano played for time, claiming he would investigate the matter, and stating that, like the British, he wanted to maintain peace, and as a last throw of his dice he suggested that the attackers might have been 'red planes'. In his diary entry Ciano was more cynical and brusquer than in his diplomatic records, stating that in his response to Ingram 'I replied brazenly. He left almost satisfied.'[69] Later in his diary Ciano amused himself with an unkind description of Ingram, writing 'that flaccid and false British functionary was so flattered that, feebly, he will do it. Touch someone in his personal vanity and you cannot go wrong.'[70] When it comes to the question of personal vanity it could be claimed that Ciano led the field.

Ciano gave the impression that he controlled events, using diplomatic smokescreens with the British, informing the Chinese they could no longer buy planes, ordering the water supply to be cut off from Santander, instructing Italian planes to bomb Valencia, and on the last day of the month sending another 5,000 volunteers to Spain. He gave the impression in his diary that he was running not only Italy but the war in Spain. He even asked Mussolini for a huge amount of money to be spent on projects in Albania, seeing it as an Italian interest, stating that 'we must be ready to grab opportunities when they arise'; most of this month he was enjoying his power. A few years before he had been a minor diplomat, but now, as foreign secretary and married to Mussolini's daughter, he was a significant figure in Italy, revelling in his position.

In September Britain and France had signed an agreement to protect shipping in the Mediterranean, where Italian submarines had been sinking ships thought to be helping Spanish republicans. Mussolini was furious, because he still regarded the Mediterranean as the *Mare Nostrum*, but Ciano was busy trying to normalise relationships with the two Western democracies. Although Ciano was constantly subservient to Mussolini there were early signs that he was not always in accord with his master.

Litvinov, the Soviet foreign minister, had complained that two Russian vessels had been attacked, and the Italians had stated they would not attend any conference alongside the Russians. Eden had demanded Italy's attendance to deal with 'this piracy' as a 'prelude to Anglo-Italian talks', and thought that Italy's best response was to attend despite the presence of the Russians, whom Ciano had argued would destroy the conference.[71] Eden, with his hatred of dictatorship, was never fooled by Ciano's smokescreens. Mussolini, meanwhile, was not concerned about the British, and explained to Ciano that he had studied British demographics and decided that there were only about '22 million men of whom 12 million were over 50 the age of bellicosity', later condemning the British for having hospitals and graveyards for animals.[72]

GERMAN FRIENDSHIP

Mussolini was preparing his speech for his proposed visit to Berlin, and Hassell was politely received, even though Ciano described him as 'unpleasant and untrustworthy.' It was dawning on Ciano that the anti-Nazi Hassell, who belonged to the old school, was not fond of fascism and had a distaste for Ciano. Hassell disliked the dictators, and he could foresee the dangers into which Europe was being driven. Mussolini, perhaps because of his portending visit to Germany, exploded according to Ciano with vitriolic abuse against the USA, accusing the country of being run by 'Jews and Blacks', which he described as the 'disintegrating element of civilisation'.[73]

It was known that Mussolini intended to visit Hitler, and the diplomatic dancing continued unabated. Grandi met Mussolini to discuss Britain, which concerned Mussolini more than France, and expressed the opinion that he could not care less if Britain continued to rearm. There was disturbing news from East Africa, with growing unrest and revolts against Italian control, but Mussolini ordered it to be crushed and to use gas. Ciano was concerned from the financial perspective, appearing better informed than Mussolini of the dire economic problems in Italy. The expense of not just the East African war but also supporting Franco in Spain, building up Italian influence in Albania, and the military expenditure, especially in naval vessels, was costing the Italian economy too much. Ciano observed that more troops were being sent to Palma ready for action, and that Mussolini's son Bruno was going. Ciano wrote that he envied him 'but I am, at least for the moment, nailed to this desk'.[74] Ciano at this stage appeared to have a romantic view of war, but the reality of the Spanish conflict was bitter and characterised by massacres, the hallmark of a civil war.

On 24 September 1937 Ciano and Mussolini travelled to Germany, where some observed that Ciano appeared to be in favour of the German relationship; yet he had told friends he needed to apply the brakes to Mussolini's enthusiasm. Ciano at this stage presents a confusing picture as to where he stood on the German relationship. The Italian Ambassador Bernardo Attolico, who was anti-Nazi, caused the suspicious Ciano to ask his brother-in-law Magistrati to 'keep an eye on the ambassador'. However, the Germans soon became somewhat distrustful of Ciano himself and his ambivalence towards them. They had noted his degree of immaturity as a foreign minister; his private gossip and thoughts were widespread; and his subservience to Mussolini was known. At times it seemed to dawn on Ciano that he had little to fear from the democracies but much from Nazi Germany.

The next day they travelled to Munich, where they watched manoeuvres, which Ciano found 'interesting but expected more' than what he saw. On 27 September they went to Essen to visit the Krupp industrial site, which impressed both Mussolini and Ciano. In Potsdam they observed a parade, which Ciano cynically noted was 'heartfully choreographed with much emotion and a lot of rain'. As an overall impression Ciano felt the trip, obviously staged to impress the Italians, had added little to their current agreements, but Mussolini, according to Ciano, managed to impress the German crowds with his voice and presence. Mussolini had addressed a massive crowd at the Berlin Mailfeld as the culmination of his visit. 'Amidst a tumultuous thunderstorm that created a truly Wagnerian atmosphere, but unfortunately also slowly dissolved his sheaf of notes, Mussolini extolled the close ties between the two countries that had in the previous year described themselves as the Axis, around which European diplomacy would henceforth revolve.'[75] He said the 'German rebirth' was inspired by the same 'spiritual force' that underpinned the 'resurrected Roman Empire' and bound the two nations 'in a single unshatterable determination', prepared to march together to the end.[76] It was a speech which clearly outlined Mussolini's wish to be associated with the growing power of Germany.

Interestingly, Ciano seemed less certain, and committed to his diary the thought as to whether Italy should consider Germany as a goal or a place to manoeuvre, adding a query as to whether the situation would 'develop in such a way as to separate these two nations' once again. On their return to Rome, Ciano was bemused by the welcome with laurels and arches, which he wrote 'were more symbols of a successful war and not a return train journey'.

Ciano was showing signs, despite his playboy lifestyle, of being able to question what was happening based on his own judgement. During this busy month he had managed to spend some family time in Livorno at a horse-race meeting with his father, plus Edda and their son Fabrizio. He barely mentioned Edda, though he did note that she did not always have popular support and was not particularly good at appearing in public. When he met a Princess Mafalda at a social lunch he noted 'she is not beautiful; she has neither intelligence nor personality. But she likes men, as all women do'.[77] This patronising view of women says a lot about his own well-known proclivities.

THE BRITISH REACTION

At the beginning of October Drummond returned to Rome, expressing regret that the Italo-English relationships had deteriorated after they had started to normalise during August. He pinpointed two areas of concern: the first related to a telegram sent to Franco congratulating him on taking Santander, and the second was Italy's refusal to participate in the Nyon Conference in Switzerland, which addressed international concerns over the shipping crisis in the Mediterranean. Italy was not accused directly, but it was generally accepted that Italian submarines had carried out these attacks. As Anthony Eden noted, the Italians were 'quite ready to hold conversations with the British government, provided they did not deflect fascist policies.'[78] This diplomatic dancing was becoming a game of bluff, pretence and deceit. The British and French knew that Italy was the source of the problem; Ciano 'knew this, and they knew that he knew', both sides maintaining a degree of politeness. As regards the British criticism of Mussolini's telegram to Franco, it was not much more than Mussolini congratulating himself, writing 'I am particularly glad that during the ten days of hard fighting the legionary troops made a valiant contribution.'[79]

The Spanish Civil War created tensions between Britain and Italy. Ciano noted that the Italian soldiers in Spain were tired, and that 'Franco cannot wait to get them out of the way, retaining the air force and artillery. He is envious of our success and fears those of the future.'[80] Ciano knew about the criticisms of Italian soldiers, but through his propaganda ensured that the problem related to Franco and not the Italian military. Franco was seeking Italian resources, not asking permission, as Ciano often implied. There is a hint in his writings that Ciano was becoming bored with Spain, and on hearing the news that Gijon had fallen, he was pleased but wrote 'let's hope to accelerate the development of this damned war'. Although Ciano was a mere observer of events in Spain he continually gave the impression that he was a key component.

This was the month when the diplomatic dance was almost becoming square-dancing, as patterns of alliances were beginning to take on a more distinctive appearance. The Japanese and the Germans looking to form an alliance, the visit to Germany by Mussolini, and the comings and goings of Göring, Ribbentrop, Neurath and Hassell never escaped the notice of the British and French, who waltzed together. In early October Ciano had met the Duke of Aosta, freshly arrived from Britain. He had explained to Ciano that the British were open to agreements, 'but if forced to do so the English can make war and make it well.'[81] This caused Ciano to reflect that Germany needed another three years to prepare, and that Italy lacked the necessary raw materials and ammunition. A week later he wrote that he spoke in a 'conciliatory fashion' to the British ambassador, and he heard that Eden was proposing to meet him in Brussels, which Mussolini and Ciano thought was a good idea – but a few days later he decided against attending. Eden had been told that Ciano was tempted by the proposal, but that 'Mussolini had vetoed the offer' (possibly because Eden was aware that the Italian volunteers were in fact troops).[82]

THE ANTI-COMINTERN PACT

The main preoccupation during October was the Japanese and German effort to enlist Italy into their alliance. The visit to Berlin the previous month had been rapidly followed by Ribbentrop's visit to Rome in October in a (fruitless, as it turned out) effort to persuade Mussolini to join with the Germans and Japanese in the Anti-Comintern Pact. It was eventually signed on 6 November, and it was a significant event in alerting the world to an alliance which might lead to conflict.

Ciano and Ribbentrop had a mutual distaste of one another, which possibly had its origins in their having much in common: both men tended to be proud of their status, egotistical, pretentious and flamboyant, and both pretended they were the powerbrokers, yet were in total subservience to their respective leaders. They had different social backgrounds, but had many similar characteristics. They both distrusted the German Ambassador Hassell, who had been in Italy since 1932. For Ciano, Hassell was too aloof, reserved, belonging to the old school of diplomacy, but for Ribbentrop there was an awareness not only that Hassell looked down on him, but also that Hassell was suspected of being anti-Nazi.[*] Hess, the Führer's deputy, visited, and taking Ciano aside told him that he had heard that Hassell's wife had been heard saying that her husband was anti-Italian. This was a clever but false construction; Hassell was not anti-Italian but anti-fascist, but Hess was preparing the way for Hassell's dismissal. Ciano had heard that Hassell was spreading the story that Julius Streicher had visited a German school in Italy and selected the most beautiful and intelligent girl, who transpired to be the only Jew there.[†] There may well have been some truth in this claim, because Hassell's diary is inundated with anti-Nazi jokes.

Even Heinrich Himmler arrived on 18 October to watch a police parade and claimed he was deeply impressed by it, hoping to woo Mussolini. It was Ribbentrop who was the main negotiator. He had been a failure in Britain, was fervently pushing the anti-Comintern alliance, and condemned the British, accusing them of not understanding communist dangers, and their refusal to return German colonies, which made mutual agreements untenable. The main purpose for Ribbentrop was to ensure that the Italians understood the importance

---

[*]   Hassell was removed from his post in Italy because of these well-founded suspicions. He became a member of the German resistance and was executed following the 1944 July Plot. Like Ciano, he left some invaluable diaries of his thoughts and activities which are referred to in this text.
[†]   Julius Streicher edited the anti-Semitic paper *Der Stürmer*.

of the alliance. Ciano, undoubtedly prompted by Mussolini, wanted to know if this alliance had further ramifications in military, political and economic interests.

At a personal level Ciano had been apart from Edda for some time, in his diary writing 'Edda is back'. At the beginning of the month he had spent the day at Ponte a Moriano with his parents and children, and had accompanied his son Fabrizio to his first day at school, recalling his first time, when he had cried; there is no doubt that despite his public vanity and playboy life, he loved his family. A week later he spent a Sunday afternoon with them playing war games, and they had the whole neighbourhood 'running for cover' with their cannon-sound effects.

Ciano received a Romanian decoration, with no idea why he deserved it – but cynically, and probably correctly, explained it as Romania's wish for a peaceful alliance. At the end of the month he attended with Mussolini a service giving medals to widows whose husbands had fallen in Spain; at the service he saw wounded soldiers, prompting him to write 'I had to examine my conscience, and I ask myself if this blood had been spilled for a just cause'.[83] He wrote the immediate answer 'Yes', which may prompt you to wonder whether this was a safety valve, in case Mussolini wanted to read his work.

November was dominated by the agreement with the Japanese expressing their sense of deep friendship with the Italians, the signing of the Treaty taking place on the morning of 6 November. Ciano later 'whetted Japan's interest in the negotiations by supplying it with stolen plans for Britain's Far East bastion of Singapore'.[84] Ribbentrop, in conference with Mussolini and Ciano, suggested that the British would be less happy with the agreement because they would regard it as an alliance between the 'aggressive nations against the satisfied ones'. The Jewish question arose, with Ciano pompously pointing out that 'we are conducting a very determined and increasingly intense anti-Semitic campaign directed by Farinacci'.[85] Italian anti-Semitism would not reach the extreme barbarity of that in Germany, and there seems little doubt it was Mussolini's way of pandering to the Nazis. During these international rumblings it was decided that the Italians should keep their rights to a military base in Majorca in case of a war with France. This was a curious statement, because the three-way agreement had initially been built on the premise of being anti-communist, yet war in Western Europe was already being projected, with Ciano stating that the next war will 'be played out in France'. Their patchwork discussion finished over the Austrian question, with Mussolini informing Ribbentrop that he regarded Austria as German state number two, which could do nothing without Germany, and Mussolini concluded on the puerile note that the 'Austrians still treat us coldly'. Ciano's diary reveals an almost schoolboy approach to major issues, based on 'who likes who'.

Russia had not appreciated Italy's signing the treaty. On 2 September 1933 Russia and Italy had signed a friendship agreement, and two days after the signing of the new pact the Russian ambassador arrived protesting, stating he had nothing more to say, and was met by a cold response by Ciano, who led him to the exit. The international reaction to the pact was worldwide, stretching as far as Brazil, which later prompted Ciano to contemplate enlarging the pact, but he eventually concluded that it was not for small countries; 'it must remain a pact of giants'.[86] This statement indicated the misconstrued sense of national self-importance prevalent in the Italian fascist leadership. Ciano wrote that 'three nations engaged down the same path which could lead to war. A necessary fight if we want to break this mould that suffocates the energy and aspirations of young nations'.[87] Mussolini and Ciano appeared to know that war was probably the outcome, feeling the alliance had made them less isolated on the world stage. But the war came sooner than they had anticipated.

The diplomatic dancing was gaining momentum as the alliances were becoming defined. The Hungarian minister, Villani, arrived to apologise for press comments in his country, claiming that the government had no control over its press, which was mainly controlled by Jews. The Yugoslavian Stoyadinovitch was equally concerned, complaining to Ciano that following a visit to the West he had received nothing from England or France, and informing Ciano that in his opinion, although the British were building up their navy and air force, the army was of little value because the British had no appetite for compulsory military conscription. The British ambassador made more overtures for a meeting between Ciano and Eden, but following a discussion with Mussolini it was denied.

At the end of the month Ciano was feeling self-satisfied, proclaiming in his diary that at least fascist governments had a 'national formula', and the Germans based their version on 'racism' and the Italians on 'Roman imperialism,' neither of which was moral or sound. Mussolini had been fermenting against the intellectual and bourgeoise classes for being weak and not entirely fascist, stating that he would form the Italian character by forging it in combat. For many of the more intellectually and politically sensitive Italians the future must have looked somewhat bleak.

At a personal level Ciano was concerned about his father's health; it was evident that Costanzo was fading rapidly, and Ciano wrote 'may God perform a miracle'. He concluded the month with his family on the beach, recording that for the first time the children ate with 'us at the same table'. His diary often mentions his love of family – but seldom Edda, who was enjoying her own private love life. Edda gave birth on 18 December to their third and final child, Marzio, Italian for Mars, the god of war, nicknamed Mowgli. Ciano was pleased to receive congratulations from Hitler to royalty 'and other minor people'. There seems little doubt that Ciano later tampered with this diary, but it could not have been a full revision, because here and in many places he appears as an aggressor waiting to light the fuse.

Most European countries were nervous, not least Poland. The Polish Ambassador Wysocki told Ciano that some form of collective security was necessary. Ciano had reflected whether Poland should be part of the anti-communist pact, but Wysocki had made it clear that he had not changed his views on Russia, but they would not consider joining. Ciano also heard that the British ambassador to Turkey, Percy Loraine, had supposedly claimed that the day would come when the British would crush the Duce. Mussolini had instructed Grandi to protest to the British about Loraine's comments; curiously, later Loraine would be appointed as ambassador to Rome.

Stoyadinovitch was also preparing to make a visit in his role of Yugoslavian prime minister, to ensure national safety. Ciano described Stoyadinovitch as 'a man who inspires confidence, he is a strong, full-blooded man, with a resonant laugh and a strong handshake' (a strange way to estimate a person's character). Ciano picked up from various intercepts that the British Embassy had noted Stoyadinovitch's love of women, which amused Mussolini, who was told by Ciano that 'beside the official visits I had prepared some dances with the most beautiful women of Rome Society'.[88] The British had been correct, but Ciano more appreciated Stoyadinovitch's love of fascism and his 'Roman salute'.

In the second week of December Italy formally left the League of Nations, to Ciano's delight when he announced its departure. Since the various sanctions this had been anticipated, but with the Alliance Pact Italy was not as isolated as previously. When the next day Grandi expressed concern that any agreement with London was unlikely to be reached, Ciano told Grandi that he agreed, adding the curious note in his diary that he concurred with 'the Duce that on a historical level the Italian–British conflict is inevitable'. This rift with the British had started with Eden's point-blank refusal to recognise the *de jure* status of Ethiopia, continuing with his irritation about the interference in Spain, deepened by the Tripartite Agreement, making Eden firmly convinced that the German–Italian relationship was dangerous. Eden had talked with the previous ambassador to Rome, Sir Ronald Graham, who knew Mussolini well, and 'like me, he regarded Ciano as then completely hypnotised by Germany'.[89] It was not a great surprise, then, when on Christmas Eve Ciano heard that the anti-Italian assault was resuming in London, though he noted that when he had had lunch with Lady Ivy Chamberlain she had drawn a different picture, as she was offering friendship and wore a fascist emblem. Lady Chamberlain had married Sir Joseph Austen

Chamberlain and helped her husband in the negotiations of the 1922 Locarno Pact; because of this she had been created a Dame of the British Empire in 1925.* She also campaigned for the relief of women and children during the Spanish Civil War and was awarded the French *Chevalier legion d'honneur* and the Italian Gold Medal of Merit. The British prime minister often used her for communicating with the Italians, which caused some annoyance to Eden.

The problems with the Spanish conflict persisted, with Mussolini more concerned about the Italian image as a fighting machine, and after a debate as to whether to withdraw or not it was decided to stay in Spain to the bitter end rather than tarnish the Italian reputation, as they perceived would happen. Just before Christmas Mussolini was ruminating on the possibility of making a sudden move to destroy the British fleet, as he hated the impunity of the British tending to dominate the 'Roman' waters. On New Year's Eve Ciano spoke with Admiral Bigliandi, who gave Ciano the impression he was confident that if a war occurred with the British the Italian fleet would be successful.

During 1937 it had become widely suspected that the Nazi powerhouse was looking towards the occupation of Austria, the now well-known Anschluss. This increased Mussolini's nervousness with Hitler's nationalistic irredentist demands, claiming Italy's lost part of the Tyrol, the Alto Adige. As Mussolini reflected on the Anschluss possibility, he told Ciano that it was inevitable and there was nothing they could do, but it gave him no pleasure. When in January 1937 Göring had appeared in Rome to persuade Mussolini to give the Germans a free hand in this possibility, this had all been part of the preparation of Germany ensuring Italy was on side. Mussolini had already discussed the situation with Ciano, and they wished the Germans would keep them informed. The Germans, however, never did, and this was going to be their continuous practice, to the aggravation of Mussolini. As it transpired, Göring had intended to speak privately to Ciano, but the Germans had already started to suspect him as something of a social dilettante who could not be trusted in matters of discretion, Hitler referring to him as a 'Viennese café ballerino'.[90] Ciano was more concerned over the British and trying to resolve the maritime conflict in the Mediterranean. He had demanded that Dino Grandi expedite the matter, but he was up against Eden, known for his reluctance to deal with dictators. Eventually a worthless agreement was signed in April 1938; it was of no value because the agreements were contingent upon Italy withdrawing troops from the Spanish conflict, and throughout this year relationships with the British were never easy.

---

*   Sir Joseph Austen Chamberlain died on 16 March 1937. Neville Chamberlain once told Mussolini that the ghost of his brother Austen had told him that Mussolini was a good man to do business with.

SUMMATION OF 1937

The year had been one of finding partners for the future, trying to keep a balance with some, while hoodwinking others. There were the usual ups and downs, with General Italo Balbo appearing to be anti-German and opposing anti-Semitism. The latter issue would not go away. When talking with Ribbentrop earlier in the year Ciano had proudly noted that Farinacci had been conducting an anti-Semitic programme, but when Ciano found himself under attack by Jews for following Hitler's racist campaign, he claimed in his diary on 3 December that 'the problem does not exist here'. This may have had something to do with the fact that the next day the Pope awarded him the Pian Grand Cross, a Pius IX award to those who had done outstanding deeds for Church and Society. Given Ciano's lifestyle and general conduct the Pope was either blinded by advisers or this was his share in diplomatic dancing.

Although during 1937 Ciano rose in importance, especially in his own eyes, he was not necessarily popular and despite his seeming obsession with Germany, the Germans were already deeply suspicious of him, not least because of his lifestyle and gossip. He had obediently followed Mussolini and they had rejected the League of Nations, regarding Italy as no longer a state in isolation because they believed that in the signed pact, they had joined the 'real powers'. They had quietly acquiesced over the German–Austrian situation, maintained the charade of wanting peace, kept a wary eye on potential allies and tried to bluff others with diplomatic courtesy. Their support of Spain was wearing them down, but they seemed indifferent to the economic cost, with only Ciano seemingly indicating concern. One thing was clear: it was during this year that Ciano and Mussolini both anticipated a war not with the communists but with the Western democracies, especially Britain, whose presence in the Mediterranean was a continuous source of aggravation.

4

1938 – TEMPO RISING

Hitler and Mussolini – primus inter pares?
(Ladislav Luppa)

BRITISH ISSUES

The year 1938 started with a visit to Rome by the British Ambassador Eric Drummond, who following his brother's death in 1937 had held the title of 7th Earl of Perth. Relations between Italy and Britain were seriously strained, with Mussolini still taking personal affront that the British would not acknowledge his empire. The irony was that many British shared the same views as Mussolini over the role of the League of Nations, which they tended to call 'Geneva-ism', and were more interested in appeasement with Germany.[91] Perth claimed the British were hoping for a 'comprehensive solution' adding that 'it is no part of British intentions to make futile efforts to put them in cold storage'.[92] This Italian–British relationship was brittle and was of concern to other countries, especially France and Germany. Nevertheless, through Lord Perth's office the British pursued this possible friendship to keep Italy within their influence and away from Germany. One issue was the Italian support of Franco, and this problem would never improve.

There was a clash of opinion within the British government. Prime Minister Chamberlain was constantly seeking a peaceful relationship, and he appeared to trust Mussolini and Ciano more did than his foreign secretary, Anthony Eden. Lady Chamberlain had been acting as a private source of influence for her brother-in-law, the British prime minister. Eden had been further annoyed when he heard from Perth that Lady Chamberlain had been reading letters from the prime minister to Ciano and Mussolini, thereby creating confusion, claiming that 'Rome is counting on her'.[93] On 17 February 1938 Lord Perth sent a deciphered message which Lady Chamberlain had sent to the prime minister, and it read: 'Count Ciano lunched with me today and asked me whether I had any further message from you. I said no. He then begged me to let you know time is everything. Today an agreement will be easy, but things are happening in Europe which will make it impossible tomorrow.'[94] Lady Chamberlain found Ciano completely changed and stated that he seemed 'intensely worried'. Whether Ciano was actually concerned at this stage or simply pushing pressure buttons remains ambiguous. Later, when Eden offered his resignation, he wrote that the prime minister's views of the dictators were 'optimistic and unreal', with which Chamberlain would agree after the infamous Munich meeting.[95] This strife within the British government was known, and just possibly Ciano was stoking the fires via Lady Chamberlain.

The press was, as always, a problem in relation to international tensions, whether controlled by the government or the free press of the democracies. The free press was both the burden and the bulwark of democratic countries, and occasionally during the war years the British had to silence it with D-notices simply for security. More pertinently the German diplomat Ernst von Wiezsäcker had written 'Hitler had embarked on a military enterprise and could not therefore withdraw from one … but unfortunate provocation by the foreign press really set Hitler going' towards Czechoslovakia.[96]

Ciano's diplomatic life

Ciano was delighted with the news from the Spanish Civil War that the strategic town of Teruel had been taken by the nationalists, but as usual the situation was never as clear as he hoped, epitomising the Spanish conflict for Ciano and Mussolini for most of that war.

Ciano, on hearing that King Zog of Albania was looking for a wife, somewhat cynically suggested one of the daughters of the Durini, an Italian noble family, not to promote their social standing but because he saw Albania as an Italian interest. A month later Sereggi, Zog's aide-de-camp, asked if Ciano would be Zog's best man at his wedding in April. Ciano decided that even though his recommendation had not been taken up he would agree on the grounds that 'I strongly believe in my programme for Albania and anything that may increase our prestige and our influence must not be neglected'.[97] (This mention of 'my programme' illustrates once more that Ciano regarded himself as an ingenious arch-manipulator on the international scene.)

On 7 January Ciano had a long meeting with the king of Italy, who was curious about the proposed visit by Hitler. Mussolini had long resented the power of the throne, but although the influence of the monarchy was limited it remained constitutionally powerful despite him: the king was more like the chess king, limited in moves but key to the game. Mussolini wanted to know about the palace involvement regarding Hitler's visit and the suggestion of a return visit to Germany. He heard from the king that the monarch had a lifelong distrust of Berlin, which in the monarch's opinion could never be trusted, and that he felt the Austrians were more honest.

A few days later Ciano met the Austrian Chancellor Schuschnigg at a meeting often dubbed the Budapest Conference. He had more meetings, both public and private, with Schuschnigg over the need for Austria's independence and making general attacks on the Little Entente. In Ciano's own mind he considered himself an outstanding success, leaving 'good echoes in Italy' and 'the Duce called me with his congratulations. This is the reward which counts the most'.[98] The conference achieved nothing in the end, but Ciano was typically more concerned about his reputation and pleasing Mussolini.

Back in Italy a few days later, the news from Spain was not improving and there was dissent over Mussolini's decision to introduce the goose step to his military, emulating Germany. Many, including the king, regarded this type of parade marching as a Prussian invention, and they objected, only to be rebuffed by Mussolini on the grounds that the king was 'a little runt' who could not manage this style of marching.

On a happier note, Ciano and Edda had their son Marzio baptised, and it was noted that during the ceremony the baby received the oils and waters in 'religious silence without shedding a tear, which according to the experts', Ciano proudly wrote, 'is quite miraculous'.[99] Only Ciano, it seems, could be at the centre of a

Divine miracle by producing a child who by not crying stood blessed in God's eyes.

February was dominated by events in Austria. Chancellor Schuschnigg, who had held the position since July 1934, had always found it difficult to resist German demands and their interference in Austrian life. Italian support for Austria was weakening as the Austrians grew closer to the Nazis, but Austria had felt reasonably safe since the agreement of 11 July 1936 that Austria could maintain its independence so long as it conducted its business as a German state. Despite this agreement Nazi Germany persisted in its efforts to subordinate Austria. On 12 February 1938 Schuschnigg had been summoned to Berchtesgaden by Hitler and confronted by further demands. These included the dismissal of the Austrian chief of staff and the inclusion in the government of Artur Seyss-Inquart, who would be responsible for security. Seyss-Inquart was an Austrian Nazi politician, and later in the year served as chancellor of Austria for two days before the Anschluss (he would eventually be executed at Nuremberg). This early move by Hitler raised the temperature, especially between Italy and Britain.

On 4 February the Italians agreed to Eden's request for greater surveillance of the Mediterranean against piracy, but Ciano added the cynical note that 'these are feeble measures'. There was no embarrassment on the part of Ciano about playing out this hypocritical charade, knowing that the 'pirate' vessels involved were nearly all Italian. The Spanish issue occupied considerable time during this month, with both Ciano and Mussolini being critical of the Spanish military leadership. Ciano was pleased to bid farewell to Hassell, in a 'cold hostile and rapid meeting', concluding that Hassell belonged to the Junker* class and did not support the Nazis. Ciano was more concerned with Mussolini's demand to beautify Rome, ready for Hitler's projected visit, having heard from the Prince of Hesse that Hitler might take a break in Italy for a few days.

RUMOURS OF THE ANSCHLUSS

On 11 February Ciano discovered that Chancellor Schuschnigg had been summoned by Hitler, which he thought gave substance to the 'silent Nazifying of Austria', but which sent reverberations throughout Europe. Ciano, in another diary entry, wrote that 'the Anschluss is inevitable. We must only as far as possible, delay it'.[100] This singular entry underlines the Italian fascist view that Germany would occupy Austria eventually, and that for the sake of the alliance Mussolini would acquiesce, but the Italians would have preferred to retain the *status quo*.

The reaction in Britain was immediate, Eden demanding to see Dino Grandi who, having received instructions from Ciano, played the waiting game. Grandi

---

*   Traditional German aristocratic

pretended he could not meet Eden because of a golfing engagement, even though this was a game he never played. However, he could not avoid the prime minister's invitation as he was most 'cordial' and suggested that Eden should be present, to which Grandi was obliged to agree. They met early in 1937 and Chamberlain questioned Grandi about the Austrian situation, explaining that it could change the balance of power. Basically, Chamberlain was trying to ascertain precisely where Italy stood in the developing situation, and Grandi was being as evasive as possible. He was conscious of Eden sitting there listening, who suddenly intervened, pointing out that Italy was ignoring the Stresa Agreement. This had been signed on 14 April 1935, when Italy, France and Britain had agreed to consult with one another over any major events in Austria. Grandi had to circumnavigate this accusatory question by stating that much had happened since April 1935. Ciano wrote that he always suspected Grandi of attempting to promote himself, which was somewhat hypocritical.

It was clear that Chamberlain was probing to discover not only Mussolini's attitude, but also what Hitler was planning. It was Grandi's opinion that Chamberlain was pleasantly accepting his replies, but there was obvious tension between the prime minister and Eden. Next, Eden questioned Grandi over the Italian contribution in Spain, the issue of the so-called volunteers, and the matter of piracy in the Mediterranean, and informed Grandi that with all these other causes of aggravation there was no question of Ethiopia being recognised. Grandi turned to Chamberlain and, using Ciano's advice, said that the Duce 'is more anxious to clasp England's hand than he was yesterday'.[101] Further talks were proposed but there was a clash over the venue, Grandi insisting on Rome and the British on London. Grandi claimed that Rome had been agreed, and produced the necessary papers to prove his point.

In his telegrammed report of the meeting Grandi outlined the difficulties and tensions between Eden and Chamberlain, the two arguing in front of him as if he were not there. Grandi wrote that 'Eden, for his part, did not scruple to reveal himself fully in my presence … as an inveterate enemy of fascism and Italy'.[102] Grandi was correct about the tussle between the two hosts, pointing out that Eden had the support of the 'man in the street', as well as of Churchill, adding that he hoped Churchill would bring 'Eden the same good fortune as … to the ex-King Edward VIII'.[103] On 20 February Eden resigned.

March 1938 was dominated by Austria, and in Britain Anthony Eden had been replaced by Lord Halifax which was soothing music for Ciano, because he was informed that Halifax was more like Chamberlain in his views: less abrasive, and more prepared to trust the dictators, especially Mussolini. Lord Perth, meanwhile, was in and out of Ciano's office on almost a weekly basis as they tried to agree the agenda for the talks between their two governments. The major sticking points, however, persisted with the Spanish Civil War and the British refusal to recognise the Italian empire, with Perth and Ciano knowing without saying it that Italy was playing a double game over Spain, which was constantly denied by Ciano. He persisted in emphasising that the Italians supported Franco, with Perth hinting that Britain's recognition of Ethiopia was dependent on Italy taking a lesser role in Spain. The Balearic Islands were part of these contentions, with Ciano insisting there were no Italian troops there, just aircraft. Perth raised the question of the number of Italian troops in Libya, and Ciano defended their presence there on the grounds that the British had the Royal Navy moored offshore. Other issues were discussed, with Ciano being evasive, occasionally protesting, or asking for the matter to be deferred while he consulted with Mussolini. Perth remained polite but persistent, and at times Ciano noted, 'he simply dropped the subject'. It was clear that Perth's efforts reflected the British hope that an amicable agreement with Mussolini might curb the Duce's political ambitions in the Mediterranean. Ciano felt the cards were in his favour, because he believed that Chamberlain's position as prime minister, following his conflict with Eden, was dependant on his success with the Italians. Ciano was still taking the self-important stance that Italy was pivotal to the European scene and that although he deferred to Mussolini he was the manager of these historical moments. Britain, however, was more concerned about Nazi Germany, with Chamberlain seeking peace at any cost, not wanting a repeat of the Great War, trying to keep fascist Italy away from German influence and to maintain the *status quo* in the Mediterranean.

THE ANSCHLUSS

The German–Austrian situation was reaching crisis level. Most other countries assumed that the Italians had no wish for Nazi troops as their immediate neighbours, and Italy's reaction was monitored with interest. Ciano had heard early in the month that Schuschnigg was considering a plebiscite for the Austrian people to choose independence, which he did on 9 March; two days later this was followed with an ultimatum from Berlin, backed by the threat of invasion. The demand was that Schuschnigg should step down and be replaced by Seyss-Inquart. Schuschnigg had considered military opposition, and had appealed to Rome, Paris and London with no results, and Austria's federal president, Wilhelm Miklas, refused the policy of military resistance. Schuschnigg had even appealed to Ghigi, Italy's ambassador to Romania, to seek Ciano's help, but was met with the rebuff that Ciano 'could not advise one way or the other'.

The Anschluss was virtually instantaneous, with Ciano writing that 'Austria is no more', and Mussolini claiming that Switzerland, Czechoslovakia and Belgium were similar ambiguities which would follow. The Prince of Hesse arrived in Rome as Hitler's emissary, saying that Hitler was grateful for the Italian silence. Ciano and Mussolini were nervous that the Anschluss might endanger Italy, thereby making the English talks more critical. Nevertheless, Mussolini sent Hitler a telegram, stating 'I congratulate you on the way you have solved the Austrian problem. I had already warned Schuschnigg', to which Hitler – at the time a great admirer of Mussolini – warmly responded, 'I shall never forget'.[104]

During the British negotiations Ciano believed he held the upper hand, writing that 'Chamberlain is more interested than we are in reaching an agreement; it is on this card he has staked his political future, as well as that of the entire Conservative Party'.[105] Evidently Ciano was not the international expert he deemed himself to be, but he had at least recognised the British struggle over what has since been called appeasement.

Lord Perth was promptly back in Ciano's office, reviving their polite discussions over the meaning of the expression 'volunteers' in terms of Spain, but he was soon asking Ciano about Italian reaction to the Anschluss. Ciano was shown a copy of the British telegram sent to Berlin, with the phrase 'protesting in the strongest terms' encapsulating the British reaction. Ciano evaded giving any direct answers, claiming that it was not the business of outsiders. The American Ambassador William Phillips appeared before Ciano, asking for help to assist German and Austrian refugees, and questioning him over the bombing of Barcelona. Ciano refused the former, and blamed Franco for the bombing (which he knew had been carried out under Mussolini's orders). The American was somewhat taken aback by the apparent hard-nosed response, telling Ciano that America was animated 'by high and noble humanitarian aims'.[106] According to his diary Ciano responded by writing it was a matter of 'political ethics', and the 'abyss of misunderstanding between us and the Americans grows deeper and deeper'.[107]

Perth, like Phillips, also asked about refugees, but with special reference to those seeking help from Ethiopia, including Italian soldiers who had deserted, some of them out of disgust. He was met by Ciano's ruthless reply that the deserters would be met by the full force of the law – execution – and that refugees would be examined individually. It could be argued that Ciano was simply following Mussolini's directions, but in his diplomatic papers as well as his diary there are few hints of humanitarian principles. However, he later requested that the Germans show some clemency for a Jewish scientist in Vienna called Neumann, who was 80 years old, but he and Mussolini soon found themselves inundated with such requests. Ciano's attitudes towards Jews seemed to depend on whether he knew them or not. He was unquestionably socially inclined against them, but not engrained with the Nazi form of anti-Semitism. As mentioned earlier, the king had informed Ciano that the Germans could never be trusted, and General Balbo was making the same noises as the king, to the annoyance of Mussolini, who wished to see the end of Balbo.*

Mussolini had to prepare a speech regarding the Anschluss, and there were many angry anonymous letters protesting at the German occupation and the lack of Italian reaction. Mussolini had the postmarks checked, and decided most of the protests came from the north of Italy and in his customary way claimed it was only the 'cowardly rich of the North', worried about their new neighbours.

Italo Balbo
(US Gov, Public Domain)

Eden concluded that some damage had been done to Italy by its silence over the Anschluss, and that Mussolini wanted to repair this damage with official conversations with Britain, to recover some of his prestige; Eden's comment was probably astute, as Mussolini regarded himself as the strong man of Europe.[108] Ciano and Lord Perth made some progress with their talks, papers were signed by Mussolini, and the more sensitive areas were deferred.

The spring of 1938 continued with the reverberations of the Anschluss, the completion of talks with the British, the French seeking similar arrangements, problems with the Alto Adige region, and Ciano fastening imperial eyes on Albania. Ciano discovered that since the Anschluss Yugoslavian opinion was turning in favour of Italy, probably out of necessity, and all these diplomatic niceties pleased him. Mussolini and Ciano ignored the growing public opinion in Italy, with Ciano noting on 5 April that some Italian shopkeepers were proving reluctant to show pictures of the Führer on their premises. It was not just the shopkeepers, though; many Italians were unhappy with the German relationship, and this unease would one day lead to internal dissent.

This German affiliation remained delicate, with Mussolini concerned about the British and French overtures for pacts of friendship, but Ciano ensured he kept the new German Ambassador von Mackensen in the picture with the necessary details. There was a growing concern over Italian commercial interests in Austria now that the Nazis were in control there, but von Mackensen informed Ciano

---

*   In June 1940 Balbo was a passenger in an aircraft which, it was claimed, was attacked by a British fighter, and then as it tried to land it was brought down by Italian gunfire, mistaking it for the enemy. At the time it was possibly suggested by Ciano that Balbo had died fighting. Because of Mussolini's views on Balbo it has been suggested that this was an assassination, a conspiracy theory now debunked.

that 'we are entirely disposed to respect Italian interests'.[109] The Alto Adige region was the main concern, where a resident German population of over 200,000 were showing signs of irredentism, the issue Mussolini had feared before he had acquiesced to the German occupation of Austria. Ciano asked Mussolini to speak directly to Hitler on this issue, informing Hitler that it was being fermented by Catholics, Masons and Jews, which he knew might activate the German dictator's interest. The problem could not be solved, and later in the month Ciano asked the Prince of Hesse to speak to Göring for help. Hitler's irredentist claims were well known – both Mussolini and Ciano, as mentioned, had feared the consequences in Alto Adige – and they were now paying for this, with Mussolini fuming with anger at his new friends in Germany.

A BRITISH AGREEMENT

In the meantime, the British talks were drawing to a satisfactory conclusion, with Ciano hoping the pact would be signed on Maundy Thursday; it became a series of eight agreements signed on Easter Saturday, to become known as the Easter Pact; somewhat ironic because Mussolini was a well-known atheist.* Mussolini was content with the arrangements, and gave the necessary permission, though he queried how Britain could arrange for the League of Nations to recognise his empire. The British cunningly explained to Ciano that they would 'recommend' it, because that only required a majority Cabinet decision, as against unanimous. Ciano regarded the 'English pact' as important in opening a new era, writing 'friendship on a footing of parity [is] the only kind of friendship that we can accept, with London, or with anyone else'.[110] He also noted that this meant the 'Ethiopian venture is truly closed'. The pact was signed at the Palazzo Chigi with the public outside applauding; Lord Perth, to whom Ciano expressed in his diary a degree of warmth, voiced his approval of the pact on signing it. The American Ambassador Philipps was, according to Ciano, 'enchanted' by the agreement. The French sought a similar pact through their diplomatic contact, Jules-François Blondel, but they were not as persuasive as the British.

The situation in Spain fluctuated as usual, there had been considerable fighting in Tortosa (Catalonia), with Mussolini ordering the bombing of the area from the Balearic Islands, despite Ciano observing that Franco did not want cities bombed, cynically adding 'in this case the game is worth the candle'.[111] Ciano gave the impression that war was a romantic notion, and paid no heed (as with many in war) to the consequences of indiscriminate bombing. At the end of the month Mussolini and Ciano met Leslie Hore-Belisha, the British secretary of

---

* In 1904 Mussolini had written a booklet entitled *God Does Not Exist*, describing priests as 'black microbes'.

state for war. Ciano, observing that he was Jewish, was bemused that he held such an important position. There were indeed some anti-Semitic attitudes in Britain towards Hore-Belisha, but none of them had any significant effect.

THE ALBANIAN SITUATION

As mentioned earlier, Zog of Albania was preparing for his marriage to the Hungarian Countess Geraldine Apponyi, who was not Italian, and some interpreted Zog's choice of new wife as his effort to move away from growing Italian influence in Albania. Many Albanians were aware that Italy was imperialistically driven and that its commercial and political interests were expanding. The Albanian military was inefficient, often guided by Italian officers, and Ciano knew that to cause problems all he needed to do was stir up trouble between the court and the people, as the latter somewhat despised the former, and the feelings were mutual.

As Ciano prepared to travel to Albania's capital, Tirana, he ensured that his envoys let Zog know he should be met personally, speaking of Albania as a protectorate (which in many ways it was, but that was a term which was only applicable after the Italian invasion of 1939; at this stage of events Albania was best described as a 'client' state). As the marriage arrangements were being prepared Ciano heard that the king of Italy wanted to send the Duke of Spoleto as his representative. Mussolini wanted to avoid arguing with the king, and Ciano noted that 'in any case the king's envoy will have a second-class reception compared to the Duce's envoy', namely himself. When Ciano arrived in Tirana, he was pleased that Zog came to meet him, writing 'the importance of this gesture going against protocol, can escape no one'.[112] It may be speculated that yet again Ciano was glorying more in his own importance than in being a representative of Italy. He also noted, condescendingly, that the ceremony was carried out with greater seriousness than he had anticipated. When he returned from his tour, he showed Mussolini some excellent copper minerals from Albania as the 'figs from Carthage'.* The idea of occupying Albania was developing fast in Ciano's mind and would lead to long-term disasters. The month of May started for Ciano with his work on the Albanian report: whether this was simply an update of his latest visit for Mussolini or plans to occupy this Balkan territory remains elusive; it was probably a mixture of both.

HITLER VISITS ITALY

For Ciano, apart from watching British efforts in Geneva, hearing the French seeking a similar pact, and observing the war in Spain and the unease over

---

* Cato the Elder had, with fresh figs in his hands, used this expression to persuade the Roman Republic that Carthage was close to Rome and ripe for invasion. This led to the Third Punic War.

Czechoslovakia, the main preoccupation was Hitler's visit. Ciano went to the Royal Palace, where Hitler would be staying, and announced that its appalling bathrooms had to be refurbished at government cost.

Hitler arrived with several trains and was greeted at the Brenner Pass, the main border post between Italy and Austria. It was a visit welcomed with caution, many resenting the Nazi regime, and some openly hostile; for example, the magazine *La Vita Italiana* had recently claimed that the Nazi racial philosopher Alfred Rosenberg was the anti-Christ. Hitler arrived in a raincoat and civilian dress, prompting Mussolini to say he looked like 'a plumber in a mackintosh'. He was greeted by fascist troops forming guards of honour and the local houses were decorated, but when he arrived at Rome's Porto San Paolo station it was dark, and he was disappointed to be met by King Victor Emmanuel rather than Mussolini. Not only that, but Hitler felt it was demeaning to travel in an old-fashioned royal carriage, asking if the Italians had ever heard of cars. The crowds met him, but his time in the palace did not go well, as the king thought little of his visitor. During a formal meal Hitler sat next to the queen and not a word was exchanged, with some observers speculating this was a deliberate act on her part.[113] 'Hitler was particularly annoyed by the huge crucifix the queen wore around her neck. She had done it, he thought, to annoy him.'[114]

Ciano commented on the rumours that Hitler had demanded a woman and that the king thought Hitler needed stimulants to keep him going. The need for a woman was probably Hitler wanting his bed 'turned down', as was his habit, and they found a hotel maid to assist. Ciano suggested the king was trying to make Hitler look like a 'psychophysiological degenerate', which post-war generations might validate. Mussolini told Ciano that Hitler put rouge on his cheeks to hide his pallor.

Hitler, uncomfortable, vented his rage on Ribbentrop, who the next day presented Ciano with a draft agreement with Germany offering a military alliance. Ciano was at this stage uncertain about it, on the grounds, as he explained to Mussolini, that he did not want Chamberlain upset prior to his (Ciano's) forthcoming efforts in Geneva to have the Italian empire recognised; but Mussolini wanted to move forward with this agreement. The next day Ciano wrote in his diary that Mussolini 'speaks of going to war left, right and centre, without a clear opponent or a defined objective', sometimes Russia, but then he would fulminate against France and Britain and even America 'before he calms down.'[115] Meanwhile, Hitler had found that his chief of protocol, Bülow-Schwante, had gone in evening dress to inspect a guard of honour; to a man like Hitler he might as well have 'dressed in his pyjamas', and this constituted an excuse for Hitler to sack him.[116]

Despite the royal insults the visit appeared to go well, notwithstanding Hitler being somewhat disturbed that the Italians had not condemned modern art. Hitler and Mussolini spoke together about the future, with the former raising the question of Czechoslovakia almost in passing. Mussolini gave the impression that 'this little country was not important to him and he would look the other way'.[117] According to the German interpreter Paul Schmidt, both Hitler and Ribbentrop continuously wanted to talk politics, which Mussolini and Ciano tended to avoid, and Schmidt noted that Ribbentrop, something of a bully, 'tried this tactic on Ciano but without success'.[118] The bond between Mussolini and Hitler seemed to strengthen, and after a visit to Florence, according to Ciano, they parted at the railway station with 'the Duce stating "now nothing can separate us", and the Führer's eyes filled with tears'.[119]

As the visit concluded the French government, through Blondel, knocked on Ciano's door again, and when he raised this with Mussolini he was told that the French had been ruined by alcohol, syphilis and journalism – which was in Mussolini's case somewhat hypocritical since he too suffered from syphilis, had been a journalist and enjoyed drinking. On 14 May Ciano travelled to Genoa, where Mussolini in his speeches adopted a belligerent approach, probably induced by an over-indulgence of confidence inspired by his German visitor and his projections for the future. He told his audience that 'when Italy is united it cannot be anything but an empire. When it is an empire it can only dominate others. From today's enthusiasm I am convinced that the Italian nation is not tired, on the contrary, it is ready for a new assault.'[120] It could have been no surprise to Ciano that four days later Lord Perth was back in Ciano's chambers, expressing the unease which the speech had caused in London and elsewhere. The British, Perth explained, had hoped that Europe would not divide itself into two blocs based on ideologies, referring to the possible French rapprochement which the Genoa speech might have delayed.

RUMOURS AND MACHINATIONS

A few days later Perth returned again, expressing concern over the rumours regarding Czechoslovakia, the Sudetenland problem and the Bohemian Germans, all by-products of the Versailles Treaty. He said the French had an agreement with the Czechs, and in a diplomatic hint to Ciano pointed out that England and France were close, but stated that Britain would not involve itself in any conflict. It was apparent from Perth's meeting that Mussolini's infamous Genoa speech had created a coolness towards Italy in British and French circles. Ciano and Perth must have both known that despite the courtesies of diplomatic exchanges they were probably sitting on a time-bomb. Perth was not the only visitor voicing concern about the future; when the Romanian Zanfirescu expressed his views Ciano noted he was empty and pompous, and wrote 'of all the diplomats the Romanians are the biggest liars'. This sharp comment underlined his assumption that diplomacy was a game only for the 'big-boys'. Ciano was concerned that following Hitler's visit and its implications of an alliance might bring Eden back as a possible prime minister, especially in May when he heard of the problems in the Sudetenland. He noted that these events gave him a sense that the matter is 'ripening, slowly and inexorably'.[121] The use of the word 'ripening' instead of 'deteriorating' gives the impression that for Ciano this was almost exciting, and Mussolini expressed no concern, apparently believing that France would not go to war over the issue. Ciano observed that the French press were not helping, and was critical of the Germans for not keeping him in touch; near the end of the month he observed that Mussolini seemed more pessimistic about the possibility of war, indicating that despite his outright belligerence he was not entirely convinced that war would be the right direction. Hitler's visit followed by Mussolini's belligerent speeches dominated May 1938 and set the cat amongst the pigeons, with every country in Europe wondering where it stood in relationship to others, and who trusted whom.

During June, in the rare moments when Ciano was not enjoying himself on the beach, he was wheeling and dealing, especially with Lord Perth, over claims and counterclaims. It was well known by foreign diplomats and Italians that Ciano preferred the beach for meetings, and he could often be found at the bar of the Acquasanta Golf Club, where the *crème de la crème* tended to meet and gossip. This social gossip was more than capable of carrying dangerous implications, and it has been noted that 'Ciano repeatedly leaked Axis decisions to friends known to be in direct contact with the British authorities'.[122] Whether at the beach, in the club or within his office the main points of contention revolved around the Spanish conflict. The Italians pretended to be cooperating with the British requests for non-involvement, yet both sides knew that Mussolini was in total support of Franco. Lurking behind this issue was the dark shadow of the Italian–German relationship, making many countries nervous as each watched the comings and goings like twitchy neighbours or greedy vultures.

On 9 June Mussolini decided to increase the strength of his reserves in Spain, and it was not surprising that Ciano wrote in his diary that 'relations with Great Britain have not become what we had hoped'.[123] He heard from Grandi in London that 'the situation was darkening', but Mussolini remained unperturbed, telling Ciano that if Chamberlain fell it was only a matter of watching who replaced him. Grandi was correct, and the British continued to be furious at the attacks on their ships by a nation with whom they had signed a pact; for many British, this was a worthless piece of paper, and they were proved to be correct.

Ambassador Phillips appeared with an American guest, McAneny,* about whom Ciano was cynical. Ciano wrote in his diary 'I played, as best I could, the tune of pacifism and collaboration. Without much conviction but with emphasis. Phillips was very happy'.[124] This particular comment underlines Ciano's hypocrisy and double-dealing, and if he carried out the speculated total revision of his diaries he either missed this or did not consider it important, or the revision was far from comprehensive.

The Germans were aware of the diplomatic comings and goings, with Ciano always informing von Mackensen of what was said, especially with the British, noting that every now and then he felt obliged to do this because 'these Germans need an injection of trust in us'. The Italian public remained uncertain about the German relationship, not least Balbo, whom Ciano described as 'acid and hostile to everything', constantly speaking derisively about the Germans, defending the Jews, and being critical of the Roman salute. Had Balbo been a German citizen he would not have survived under Hitler, and there are hints that Mussolini would have preferred him removed.

Between the beach and his office Ciano continued to plot the possible occupation of Albania. He met an Albanian called Giro who was head of the Working Men's Club in Albania; Ciano, knowing that the working classes were unhappy about their king and 'his thugs', used Giro to help stir up feelings of discontent. A week later Ciano was busy organising grain to be sent to Albania, which was suffering from a harsh famine; by his own admission it was not from altruistic motives, but a gift from the Italians that the 'ordinary Albanians' would most appreciate. A week later he met the Italian politician Natale Prampolini, who was going to Albania to study land reclamation, and informed him of the 'political objectives'. He did not expound on this in his diary, but it takes little imagination to understand his intentions. During the next month, August, Prampolini would return with the news that there was plenty of land which could be turned over to food production, but rumours were already accumulating about Italy's intentions.

July started with renewed tensions over the Anglo-Italian pact, with constant visits from Lord Perth regarding Italy's support of Franco. It was clear that a warmer relationship had developed between Perth and Ciano, and he noted that 'Lord Perth expressed all the heartbreak he felt at this moment' that the British public would be disappointed, and he left the room looking depressed.[125] Perth returned with a list of formal requests from the British government, the most pertinent stating that 'it was clearly laid down in the documents exchanged in April that the British government considers the settlement of the Spanish question as a condition *sine qua non*[*] [of entering] into force the Anglo-Italian pact.'[126] Mussolini and Ciano were evidently breaking all their promises and affirmations about Spain, and this could not be concealed, making the April pact a mere diplomatic game. Nearer the end of the month, as Perth informed Ciano he was taking annual leave, he forlornly expressed his hope that the Italians would place a rigid embargo on men and arms to Spain.

If the British and French were uneasy about German developments and Italian machinations, this was also true in central Europe and the Balkans. The Hungarian prime minister, Béla Imrédy, had an interview with Mussolini with Ciano present.[†] Imrédy expressed concern over Yugoslavia and raised the possible revision of the Treaty of Trianon. This had been signed at the Grand Trianon Palace in Versailles in June 1920 and had generally defined Hungary's borders at the point of ceasefire; it had diminished the Hungarian population to the benefit of Romania, Czechoslovakia and Yugoslavia. This irredentist Hungarian nationalistic impulse, encouraged by Hitler with his possible reclamation of territory, had not only raised fears but also some hopes in Hungary and elsewhere. Mussolini suggested that Hungary would have to react with speed, but it was essential there be no conflict between Hungary and Yugoslavia. All parts of Europe were nervous about the future.

MUSSOLINI: CHURCH AND JEWS

For much of the summer Ciano was not feeling well, and at the end of July was confined to bed with tonsillitis. He was not the only sick member of his family, as his daughter had to undergo an operation on her ear. In his diary he rarely mentioned his family unless something important had occurred. On 4 June while unwell at home he heard Mussolini's speech on the radio, noting that when he heard his voice 'I began to cry like a baby'. This curious statement seemed to underline that at this stage he felt some affection for Mussolini, not just familial but a genuine love. It was becoming clear during July that Mussolini was again on the warpath, criticising the French, raising the subject of Jews, preparing the Italians for war, and ensuring their support of him as leader.

Although Mussolini was fundamentally an atheist, he had come to terms with the Vatican, but suddenly started an attack on what was called 'Catholic Action'.[‡] Back in 1925 he had realised that he needed the support of the Catholic Church, and on 11 February 1929, after three years of negotiations, signed the Lateran

---

[*]   '*sine qua non*' is a necessary condition without which the rest cannot happen.
[†]   Béla Imrédy later suggested a Hungarian government based on totalitarian lines; at the end of the war he was found guilty of war crimes and collaborating with the Nazis, and was executed in Marko Jail, Budapest, in 1946.
[‡]   This was a group of lay Catholics intent on spreading Church influence.

Pact with Pope Pius XI. However, by 1931 the Pope had issued the Encyclical *We Do Not Need*, which tended to focus on an attack against the pagan worship of the state. As with the monarchy, Mussolini had to live with the Vatican, which he deeply resented, but in the following month he continued with his monthly tirades against the Catholic Church. He remained irritated by Catholic Action, and 'angry' about the Pope, threatening to unleash a wave of anti-clericalism to a nation which 'has had great difficulty in swallowing a Jewish God', and according to Ciano repeating his theory that 'Catholicism was a paganisation of Christianity'.[127]

Ciano met Father Tacchi-Venturi, a Jesuit priest who was the official intermediary between the Pope and Mussolini. Ciano was less rancorous about the Church than was his master, and after this conversation he thought that with some goodwill there should be no problems. However, in mid-August the Pope made what was, as far as the fascists were concerned, a disagreeable speech on 'exaggerated nationalism and racism'. This may have been welcomed by the more discerning, but Tacchi-Venturi was sent for by Mussolini, who threatened that he would 'destroy the church'. Again, Ciano expressed a hope that this current bout of friction would soon end. As this conflict developed the Pope sent his Papal Nuncio, Francesco Borgongini-Duca, to Mussolini, seeking a resolution. Ciano sat in on the conversation with his inimitable style of feigned friendship, and managed to make his guest tell them more about the Pope. Borgongini-Duca was evidently not a good envoy, however, because he complained that the Pope was 'too authoritarian, awful, and often insolent'. He further claimed that the Pope even treated his most distinguished cardinals as mere secretaries, including Cardinal Pacelli (who was to become Pius XII), and complained that the Pope, 82 years old, was still insisting on running the Church down to the smallest detail (in 21st-century parlance, micromanaging). Mussolini had recognised that he needed to come to terms with the Vatican, but as with the monarchy he detested its members, not least because of their inclination to criticise him.

Mussolini was also launching himself into a series of racial tirades, ordering the burning of writings by Jews and Masons, and any Francophile works. It was of course an unpleasant reflection of Nazism, especially when Mussolini proclaimed that 'Italians must learn to be less sympathetic, to become hard, implacable, hateful: i.e., masters'.[128] Grasping the moment, Ribbentrop sent the Prince of Hesse to apply more pressure on Mussolini to join a German military alliance.

Mussolini's effort to ingratiate himself with Hitler led him and therefore Ciano down a route which would not normally have grasped their attention, namely the infamous question of anti-Semitism. Laws forbidding intermarriage and prohibiting Jewish people working in various professions were projected, and Mussolini went so far as to suggest that Italian Jewish populations should be removed to countries with large spaces, such as Brazil, Russia and the United States. This was a strange and significant change of attitude for a man who used to deride the 'anti-Semitic drivel' of the Germans. During 1938 his focus was changing, undoubtedly in line with currying Nazi favour. He warned his cabinet that it was necessary to introduce racial matters, and if the left wing had Jews there would be a tendency for a wave of anti-Semitism to arise, as with Prime Minister Léon Blum in France, the first Jew to hold this position. As mentioned earlier, Ciano did not appear to like Jews, suffering from the then usual social bigotry of not wanting them in his golf club, but he was not a rabid anti-Semitic.

As a matter of curiosity Italy had less than 50,000 Jews, which made them some 0.1 per cent of the population, and in that country they were amongst the most integrated in the whole of Europe. Nevertheless, 'a latent element of anti-Semitism did exist in Italy, especially on the Catholic right, and a smattering of prejudice lurked in the minds of many Italians.'[129] The *Protocols of the Elders of Zion* was widely circulating in Italy, as in many other countries.* However, there were also many mixed marriages, with some Jews sitting on the fascist Grand Council. It has been claimed that a third of the Jews were fascist, and some 229 certificates had been awarded to Jews for participating in the March on Rome. Nor could Mussolini forget that 'four of the seven founders of Italian nationalism were Jewish.'[130] In 1933, after the rise of Nazism, Mussolini had granted asylum in Italy to fleeing German Jews. However, within a mere few years he was seeking Hitler's goodwill, and on July 1938 Mussolini announced a Charter of Race, an anti-Semitic paper stipulating that Jews who had arrived after 1919 were to be expelled from all professions, and that their children were to be taught in segregated schools.† Ciano claimed it was a mild policy, and it appears he was less strident than Mussolini, but as usual was subservient to his master's demands. On 24 July he noted that 'the Jews were the leaders of anti-fascism and were therefore to be suppressed along with it', written to go with the flow of Mussolini as he pandered to the Germans whom he had once found distasteful. Mussolini was endorsing the nonsensical belief of Aryanism and believed that the Italians were part of this so-called ethnic strand.

Ciano's birthplace of Livorno was the area with the largest number of Jewish residents. Mussolini demanded that all Jews were to be removed from the diplomatic service, but from available evidence it appeared that leading Jews did not regard Ciano as overly vociferous in this anti-Semitism. Later, during the war years, it has been claimed that Ciano was behind the resistance to have

---

* This was a fabricated anti-Semitic text plagiarised from earlier sources and published in Russia about 1903, and widely believed by those who were prejudiced against Jewish people.

† Later in 1941 Mussolini tried to prevent Christmas because it was a celebration of a 'Jew who gave to the world debilitating and devitalising theories'.

Jews removed from their small area of occupied France to be 'sent east', but this remains unconfirmed and is questionable.

Anti-Semitism was and is a wicked form of racism beyond reason or redemption; at the time it was widely prevalent, ranging from English golf clubs through to the Nazi liquidation camps, and with a long unfortunate history in Europe. Mussolini was not an extreme anti-Semitic in Nazi terms, and probably exaggerated his usual social bigotry to please Hitler. In his subservient way Ciano followed Mussolini, but his attitudes remain ambivalent. On 3 August foreign Jews were banned from schools, and although Mussolini later welcomed the news of the Nazi Kristallnacht, he retracted much of his approval when he realised that Italian public opinion was against such brutality. Later in the year, when anti-Semitic legislation would be promulgated, somewhat similar to the Nuremberg Race Laws, it was not well received by everyone; for example, Farinacci wanted his secretary, Jole Foà (who was Jewish), exempted even though he (Farinacci) was personally otherwise rabidly anti-Semitic. The Prince of Hesse later approached Ciano on the Jewish question on behalf of the queen of Italy, who was worried that she might lose her Jewish Doctor Stuckjold. Ciano's response was all too cynical; he informed his German visitor 'that the Führer would not appreciate that such a mission was entrusted to him, a German and a Nazi. [The Prince of Hesse] turned pale'.[131]

The anti-Semitic policy grew to unpleasant proportions and the Charter of Race or Racial Manifesto (Italian: *Manifesto della razza*) of 14 July had been the preparation for the enactment of laws to be published in November 1938; this clearly demonstrated Hitler's influence over Mussolini, as prior to this there had been no race laws in Italy. It has been alleged that there was a secret pact made with the Vatican not to criticise the anti-Semitic measures, but this is dubious, and the Pope had expressed reservations. It was even claimed that Italians were descendants of the Aryan race, which encouraged thoughtless Italians to be racist. Many others, including some Italian fascists, never appreciated biological racism, and many of these racial rules were met by the disapproval of men like Balbo. The king had objected, but Mussolini persisted – and even ordered the anti-Semitic campaign to be conducted in Tunisia.

When challenged once by a fascist friend, Mussolini agreed he was not a believer in this form of racist thinking but did it for political reasons (as if that justified his actions). How far Mussolini was anti-Semitic is difficult to fathom; it is generally believed he was pandering to the Nazis, but the claim that he protected Jews from Nazi oppression because of humanitarian reasons or as a way of standing up to Hitler remains ambiguous. 'The official line adopted in "legal Italy" was not always followed in "real Italy." Whatever the case may have been among Germans, the Italians showed few signs of being the "willing executioners of Jews." '[132] It seems possible that Mussolini and Ciano had failed to understand the horrendous ramifications of Nazi anti-Semitism. There is a hint of confusion, and although the year 1938 had these anti-Semitic overtones, which carried through to 1939, thereafter it tended to quieten down. It was certainly safer to be a Jew in Italy than in Germany because in Italy there was no governmental intention of liquidating them.

It is curious that in his diary when these measures became law Ciano noted that 'naturally the law, which is very harsh against the Jews, will pass tomorrow as planned.'[133] Equally curious was that when Achille Starace, secretary of the Fascist Party, wanted all Jews expelled from the party Mussolini objected; it is inconceivable, of course, that Hitler would have made any exceptions. Ciano raised the issue of a Jew married to an Aryan wife, who under the laws would be treated as inferior even to his own children. Here is yet another hint that for Ciano this anti-Semitism was a matter of political expediency.

THE DIPLOMATIC MACHINATIONS CONTINUE

For the first week of August Ciano was still unwell, but he recovered and had an easy month, his diary indicating that most of his time was spent on the beach and on holiday with his family in Venice. The British *chargé d'affaires* and the Russians knew where to find him as he enjoyed his leisure time by the sea. Lord Perth was on leave and Sir Noel Charles, taking his place, was continuing to express British concerns about Italian activities in Spain, which Ciano avoided, claiming he must speak to the Duce. Ciano realised that the British knew the facts, but he tried to explain that his 'volunteers could not fight waving olive branches at their attackers'. After their first meeting Ciano claimed that Sir Noel Charles in his personal capacity considered the Italian actions both 'logical and sensible'.[134] This statement was recorded in his diplomatic papers, but whether the British representative meant this or was being overly polite is difficult to understand or verify. Perhaps he would not have confided such thoughts had he known Ciano's propensity to record everything, even when conversations took place on the beach. The ambiguity was probably caused by the usual British ploy of politeness, and the main issue for the British was to remove Italy from German influence. Sir Noel Charles was equally concerned about Czechoslovakia, but although Ciano brushed this aside, the question of Czechoslovakia was constantly lurking in the background, with Ciano picking up rumours that the Germans were keeping Italy in the dark, as they always would.

Ciano was constantly busy with plans to occupy Albania. It was apparent that he had shared his feelings with too many people, because rumours were rife about his intentions to invade a country which the Italians already dominated. He demanded that a Lieutenant-Colonel Mondini, their military attaché in Greece, should keep an eye on the borders in case the Greeks caused problems when the Italians occupied Albania. He studied plans for a new sports club complex in Tirana, all part of his effort to bring the Albanian population on side. It was by now apparent that Albania was Ciano's personal plan, and all he needed to do was convince Mussolini of it.

RUMOURS ABOUT CZECHOSLOVAKIA

The most disturbing rumour of the summer related to the German intentions regarding Czechoslovakia. Ciano was picking up fragments from the Italian embassy in Berlin, and of course he and Mussolini were still feeling angry that the Germans never corresponded with them. Ambassador Phillips, before returning to America, was asking Ciano for his estimation of the problem, and although Ciano was able to indicate Italy's view on the subject, he knew little more than the speculations of the other bewildered international diplomats. Given the way gossip abounded in Italy, the Germans were alert to this problem.

On 28 September 1938 Hitler presented his ultimatum to Czechoslovakia, and there was panic in the diplomatic dovecotes. A few hoped that Mussolini could broker a deal avoiding conflict, many still regarding him as a person with whom the democracies could work, and this undoubtedly flattered him. From the beginning of the month Konrad Henlein, the leader of the Germans in the Sudetenland, had been stirring up trouble after his visit to Berchtesgaden, and Hitler was clearly indicating his intransigent attitude towards Czechoslovakia.

Nearly everyone wanted peace, whatever the cost. At the beginning of the month *The Times* had published a leading article which had created a sensation because it gave the impression that Britain had abandoned the notion of Czechoslovakia's territorial integrity.[135] The Belgian ambassador suggested to Ciano that he was proposing that Czechoslovakia should commit suicide; this was becoming the prevailing attitude across Europe, if only to try and stop a major war.

This was the dominating issue on the diplomatic front across Europe and beyond. However, in Italy Mussolini and Ciano were more engaged, as always, with Franco's conduct of the war in Spain, and the so-called Italian empire; General Ugo Cavallero sent a report that he expected all revolts in the empire to be crushed by Christmas. He also suggested that with more troops he would soon be able to take Egypt and even seize Aden from the British; Hitler appeared as the bully boy, but Mussolini had his own ambitions. In internal matters he was preparing the Council of Ministers to take measures against foreign Jews.

Ciano, in an obsequious fashion, extolled Mussolini, writing that 'the Duce, when he believes it necessary, has the courage to be unpopular, and he ends up being right'.[136] As noted above, Ciano's diary was known to Mussolini, who often referred to it as 'your book', and again there is a hint that Ciano was aware that one day Mussolini might ask to read his observations.

The Spanish question and anti-Semitism may have dominated Mussolini's mind, but it was the threat of war over Czechoslovakia that occupied the minds of those in the rest of Europe. As early as 5 September Ciano openly expressed his annoyance at the Germans for not keeping to their agreement to keep him and Mussolini informed. He had received little information from Bernardo Attolico (the Italian ambassador to Germany); and even the Prince of Hesse, when asked, replied that what he did know he could not disclose. He soon, however, returned with the news that Hitler could not specify his programme, but he would attack if the Czechs provoked him. Hitler suggested that he and Mussolini could meet at the Brenner, which Mussolini welcomed – but he then demonstrated his own importance by answering that he was too busy for the moment, touring the country giving political speeches.

There was a palpable and growing degree of uneasiness around Europe, and Grandi in London contacted Ciano on behalf of Chamberlain to ask if Mussolini could consider talking to Hitler, seeking a more moderate approach. Mussolini poured scorn on the request, claiming that the English 'had unbalanced hormones', and obsequiously told Ciano to let the Germans know that if they needed any more favours, to inform him.

The Yugoslavian Bochko Christich arrived on 13 September, asking where Italy stood if war came, stating that Yugoslavia would want to stay neutral, standing alongside Italy. It was a predictable response of many in Europe: whatever happened, they wanted to stay neutral. Within weeks Franco would be making the same move, but Henlein was becoming more proactive, claiming that he wanted the Germans in the Sudetenland to 'return to the bosom of the Reich'. France started a partial mobilisation, the British moved their fleet around and, as Ciano later noted, 'there is the smell of war in the air'.

On 22 September the Hungarian minister arrived, and according to Ciano he was full of unctuous congratulations on the role the Duce was playing. The Hungarian referred to their claims on retrieving their populations lost in the Trianon Treaty (referred to earlier), pointing out that Hitler had also encouraged this wish, which was not surprising. The Romanian minister arrived on the same day, and after a tussle over press attacks and the Romanians being asked by the Russians for free transit for their troops, Ciano concluded by congratulating the minister for being free of the Little Entente. The Romanian was followed by the

German ambassador, who expressed Hitler's gratitude for the Duce's support, and announced that Attolico would be contacting Ciano with the items that Hitler wanted Mussolini to mention in his speeches; all part of the Italian subservience.

The British Ambassador Lord Perth, back from leave, informed Ciano that the French would support Czechoslovakia and that Britain would probably follow the French, but that Chamberlain had done his best to maintain peace. Ciano replied that Mussolini also wanted a solution, but one which bore in mind the situation for the Hungarians, thus indicating that Italy was in support of the German demands. Lord Perth had been asked by the British government to contact Ciano in the hope that the Italians might use their influence to resolve the impending issues, and everyone was trying to find out if Ciano knew more than he did, even the French and Russians contacting him while he was enjoying the beach again. Perth also brought Chamberlain's personal good wishes and news of the implementation of the Italian–British treaty.

News of the German reactions became unsettling, and Ciano gathered that Hitler had found Chamberlain's suggestions too vague. Hitler had responded in a four-part statement with his demands, and followed this with an ultimatum to the Czechoslovakian Edvard Beneš, with the sinister threat that if there were no response by 1 October Germany would attack. On 27 September Mussolini ordered mobilisation to form a basis of what he expressed as 'armed neutrality'. Ciano noted that there was nothing new on the 'diplomatic chessboard', as if the waves of fear sweeping across Europe were irrelevant. Since he had been elevated to the position of foreign secretary he had treated many of his meetings as chess, involving cunning and deceit; clearly his job was for him almost entertainment at times as he tried to elevate himself to Grandmaster status. It would not be long, however, before he realised that this version of chess had deadly consequences.

Lord Perth phoned Ciano with a request from Chamberlain that Mussolini should be approached with an official request to act as a mediator. Mussolini's immediate response was to reject the suggestion, and he asked Attolico to let Hitler know that he always stood by his side. Hitler, however, responded in favour of the suggestion, and Perth was cheered by the prospect of a meeting of the four leaders of Germany, Italy, France, and Britain, which would take place in Munich; Hitler, meanwhile, was happy so long as Mussolini was present. Ciano arrogantly warned Lord Perth to make sure the French behaved themselves, which Perth, in his hope for peace agreed with, at least to Ciano.

MUNICH CRISIS AND MORE IRREDENTISM

Ciano enjoyed his trip to Munich with Mussolini, who obsessively talked about English demographics, observing that Britain had 4 million excess women. At the formal part of the meeting Ciano was pleased to note that when Hitler with his entourage arrived, they gave Mussolini and himself a very warm welcome, whereas Chamberlain and the French prime minister, Daladier, received 'cold handshakes'. During the meeting Ciano watched Mussolini saunter around the room, unable to bear 'the almost parliamentary discussions' describing him as 'a great genius'. In a private conversation with the talkative Daladier, Ciano gathered that the way the meeting was heading when Daladier confided to him that the problem was down to Beneš, who was proving 'obstinate'.

The well-known Munich Agreement ended with, in Ciano's words, 'signing, handshakes, departures'. On the way back to Rome Mussolini was, according to Ciano, greeted by adulation, from the peasants to the king, greater than he had experienced before. This praise was because Mussolini was regarded as the mediator who had accomplished peace in Europe. Mussolini had managed to appear in what he regarded as a lead role on the international stage – which of course we can see now was sheer nonsense. Unquestionably both Mussolini and Ciano enjoyed their sudden important international status, Mussolini had emerged as the peacemaker of Europe, but the playboy Ciano was never far away, and according to the SS officer Eugen Dollmann,* Ciano asked him to show him the nightlife of Munich![137]

They had barely arrived home when Ribbentrop sent Ciano the projected plans for a new tripartite alliance which he claimed would be 'the greatest thing in the world'. Mussolini and Ciano basked in their perceived success, but the Germans saw it as an act of confirmation that the Italians were prepared for war. Mussolini's pandering to Hitler had worked, Ciano was pleased. Both would at different times come to regret this development.

October was dominated by German pressure for the Italians to join the Tripartite Alliance, and by the rumblings created by irredentist claims to the east of Czechoslovakia and elsewhere by Hungary and Poland, which had been encouraged by the German success in the Sudetenland crisis. As a brief introductory oversight, this would result in what is sometimes called the Vienna Agreement (or Award, or Diktat). These claims arose because of the multi-ethnic territory divisions caused by the Trianon Treaty; as mentioned earlier, Hungary had lost considerable swathes of its population, but in addition claims were made that the Magyars were left in isolated pockets outside their own country. All these machinations involved the question of natural resources and an inflated sense of nationalistic importance. In brief, Hungary regained part of Czechoslovakia known as the First Vienna Award

---

* Dollmann always acted as Ciano's interpreter, when available, on his visits to Germany. Dollmann could hardly conceal his contempt of Ciano, and Ciano thought Dollmann 'lacked zeal'. See Salter Michael, *Nazi War Crimes, US Intelligence & Selective Prosecution at Nuremberg* (Oxford: Routledge-Cavendish, 2007) pp.68 and 71.

in 1938, and again in 1939. The Hungarians had especially resented that most of Transylvania had been ceded to Romania. The Second Vienna Award (better known as the Diktat) was settled in 1940, when much of northern Transylvania was removed from Romania and awarded to Hungary.

The Trianon Treaty had created these problems, but the emergence of the successful German action in September and October 1938 precipitated this renewed sense of irredentist nationalism, with Germany and Italy regarded as the powerbrokers. The treaty had done nothing except worsen relations between Hungary and Romania. (Eventually, in the 1947 Paris Peace Treaties, the borders between Romania and Hungary were reaffirmed according to the delineations defined by the Treaty of Trianon nearly three decades before.)

Ciano assisted the Hungarians in their irredentist claims that parts of Czechoslovakia should be returned, which eventuated in closer relationships between Horthy's Hungary, Mussolini, and ostensibly Nazi Germany. On one occasion Paul Schmidt watched Ribbentrop and Ciano with large maps spread out, drawing new borders: 'seldom have I been so acutely aware of the contrast between the light-hearted decisions taken by statesmen ... and the consequences of their decisions in terms of the everyday life in the territories affected'.[138]

This seemingly effortless changing of territories prompted Mussolini and Ciano to look avariciously towards portions of French territory; this was naïve of them, and arrogant. When the new French Ambassador André Françoise-Poncet arrived in Rome, it was to hear that Ciano, undoubtedly prompted by Mussolini, was proposing to make a demand for some French territories, such as Tunisia, Corsica, Savoy and Nice, to the Chamber of Deputies. The sell-out of Czechoslovakia and all the potential dangers now preoccupied the powers of Europe and raised a degree of anxious curiosity across the world.

First Vienna Award. Ciano and Ribbentrop in centre
(Naučný slovnik Aktualit 1939)

Therefore, during October Ciano was continuously occupied by those seeking help over territorial claims. On the first day of the month, just after Munich, Jócef Beck, the Polish foreign minister, was demanding the return of land, with Ciano noting that the Poles were 'intransigent because they had not been invited to Munich'. Times were changing, because Hitler had demonstrated that it was possible to adjust borders without a major conflict. By 10 October the Hungarians claimed they were considering mobilisation, but Ciano found this difficult to believe. Mussolini told Ciano to put pressure on Prague, especially in relation to the areas where the Magyars were in the majority. This activity created tensions between Prague and Hungary, which had gone on to a war footing, bringing Count Czaky, a Hungarian politician, to Ciano's desk asking for a four-power conference as had happened in Munich. It does not seem to have crossed Ciano's mind that the Munich Agreement had unleashed a crescendo of irredentist nationalism. Ciano was inclined to agree with a four-power conference, but not in Berlin, and Mussolini and Ciano realised that in this new climate no one dared upset the Germans. Therefore, when the Polish Villani was back, asking for the Axis to help in the Poles' claims, Ciano noted that 'the Duce agrees, but advises to feel Germany's pulse before inviting Poland'.[139] On 22 October Ribbentrop made contact by phone, wanting to discuss the Hungarian claims, with their proposal for an Axis arbitration after he had consulted the Führer. Ciano explained that he and Mussolini were happy but would not move until Germany and Italy agreed.[140] Ribbentrop suggested he come to Rome, which Mussolini was prepared for, warning Ciano that Ribbentrop 'had a very small brain'. This would have been music to Ciano's ears, making it tempting for him to wonder if he had put these words into Mussolini's mouth to please himself.

Ribbentrop's machinations

When Ribbentrop arrived, the discussions over the projected Vienna agreements were brief, and Mussolini, always fond of the Hungarians, was pleased. According to Ciano 'he predicted a period of relaxation in Europe'. He was not alone in this, with Chamberlain's well-known cry, 'Peace in our time'. Politicians across the borders and boundaries of Europe were behaving like schoolboys, arguing over who owned which part of the playing fields, with no consideration for the people who lived there or for the dangerous consequences for the future. The rampant irredentist claims released by Hitler were volatile because they gave a sense of justification, and were always leading to further aggressive expansionism.

Ribbentrop was pressing for the proposed Tripartite Agreement between Germany, Japan and Italy. Mussolini, possibly at Ciano's suggestion, demurred for a time, explaining that he needed wider support. It was clear to Mussolini that

Ciano was not entirely happy with the proposal, finding the Germans, especially Ribbentrop, arrogant in their demands and manners. On 27 October the Japanese were knocking at Ciano's door, applying their form of pressure for the alliance. The pressure was continuous, but Ciano was conscious that the British pact was close to being signed, and he wanted 'to keep both doors open' in this game of diplomatic chess he was playing.

During the 28 October consultation between Mussolini and Ribbentrop, with Ciano present, the German foreign minister explained Hitler's thinking about the future. Hitler based his forecast on the premise that within a few years the Axis would be at war with France and Britain, and that the USA would do its best to avoid conflict, especially with the Japanese threat. Hitler also believed that those who sought peace in Britain would become weaker. Ribbentrop explained that the Munich Agreement had demonstrated Axis power, and that 'Czechoslovakia was virtually liquidated' – an unpleasant phrase which should have rung warning bells.[141] Mussolini tended to agree with Hitler's forecasts, but replied he had to establish full public support, especially from the bourgeoise middle class (whose opinion he was known to ignore).

At the end of the month Mussolini wrote to Hitler with a provisional acceptance. Ciano noted, correctly, that Ribbentrop wanted a war which did not specify the enemy or objectives, and Ciano had done his best to 'kick him for touch'. Ciano believed that the British were about to implement the April pact, and he had cunningly used a Spanish–Italian agreement to return troops as a way of proving to Lord Perth that the Italians were making a serious effort, demonstrating Italian willingness to fulfil obligations over the pact. He met Perth, only to have the British ambassador ask questions about aircraft, but Ciano asked him 'not to raise more difficulties'.

Sereggi arrived again, on behalf of King Zog, who was evidently concerned about the rumours of Italy's intentions in Albania. Sereggi conveyed the king's concern that Albania was virtually under Italy's control, and that although the people were grateful, and the king was devoted to Italy, he was asking the nervous question as to what more did the Italians want? Ciano pretended he 'was affable', as he obviously brushed the Albanian concerns aside. Two weeks later Ciano held a meeting with General Jacomoni, the Italian minister to Albania, impressing on him that speed was essential because of the growing alarm in the Albanian court, and there was even some discussion about the possible assassination of King Zog. Mussolini had already made some veiled public statements to his fascist colleagues about possible intentions in Albania, and Zog's apprehension came as no surprise.

TO VIENNA

At the beginning of November Ciano travelled to Vienna to hold further discussions on the irredentist claims by Hungary. He passed through Innsbruck, suffering from the loss of its tourist trade, and the next day his destination was Vienna. There he first met Göring in civilian dress bedecked with large jewels, who, according to Ciano, 'vaguely resembled Al Capone'. He discovered that Göring had no love for the Hungarians, believing they were in cahoots with the West, and on meeting Ribbentrop heard he tended to be in favour of the Czechs. The next day they met the Slovaks, who Ciano thought presented their case better than had Hungary. In the end, either Ciano managed to persuade Ribbentrop to change his mind, or Hitler had instructed Ribbentrop not to upset the Italians, and the deal was signed.

The Hungarian minister brought Ciano a present of a statue of Hercules as a courteous bribe before he mentioned that there were problems of disorder in Ruthenia, which was a critical area for Hungary's unity. Sensing that the Hungarians were ready to act, Ciano advised against any premature reactions. Only nine days later, when he was out hunting, his head of cabinet office, Filippo Anfuso, called and informed him that Mussolini had accepted Hungary's request for 100 planes, on the grounds that Germany was happy for this – which Ciano immediately knew was a 'pack of lies'. He rushed back to put a halt to the transaction, telling Mussolini what was happening, who then phoned Berlin to explain.

Although after the Munich Agreement there was still hope of peace, for the more astute there was also a fear of instability due to the precarious nature of the relationships between the great powers. This was not helped by Mussolini's distaste for France, and since 1936, when Ambassador Chambrun had been recalled, there had been no diplomatic links between France and Italy, and any sense of a détente between the two countries seemed unlikely. It was therefore a placatory move by the French when they asked André François-Poncet, their Berlin ambassador, to move to Rome. It was somewhat unfortunate that he arrived on the very day Ernst vom Rath was assassinated.* François-Poncet explained to Ciano, when they met, that French public feeling mainly veered towards the Republicans, then asked Ciano if he considered some sort of armistice possible, but Ciano explained that Franco would not agree to this and that the Italians backed Franco. From this, François-Poncet knew that the Spanish war would always be a problem.

Within days Ciano received a letter from Grandi in London, mentioning the signing of the Anglo-Italian Pact on 16 November, and reminding Ciano of what

---

* Ernst vom Rath was a German diplomat assassinated in Paris by a Polish Jewish teenager to avenge his parents; the immediate repercussion was Kristallnacht, the Night of Broken Glass. As a matter of sheer curiosity, vom Rath was being checked by the Gestapo for opposing anti-Semitism.

Italy required from France, and of the difficulties with that country. The main problems, which Mussolini would announce later to his Chamber of Deputies, involved Tunisia, Corsica, Djibouti and the excessive payments on the Suez Canal by the Canal Company, the last of which even the British complained about, demanding a revision of the tariffs.* It was evident that there was little likelihood of any form of rapprochement between Italy and France. When on 29 November Mussolini met François-Poncet, Ciano wrote that the 'reception was glacial'.

Mainly due to Lord Perth's persistent efforts the British relationship was to result in the formal signing of the April Pact in mid-November, when Perth arrived with the necessary credentials 'directed to the King Emperor', and according to Ciano Lord Perth was quite emotional. For Perth this had been an exhausting effort, but he knew that the main issue was the attempt to entice Italy out from the German sphere of influence, which the more realistic recognised as unlikely. Lord Perth also suggested that Chamberlain and Lord Halifax wanted to visit Italy, again with the idea of cementing this friendship; Mussolini was somewhat reluctant, but Ciano managed to persuade him.

In the meantime, Albania watched and waited to see what the Italians planned; this was more the initiative and project of Ciano, and he admitted in his diary entry of 14 November that 'the Duce, for a long time, has had reservations about Albania'. Later Ciano would be blamed for the invasion of Albania, with good reason. In a hypocritical moment Mussolini expressed concern about the German violence against the clergy, treating its members as they did Jews; it seemed to dawn on him that this behaviour gave the Axis a poor reputation overseas. On 23 November Ciano was pleased that Italy had also signed a cultural pact with Germany, to open the doors to Italian culture – but in the week before he had added a telling comment to his diary that 'the Germans have liked us, without respecting us. We have respected them, without liking them'.[142] This revelatory view by Ciano in late 1938 was setting the stage upon which he would strut.

THE EUROPEAN ORCHESTRA

Ciano ended the month with his nationalistic address to the National Assembly on international matters, focusing on Italy's demand for consolidation. He knew he had provoked powerful sentiments from his fascist peers when they rose, shouting 'Tunis, Djibouti, Corsica!', all of them places under French control.†

---

* Djibouti, a major port in East Africa, was considered essential for the Italian Empire but administered by the French.

† Monelli (a journalist friend of Ciano's) returned from Corsica, warning that there were no irredentist feelings in Corsica. In 1767 the Republic of Genoa had sold Corsica to France, ceding all rights in the 1768 Treaty of Versailles. It had been incorporated into the French state in 1789, and by that time its population felt they were French.

Ciano was pleased with himself, as he thought the speech demonstrated that the Axis had objectives which were not solely German, and Mussolini was happy for the 1935 French–Italian agreement to collapse.

Two days later François-Poncet was back, demanding an explanation of the excited eruptions caused by Ciano's speech. It was a typically polite conversation, with Ciano noting that François-Poncet appeared cordial as Ciano explained that they could not control such outbursts and protesting there was nothing provocative in his speech (which was blatantly untrue; it had been a series of threats against France which almost amounted to blackmail). In some ways these attacks were merely theoretical, and Ciano knew there were no signs of irredentism in Corsica, and Tunisia was stable. The problem with the French would not diminish, because they were acutely aware that Italy was looking to expand at their expense. The debate continued, with Ciano noting in his diary that his father spoke well in the Chamber 'with a few simple phrases, full of life, as is his nature'.[143] In terms of internal politics Ciano was beginning to regard the Party Secretary Starace as something of a problem, creating bad feelings and a sense of persecution. The Papal Nuncio claimed that Starace was 'a dangerous pagan and a vile example of immorality in his private life'. This may well have been true, but Mussolini's and Ciano's private lives were not that much better.

On the diplomatic front, Ciano claimed that Perth thought the French were wrong and told François-Poncet not to overdramatise the situation, but Perth was probably doing no more than trying to persuade the French to keep matters calm. Perth did not want any significant eruptions to spoil Chamberlain's projected visit the following month. Perth then announced his departure with Ciano claiming he had tears in his eyes, and 'he is sincerely fond of me and I of him'.[144] Later in the month Percy Loraine was approved as the new British ambassador to Italy; Ciano noted that Loraine had a record of saying 'nasty things' about Italy.

Despite the French debate, which Ciano cynically referred to as the European orchestra, his main interest focused on devious machinations over Albania. He observed that the 'Zog regime' appeared more unstable, adding that 'we must act decisively and unscrupulously. Besides, it is humanitarian to take one life if by doing so hundreds and maybe thousands can be saved'.[145] The use of the word 'unscrupulously' underlines the immoral intentions and was promptly followed by the traditional excuse that the 'end justifies the means', though in this case it did not seem to cross Ciano's mind that it was both the end and the means that were immoral. He received Jacomoni, accompanied by one Jake Koçi, an Albanian leader who was prepared to carry out the necessary coup. Koçi had fallen out with King Zog, and had for safety reasons moved his family to Italy. Ciano observed that the death of Zog would remove all centres of resistance and 'enflame the country'.

Mussolini had examined the plans and approved them, but he was concerned about the reactions in Yugoslavia, and suggested that Stoyadinovitch should be consulted. The intrigues and political plots were almost medieval, reflecting the same ancient motivations of power and expansion, both national and personal.

Just before Christmas Ciano accepted an offer from the Hungarian prime minister to visit him for a hunting holiday. Ciano knew he was being courted but was nevertheless thrilled by his reception. He spoke about the new Magyar policy as being 'open, certain, not equivocal, joining with the Axis', and was pleased that he could see a union bloc between Italy, Yugoslavia and Hungary, but observing that 'nothing must be done which can acquire an anti-German flavour'.[146]

SUMMATION OF 1938

The year 1938 had witnessed the Anschluss, the Munich crisis, the rise of irredentist claims, diplomatic manoeuvrings, the rising threat of Nazi Germany, and signs of official anti-Semitism in Italy. Ciano was Mussolini's obedient servant and was at the centre of these events, which were the foreshadow of the impending disaster of World War II – but he was becoming slowly aware of Nazi power, and some embryonic questions about Italy's German partners were mounting in his mind.

5

1939 – CRISIS

Ciano signs Pact of Steel, May 1939 (Istituto Luce Id: A0013852)

THE CHESSBOARD

The year 1939 is highly significant, marking the point at which of the outbreak of war in Europe rapidly developed into a global conflict. It transpired to be a war of sheer carnage, adding to international vocabulary words such as 'genocide' and 'crimes against humanity', arising from Nazi behaviour under Hitler, while under Mussolini's leadership Italy was plunged into a bitter internal strife which continued post-war. From the start of the year Ciano and Edda continued to lead the lives of socialites, pursuing their own questionable pleasures, and on New Year's Day, when Mussolini had returned to Rome, Ciano sat with his master and reflected on their major problems. These amounted to continuing revolts against their occupying empire in East Africa, the Catholic Action (which Mussolini blamed on the Vatican), the proposed military alliance with Germany, and the annoying visit by Chamberlain and Halifax, due for the following week.

Following Mussolini's instructions Ciano drafted a letter to Ribbentrop, proposing that the end of January would be a 'good time' to start the military pact. Uppermost in their minds was the question of France, over which Mussolini and Ciano had fanned the flames of aggression. France had tried to follow Britain's policy of seeking friendship, but the Italian responses had been aggressive, with irredentist claims over French territory which Ciano raised in his letter to Ribbentrop; Ciano wrote that there was certain evidence of a military agreement between France and Britain, that some in France predicted a war, and America was undergoing a military build-up.[147] He explained to Ribbentrop that Mussolini thought the time had come to change the 'Comintern triangle into a military system'. Ribbentrop was relieved to receive the letter, because the Italians had prevaricated far too long in his opinion.

There was ongoing friction over the Vatican's Christian Action, Ciano noting in his diary that 'not-withstanding Starace, I should like to avoid a clash with the Vatican which I would consider harmful'.[148] This and other references imply that Ciano had some affection for the Catholic tradition, compared to his atheistic father-in-law who saw the Vatican merely as an intermittent necessity. In Spain there was growing anticipation that the war raging in Catalonia was ending, and Franco had written a letter to Mussolini about his progress, which pleased the Duce because he told Ciano that it read 'like a report of a subordinate'.[149] Unaware of the bleak future, Mussolini and Ciano continued playing on their international chessboard and looking to an unrealistic world status for their so-called 'Italian Empire'.

CHAMBERLAIN IN ROME

Part of the 'game' was having to be courteous to Chamberlain and Halifax, who arrived on 11 January, a visit noted by Ciano 'to be kept in a minor tone', which was held 'in a tired manner', and for which Mussolini and Ciano could 'see no use'. Mussolini told Ciano that Chamberlain was no Sir Francis Drake but reflected the 'tired sons of a long line of rich men who would lose their empire'.

There were two formal sets of talks in which both sides explored issues and tested the waters. Mussolini told Chamberlain he sought peace, only wanting to reap the benefits of his empire, he was firmly convinced of being an Axis partner, grumbled about the French, informed his guests that Franco was winning, and rebutted Chamberlain's hope for disarmament, suggesting only that a limitation of arms could be possible.[150] Chamberlain agreed that the four-power proposal was a 'good thing' but added the ominous note that Russia should be included, otherwise there would be little point in arms limitations. Chamberlain then raised the questions of the persecuted Jews, only to have Mussolini respond that Germany should not be pushed on this matter because they had 'suffered greatly because of the Jews'. Whether Mussolini and Ciano actually believed this is questionable, but their support of the Nazi policy appeared unwavering.

In the second meeting Chamberlain expressed concern over the Italian relationship with France, confiding that he was concerned about the stability of Daladier's premiership, dropping the less than subtle hint that if Daladier fell it might lead to another Blum left-wing government. Chamberlain moved on to his major point, hoping for more post-Munich cooperation, asking about Hitler's intentions (which Ciano and Mussolini were not privy to), and raising the question that Germany was arming and might be looking towards the Ukraine. In his self-assured style Mussolini argued that Germany needed to rearm for defensive purposes and had no ambitions in the Ukraine. He was accentuating his weak estimation of international matters and lack of knowledge about Hitler's intentions.

Ciano noted that the British press defined the meeting as a 'game ending with no score', was bemused that Chamberlain had no idea how many Jews lived in Britain, and baffled that Chamberlain left 'with tears in his eyes' while his countrymen sang 'for he's a jolly good fellow'. Ciano presented Mussolini with Chamberlain's preparatory parliamentary speech, a copy given to the Italians to ensure they were happy with the contents, and later Ciano heard from Grandi that it had been well received.* Naturally Ciano ensured that the Germans were kept informed.

PAWN MOVEMENTS

Ciano was preparing for a week's visit and hunting holiday in Yugoslavia, and on arrival was pleased with the welcome and the private conversations. These hunts were often regarded as a diplomatic cover for off-the-record *tête-à-têtes*. In his report to Mussolini, Ciano described Stoyadinovitch as 'calm' and winning a close election with his party, supported by young armed followers dressed in green, and based on the fascist model, but Stoyadinovitch had not convinced the Croats. Ciano spoke to Stoyadinovitch about Albania, raising the question of Zog's unpopularity and the possibility that Zog might well try and involve France and Britain, and tentatively raising the possibility of Italian occupation.[151]

---

* Chamberlain, prompted by a Sir G Mitcheson, gave a brief account of his visit. He said they had been made welcome and that 'the arrangements for our comfort and convenience throughout our stay were carried through with a thoughtful consideration and an efficiency which could not be surpassed ... the Foreign Secretary and I had two long conversations with Signor Mussolini and Count Ciano ... in an atmosphere of compete frankness ... our discussions were exploratory and informal ... and I would remind the House that Signor Mussolini gave proof last September both of his willingness and his ability to intervene in favour or peace.' See Hansard, HC Debate 31 January 1939, Vol 343 cc36–41.

Here their conversation appeared to stall when Stoyadinovitch, having taken on board Ciano's proposal, suggested a joint partition. Ciano immediately had to 'kick for touch', and suggested it was sufficient that 'they had made contact on the subject'. As Ciano left for Belgrade to meet the regent, Stoyadinovitch asked Ciano to speak to the regent, causing Ciano to note that relations between those two men were not happy. (He was correct in this appraisal.) Stoyadinovitch had not convinced the Croats, and Prince Paul had recognised a fascist potential who might challenge his position.

On his return Ciano, while at the bar in his golf club, heard the news that Barcelona had eventually fallen to Franco, prompting him to write in his diary the sycophantic lines that 'Spain hears only one name, that of Mussolini, who conducted the campaign bravely, firmly, even at a time when many people who cheer him now were against him'.[152] It should be asked whether Ciano meant what he was saying, whether he intended to show it to Mussolini, or whether Mussolini had expressed a wish to see his book. The key concern was that the war had reduced Spain to starvation and food supplies were being sent from Italy; one of its better incursions. The month concluded with Ciano observing the Duce standing behind his office curtains watching the military practice for an important ceremonial; he had even chosen the bandleader's baton and taught them some of their movements in person. Meanwhile, Europe was rapidly descending towards war. It has often been believed that Ciano was reaching a level of power control, especially over Mussolini, causing Hassell to note a few months later that 'Mussolini was coming more and more under Ciano's influence and was being hamstrung by Signora Petacci' (his long-term mistress), and even a year later noting that 'Ciano is looming larger in the picture'.[153] It was more rumour than true, started because of Ciano's projection of himself.

The Pope was intending to hold a ceremony to celebrate the tenth anniversary of the Lateran Pact, but as Mussolini was not responding to him Ciano was selected to represent the state, and Prince Umberto the monarchy; if the king shared anything with Mussolini it was their mutual suspicion of priests, and the monarch was happy to send his number two. When Pius XI died a few days later, on 10 February, it was Ciano who went to the Vatican to pay his respects. Mussolini agreed to attend the Pope's funeral, probably induced to do so by public opinion. Cardinal Pacelli (who became Pius XII) was well-known for his anti-communist views, which were welcomed, and Ciano even suspected the new Pope might be warmer towards Germany. Until the Papal archives are made more public, the role of Pius XII during the war seems to have been one of Church institutional safety.

Ciano and Edda were well known internationally, with Ciano appearing on

Pius XI (as a cardinal) / 1932, Pius XII
(Politisch-Wissenschaftlicher-Verlag-Berlin) / (Breit-Der-Weg-Kirche-Wib-belt-Essen)

the cover of *Newsweek* on the day Pope Pius XII was enthroned in the Vatican. Ciano had attended this occasion but had made a fool of himself, arrogantly marching down the aisle giving the fascist salute as if everyone had gathered to see him. A few months later (24 July) Edda appeared in the magazine *Time* under the dubious heading of one of 'Europe's most successful intriguers and string pullers'.

Meanwhile the French were making clandestine overtures, proposing concessions in Djibouti with a free zone and a share in administration, and offering the necessary railway tracks from Ethiopia to the coast. They suggested they would support the Italians over the Suez issue and re-examine their claims in Tunisia. When Mussolini was given this information, he accepted it as progress. The French were pleased, but Ciano insisted that the French should keep these talks at ambassadorial level. Ciano's demand for discretion was questionable, however, the very next day he explained everything to the German ambassador. The Italian–French relationship was constantly tainted with mutual distrust, and later in the month Mussolini had another outburst, claiming that when he waged war with the French and had beaten them, he would show the Italians 'how peace in Europe should be made'.[154]

EMBRYONIC PLANS FOR ALBANIA

Ciano was stunned to hear that Stoyadinovitch had apparently offered his resignation, causing him to wonder what had happened, noting in his diary 'in any case it disturbs me'. Later he wondered whether Stoyadinovitch's party was not strong enough, but Mussolini heard, more correctly, that it was a straightforward *coup d'état*. The concern for Ciano and Mussolini was what would happen to their Albanian project with Stoyadinovitch's departure. They decided that speed was critical, and established the first ten days of April as the target for action by starting a revolt as soon as possible. There were complications, because it was clear that King Zog was aware of their intentions, Belgrade had leaked rumours of partition, Zog was considering mobilisation, and Ciano heard from Jacomoni that Zog 'and his men' were seeking greater cordiality; as in all European countries, it was a year of nervous tension.

Franco was appearing more successful, and when Ciano was once again propping up the bar in his golf club he heard that the Littorio Division had occupied Gerona, which meant that Catalonia was now effectively occupied by Franco's forces. It would take years for Spain to recover from its civil war, though, and Franco would remain doggedly neutral throughout World War II for economic and safety reasons. Spain was regarded as a pariah state. Not until it was needed for ICBM bases in the Cold War, and its entrepreneurs discovered the benefits brought by the tourist trade, did the country return to some form of normality. When General Gastone Gambara mentioned the problems of captured republican Italians, Mussolini told him to 'shoot the lot', because 'dead men don't write history'. One good result for Ciano was that Franco agreed to join the Anti-Comintern Pact, but he never took it a step further; Franco just hated communists and any opposition.

Ciano was discovering that his popularity was not as widespread as he thought, and he heard that Starace had caught a senior fascist party member called Egilberto Martire 'in the act of bad-mouthing me', claiming 'I had the evil eye'. Martire was handcuffed and landed up in jail. Mussolini pleased Ciano by stating that he would have personally liked to have 'belted' Martire and that he missed his duelling days.*

CIANO IN POLAND, AND INVASION IN CZECHOSLOVAKIA

On 24 February Ciano left with Edda for Warsaw, which he found 'rather sleepy and tired' and they were greeted with 'curiosity and perhaps lukewarm sympathy'.[155] The British Pathé newsreels revealed Ciano looking like a pompous senior uniformed officer with a high protruding head like his master, relishing the ceremony with Roman salutes, but met by civilian politicians.[156] Ciano later reported to Mussolini that he found Poland anti-German with a strong Catholic tradition and large Jewish communities, but 'sprinkled' with strong German

---

* The young Mussolini had often been embroiled in duels, and Edda recalled him having shirts with only one sleeve for this purpose. See Ciano Edda, *My Truth* (New York: William Morrow, 1977) p.34.

centres. Ciano had the further impression that the Poles liked Italian artists, sculptors and architects, but did not understand Italy as a world power. It was clear that Danzig was their chief concern, and that Prime Minister Beck preferred the situation to be dealt with diplomatically. Ciano noted that Poland was 'not an outright enemy', without realising that Poland's sole wish was to retain its integrity. Ciano's perceptions and behaviour revealed he was still an amateur. The newsreel footage pictured Ciano as appearing arrogant and condescending. In one conversation Beck informed Ciano that he was friendly with the Polish Ambassador General Wieniawa, to which Ciano rudely remarked that this friendship had cost Beck his own reputation.* Beck promptly responded by saying 'I think your reputation needed no help for Wieniawa to decline'.[157] This was not the way for Ciano, holding high office, to conduct himself as a guest, and, still an inexperienced youth, he behaved with unbecoming arrogance. A diplomat may dislike the person to whom they are writing, be it at a personal level or from political principle, but diplomacy demands frankness when necessary and politeness always, even if it means signing a letter of protest as 'Your Obedient Servant'.

The crisis growth of 1939 reached another peak on 15 March with Hitler's well-known occupation of Czechoslovakia, when that country was removed from the map and replaced by the protectorate of Bohemia and Moravia, effectively destroying the Munich Agreement and overturning the Treaty of Versailles. The rump had been seized, and Slovakia was now under Jozef Tiso, a priest turned fascist with Hitler as his patron.† Hitler's action, making his belligerent intentions crystal clear, shook the world. In Britain Chamberlain was dumbfounded by promises broken within months, the West was disturbed, and all nations were fearful about the future.

Ciano and Mussolini had no advance information on these events, and when they met their discussion was about Ciano's visit to Poland which Mussolini described as an 'empty nut', the fact that they were happy with the new Pope, and that the Japanese were hesitating to sign the Tripartite Agreement. A week later the American ambassador asked Ciano about the agreement, to which Ciano responded with the evasive 'I said that for the time being there is nothing in all this'. The rumours were rife, and the American would not have been fooled, he was probably testing Ciano's integrity.

Even before the German invasion of Czechoslovakia the world had been feeling on edge, and Lord Perth was asking Ciano to ensure there would be no war

---

*   His full name was Bolesław Ignacy Florian Wieniawa-Długoszowski.

†   Jozef Gašpar Tiso was a Slovak politician, a Roman Catholic priest who was president of the Slovak Republic from 1939–45; he was to be executed for war crimes and crimes against humanity in Bratislava in 1947. He was known as the 'clerical-fascist'.

with France; Ciano, playing his diplomatic rebuttals, countered that the British had too many troops in Egypt. Europe was anxious, and France, following the British example, was desperately trying to keep Italy within the western sphere of influence. On 26 March Madrid fell to Franco; although there was some opposition, Spain was now under his control.

There were tensions between Croatia and Serbia, which was a constant concern for Mussolini as the plans for Albania were still being pursued, and Croatia had a long coastland in the Adriatic, stretching down towards Albania. It was also obvious that Germany was keeping a careful eye on maintaining good relationships with the Italians while keeping them in the dark. Attolico informed Mussolini that Hitler was happy with the Italian alliance and Germany 'is fully committed to solidarity with Italy and is ready to march with us'.[158] A few days later Ribbentrop accepted the Italian proposal that there should be a conference between the two general staffs. Ciano suggested Innsbruck as the place, and it was arranged for Wilhelm Keitel and Alberto Pariani to meet for initial conversations.* Ciano wanted this event to be surrounded with 'considerable publicity' to impress the wider world of the two superpowers being a co-equal structure.

When the Germans had crossed the Czech borders, Mussolini had been furious at being kept in the dark, as if he had been precluded from the prefects' common room, and a 'chagrined Mussolini muttered: the Italians will laugh at me. Every time Hitler takes a country, he sends me a message'.[159] Ciano felt the same, but pretended to the American ambassador that they had been kept informed. He had noted in his diary on the eve of events that 'the Axis functions only in favour of one of its parts, which tends to acquire overwhelming proportions, acting entirely on its own initiative with little regard for us'.[160] The Prince of Hesse provided a shopping list of excuses from Hitler, claiming the Czechs had refused to demobilise, that they were in contact with the Russians, and that they had mistreated German speakers. Mussolini was more than aware that Hitler's act had received a hostile reaction from the Italian population, but his initial response was to tell Ciano that the German 'trick' had to be 'taken in good grace'. He also told Ciano that the proposed invasion of Albania would look like nothing compared to occupying 'the old and rich territory of Bohemia'.

The next day, however, Ciano found Mussolini depressed and expressing unease, suggesting that the Albanian project should be postponed because he was concerned about Yugoslavian unity, and anxious that Germany was looking towards Croatia, which was uncomfortably close to the Italian borders. Ciano contacted the German ambassador, who assured Ciano that Germany had long

---

* Keitel met at Innsbruck with Pariani, where only general issues were discussed, but they did agree on the need for three or four more years to prepare for war against the West.

agreed that the Mediterranean was an Italian concern, and the next day was back at Ciano's desk confirming this directly from Berlin that the 'Croatia rumours' had no substance.[161] On 20 March Ribbentrop waded in to comfort the Italians, thanking them for their response over Czechoslovakia, and asserting that Croatia was of no interest to the Germans and that he had managed to track the rumours down to 'certain Croatian personalities' who had been in Berlin.[162] This prompt interchange at the diplomatic level settled Mussolini's nerves, but he explained to Ciano that German hegemony was established in Europe, and although others thought they could check it they would never be able 'to roll it back'. Ciano felt that the German actions had betrayed Italy, writing 'the events of the last few days have renewed my opinion of the Führer and Germany; he is unfaithful and treacherous, and we cannot carry on any policy with him.'[163] He even reflected on cooperating with the Western powers and decided to revitalise the negotiations with the French. Such was Ciano's *volte-face* that some have believed these lines may have been part of the revision process of his diary in later years; but his distaste for the Germans had already surfaced, and the immature diplomat and playboy was now starting to glimpse reality. This may have been a cause for some early reflection, but it did not stop his own ambitions.

ALBANIA

On 21 March Mussolini addressed the Grand Council Meeting, instructing its members that they 'must adopt a policy of uncompromising loyalty to the Axis'.[164] He was opposed by Balbo and Marshal Emilio De Bono, who never trusted the Germans, and the former accused Mussolini of 'shining Germans' boots', which Ciano attacked, defending his master. Mussolini turned his attention to the Albanian project, saying that speed was of the essence and that King Zog had to accept the Italian conditions.

In 1926 Albania had signed a defensive alliance with Italy, mainly to avoid being carved up by its Balkan neighbours, but in doing so had virtually become a feudal relation of Italy, a client state. The Byzantine methods deployed by Jacomoni ranged from attempts to poison King Zog to arming bandits. (After the war Jacomoni denied there had been 'any serious plot' to assassinate King Zog, but given he was on trial at the time this denial remains problematic.)

Ciano, convinced that King Zog was playing for time, wrote that 'if Zog does not yield it will be necessary to use force resolutely'.[165] He later added the line that one 'matter which annoys me greatly is because I consider it rather dangerous to fire the first shot in this disturbed and inflammable Europe'. The hypocrisy of these statements serves as an indicator that the future revision of the diary had not been overly extensive. However, his enthusiasm may have been dampened when he heard from Jacomoni that the army could not even arrange a motorcycle unit, that they were having trouble over the landing plans, and Zog was refusing to sign.

Meanwhile, the world elsewhere stood on the brink of disaster, and when the British *chargé d'affaires* Sir Noel Charles informed Ciano that Chamberlain had given Poland the promise of British support, and the Polish Ambassador Wieniawa told him that the Poles would fight, these warning bells were not enough for Ciano. For him, April was consumed with the planned occupation of Albania. The historian Patrick Finney wrote that Mussolini's invasion of Albania in April 1939 was partly motivated by pique at the Nazi occupation of Bohemia-Moravia in March; Hitler had neglected to inform Rome until the last minute of this annexation, even though it entailed the destruction of the Munich settlement which Mussolini had proudly regarded as a product of his own mediation, and publicly relegated him to humiliating subordination within the Axis.[166] Mussolini had vacillated over Ciano's idea of occupying Albania, which had been planned for a long time, and the historian Finney was probably right in saying that Hitler's behaviour was the impetus which provided Ciano with the opportunity to perform his longstanding dream.

On 1 April, the date originally proposed, the Italians organised the ultimatum for King Zog to sign. If Zog refused, Ciano intended to arrange public revolts to provide the excuse for invading a land over which the Italians already had virtual control. The whole episode reflected Byzantine days of plots within plots. Ciano had organised that disorder would be started, but that the queen of Albania and her child, soon to be born, should be kept safe and the troops were to stop Zog fleeing towards the Mati (Zog's home district) to organise resistance. On 3 April Ciano spent time with General Alberto Pariani 'fine tuning'. Their meeting was obviously not militarily secure, because they discovered that the airfields were defended and that armed Albanians were threatening resident Italians. Later the landings and move toward Tirana would be plagued with problems such as the supply of the wrong fuel, landing problems and a lack of communication between radio operators, making contact impossible. Ciano also heard that 'at Bologna a Bersaglieri battalion about to leave for Albania was singing "we want peace and not war", and the officers present did nothing ... so Mussolini was angry'.[167] Both at that time and later on there would be many ordinary Italian soldiers wondering why they had to fight in a war they felt was unnecessary and not part of Italian business.

Ciano regarded himself as the key to events and gave what he called the 'invasion speech' which he hoped would be to a spellbound and not a shocked public, ensuring the best personal propaganda. The Italian secret service recorded his telephone message with the editor of the newspaper *Il Telegrafo*, in which Ciano told the editor to make sure the speech and applause was prominent. When the editor responded, 'Without fail, Excellency,' Ciano replied, 'Especially the finale. The final applause. You will see that I have really received a lot. Make it stand out in big type. Don't be stingy with the big type.'[168] He was dictating his self-promotion.

When the next day Jacomoni communicated that a peaceful solution was a possibility, Ciano noted that Mussolini was upset because he wanted 'his own war'. Two ships were sent to Albania to evacuate Italian citizens, and Ciano was pleased to hear from Attolico that Berlin was happy with the plans, causing Ciano to write that 'Germany is marching correctly'. Ettore Muti took a quick trip to Tirana and returned with the news that Zog would resist, and Mussolini sent Zog a warning that the ultimatum was running out, namely at noon on 6 April. It was the same day that Zog's wife gave birth in the early hours to a son, prompting Ciano to note 'how long will he remain heir to the throne?'

On the day of operations Ciano, feeling unwell (or perhaps with the proverbial attack of butterflies), had to rise early, noting that Mussolini was up in the night, which 'was unusual for him'. At the last moment, the Yugoslavian Christich was demanding an appointment, and Anfuso recorded the meeting. Christich was asking about the aims of the occupation, to which Ciano responded that it was of a 'temporary nature' and to bring 'peace and order to Albania'.[169] Ciano further explained that the motive 'was inspired by respect for Albania's independence and integrity'. None of this pretentious verbiage could have rung true, Anfuso noting that Christich was unquestionably concerned about stability in the Balkans. For Ciano it was the time to fly and observe the beaches where he saw some action which he described as a 'beautiful spectacle', before flying over Tirana where he claimed the crowds looked calm – but how he measured the feelings of a crowd from a plane defies belief, as does his treating it as a show to be watched, the irony being that they started the assault on Good Friday.

There was total confusion as to Zog's reactions, and delays, which annoyed Mussolini because they allowed the French newspapers to claim that the Albanians were winning. On 8 April an early morning call announced it was safe to land in Tirana airport, which Ciano promptly did, writing that he was 'overcome with emotions'.* Ciano claimed the Albanians greeted him with warmth as he spread largesse amongst the poor (it was of course not an altruistic act but an effort to endear himself). He heard that the occupation of the country was going well, and on 12 April he wrote that in Tirana the crowd received 'me triumphantly; there is

---

* Anfuso later wrote that if the Albanians had had a well-armed fire brigade they could have 'driven us into the Adriatic'.

a certain amount of coolness especially amongst high school students. I see they dislike raising their arms for the Roman salute,' but no doubt the money flowing from his pockets helped as he spoke to the crowd from the balcony of the Italian legation.[170]

On the same day, the Albanian parliament voted to depose the missing King Zog, and looked for a union by offering the crown to King Victor Emmanuel III; in the interim they elected Shevket Vërlaci (politician and the largest landowner in Albania); he served as head of state for five days. Victor Emmanuel appointed Francesco Jacomoni as the lieutenant-general of the king. Curiously, the Albanian exiles had proposed Amedeo, the Duke of Aosta, as their king, and Mussolini was inclined to agree with this request until Victor Emmanuel decided he should be their royal, which put the lie to the Italian claim they were only seeking Albanian independence, and made it clear that the king was greedy for imperial power. It has even been implied that Ciano was offered the crown, but he certainly treated Albania as his own fiefdom, as being the prompter of the occupation. Despite his misgivings about attacking Albania, Victor Emmanuel was all too happy to accept the throne, and on 16 April an official ceremony was held at the Royal Palace, where Ciano was somewhat bemused by the 'tough Albanians looking at their new diminutive king'.

The taking of the crown confirmed that Italy had occupied Albania not out of interest for that country's integrity but for greedy nationalistic ambitions. On 19 April the British Ambassador Lord Perth challenged Ciano, informing him that the title of a monarch was a dynastic affair and entirely internal; Ciano brushed this aside by changing the subject. The British ambassador had the same experience as the American Phillips, who wrote that 'I wondered only why Ciano had gone to the trouble of giving me and my other colleagues formal assurances that Albanian independence could be respected, when he knew the contrary was about to happen. Certainly, he lost the respect of all of us by this futile and unnecessary deception.'[171] No one was fooled by Ciano or Mussolini as to their intentions and motives. Ciano noticed that the Serbs were in 'a sense of panic,' and they needed a 'dose of chloroform'.

CIANO'S PERSONAL LIFE

Although it was Mussolini who had given the order for the takeover of Albania, the plan had been in Ciano's calculations long before Zog had asked him to be his best man at his wedding, and Ciano was unquestionably the main instigator. He now had an even more overly inflated view of his own importance; in his diary he pondered the advisability of accepting the title of Prince of Kruia, which he claimed the Albanians wanted to bestow on him for 'having given Albania to

Italy'. He treated Albania as his own fiefdom, and he spent time searching for new homes and hunting lodges, renaming places, for example changing Santi Quaranta to Port Edda.* The Albanian enterprise did nothing for Italy. Albania had no useful resources, and Italian money, previously poured into Spain, was now being consumed in Albania. It has been suggested that only Ciano benefited; he was already a shareholder in two oil companies, and like his father was swift to benefit from national enterprises.

Ciano may have renamed an Albanian town after Edda, but the marriage was not going well, and there were seriously bad-tempered interchanges between the two of them. Mussolini was approached by his daughter telling him that she wanted to leave Ciano, but was told that the nonsense had to stop. There was talk of separation, but divorce in Italy during this period was illegal. It was widely known to be a 'goose and gander' situation, with Ciano having a reputation for many mistresses. This was well known on the gossip circuits, especially in his favourite salons and golf club, where the women were known as 'the widows of Ciano'.[172]

According to Edda's memoirs there were two well-known salons, one called Princess Colonna's where the gossip included 'who was in and who was out', and another run by a Countess Pecci-Blunt, who claimed Pope Leo XIII as a great-uncle. 'It was said at the time that the true Ministry of Foreign Affairs was not Palazzo Chigi but the Palazzo Colonna'.[173] The social circuit and sexual habits would have shocked the puritans and many others. Edda later noted that 'I must say that none of Galeazzo's mistresses ever placed me in an embarrassing position', and 'contrary to my father, who appreciated women only as a physical outlet, my husband enjoyed them for aesthetic reasons also'.[174]

Wherever he travelled Ciano was known to arrange women for company, and they apparently doted on him. This was widely known not only in Italian social circles but internationally. Ciano was unabashed about his sexual appetite – and the Germans were aware of this weakness. It has been alleged that they sent agents to try and discover the nature of the gossip; there is little evidence of this enterprise, but it sounds plausible. The danger was the so-called pillow-talk and general gossip, especially at his golf club, which had been started by an Englishman and where British sympathy still tended to dominate. The only German that Ciano appeared to trust as a confidant was Prince Otto von Bismarck, who was rumoured to be anti-Nazi.

Himmler and Reinhard Heydrich had established a night-club type venue, Salon Kitty, which would encourage foreign diplomats and their entourages to meet, and then record their private conversations. The SS officer Walter Schellenberg

* Now Sarandë.

75

claimed post war that one of the 'biggest catches was the Italian Foreign Minister Count Ciano, who went there with other important diplomats'.[175] Edda, meanwhile, was developing a similar reputation to that of her husband, enjoying the company of young men and the social life, especially sex and drinking. At one time, Sir Percy Loraine informed Chamberlain that Edda had become a nymphomaniac and led a life of sordid sexual promiscuity in an alcoholic haze.[176] As mentioned earlier she had a long-term lover, the fashion designer Emilio Pucci, and Ciano would often tell his friends that he was worried about her indiscretions. This was certainly a case of the pot calling the kettle black and their well-known lifestyle reflected those of the Borgian and Versailles Courts.

BACK TO THE CHESSBOARD

Ciano was so immersed in Albania that there are hints that he took his eye off the ball as to what Hitler was planning. The Tripartite Agreement was being delayed by the Japanese, and Göring arrived in Italy dropping hints about Poland, which Ciano immediately picked up as being similar to those once issued in relation to Czechoslovakia. Mussolini was interested, but Ciano was now on his guard, developing reservations over the German intentions. Göring had been sent to persuade the Italians to join their military alliance, and when Ciano told Göring Italy needed peace, Göring informed him that it was the same with Germany. How far Ciano was taken in by this apparent deceit is ambiguous, but it apparently convinced Mussolini, who ordered Ciano to cooperate. Ciano seemed to have a better understanding of Italy's lack of military resources than Mussolini and was wary of German pressure, but because he was subservient had little choice but to follow Mussolini's orders. The Polish ambassador arrived, telling Ciano that the Poles would fight; he was revealing this because he knew it would be fed via Ciano to the Germans. The Dutch minister expressed concern that many were alarmed that Germany and Italy were dividing Europe into two sectors, and that the Netherlands would become part of Germany. Ciano privately scoffed, writing 'they are the ideas of an official who is a little stupid and very timid, but they are nevertheless, indicative of a state of mind spreading around the world'.[177] But in fact the Dutchman was far from stupid, and far from timid in telling the fascist foreign minister what he thought; it is apparent that Ciano's diplomatic antennae were not as focused as those of his Dutch guest.

Europe's confusion was increased by the Albanian occupation, and in Italy there were sceptics. As the political temperature rose in Europe, Mussolini and Ciano seemed oblivious, failing to foresee what others felt was unavoidable. Mussolini wanted Italy to be a 'great nation' on the world stage, but economically it was an impossible task. Mussolini had recognised that 'German industrial production outperformed Italian by twelve to one', and his frequent claim that economic issues had never dictated a country's history were erroneous.[178] After the expenses of the war in East Africa and the support of Franco in Spain, after pouring money into Albania and with the overall weakness of the Italian economy it was evident that Italy could not afford an international conflict. Even so, it was evident that during these months Ciano's influence appeared to be growing.

PACT OF STEEL

The month of May 1939 was highly significant for Italy's future, because of the signing of the Pact of Steel. Mussolini and Ciano treated the map of Europe like a chessboard, working out who was placed where, and Ribbentrop played the same game with his habitual deceit of talking of peace when he knew war was inevitable. This continued when he arrived at a staged welcome in Milan (the Germans were not appreciated, especially in northern Italy) and he and Ciano discussed the European situation.

There had been no serious repercussions regarding the occupation of Albania by the major powers, although Yugoslavia and Greece were understandably nervous, and in Britain, given the gathering storm in much of Europe, Albania's troubles were of secondary importance. On 13 April the British and French had offered a guarantee to Greece and Romania which was utilised by Hitler as claiming the Axis powers were being 'encircled'. Hitler had conveyed to Mussolini that Germany and Italy were numerically outnumbered, which in military terms was unlikely, but he knew that Mussolini was obsessed with demographics. Like Göring, Ribbentrop started their conversation with an attack on Poland, and he and Ciano agreed that the Poles were in a 'hysterical state of mind' and were 'by nature megalomaniacs'.[179] Ribbentrop, having arranged his pieces on the chessboard, then claimed that the Führer wanted peace, but also wanted the Danzig corridor, which had divided Prussia. Ribbentrop then stated that 'England and France were showing signs of fatigue', that Germany 'needed four or five years before being ready for war', but also that 'Germany could start if necessary'. In all this kaleidoscope of contradictory statements it must have been clear to Ciano that Poland was next on Hitler's shopping list, but giving the impression he missed the obvious. It seems unbelievable, with the rumours about Hitler's intentions in Eastern Europe, long established since *Mein Kampf*, Hitler's tedious political manifesto, that Mussolini and Ciano could be taken in by the German pretence that they sought peace.

The two foreign ministers surveyed the European chessboard, with Ribbentrop agreeing with Ciano over the French but warning that Italy could not fight France without involving Britain. They agreed that Yugoslavia should remain neutral and support the Axis economically, and now that Albania was occupied, Greece was less important. Bulgaria had to be kept close in a spirit of collaboration, Russia should be stopped from joining the anti-totalitarian bloc, and all these sweeping statements were eventually underlined by the need for the signing of the military alliance. This was Ribbentrop's fundamental purpose, because Hitler wanted Italy alongside before he attacked Poland, with Ribbentrop suggesting it should be signed in Berlin 'and in the most solemn manner'.[180] It was a German ploy to ensure they had the Italians bound to them, and they wanted the alliance made public as soon as possible. Mussolini agreed with all that had been said, but wanted further details, leading to Ciano cynically noting that 'as usual with Mussolini, when he has obtained something, he always asks for more', a statement later utilised by Eden in his memoirs to depict Mussolini's character.[181] Somewhat amusingly he wrote that the men in Ribbentrop's company were 'not the usual wooden and somewhat boring Germans; they are likeable young men, who speak foreign languages well, and who, in the drawing room, are able to forget all their heel clicking when addressing a lady'.[182]

An early war would be disastrous for Italy, and Ciano knew that although Mussolini was aware of the precarious situation, especially in the army, 'he does not seem to care'. This posed the question as to whether the Duce was a realist or merely living in his own fantasy world, hoping to restore Rome's historic grandeur. For the first time in his diary Ciano opened a cynical attack on his master, writing: 'his attention seems to be spent mostly on matters of form; there is hell to pay if the "Present Arms" is not done right or if an officer doesn't know how to lift his legs in the Roman steps'.[183] However, a few days later Ciano was himself feeling proud as he watched Albanian soldiers parading in Rome for the first time; he was at this stage little better than his master. He was considering sending a warning to Greece for accepting the Anglo-French guarantee, and in Albania ordered the imprisonment of some 20 intellectuals who had disagreed with the occupation.

By mid-May the treaty with Germany was developing in outline, with 24 May suggested as the date. Ciano pointed out that this was inappropriate, because it was on that day in 1915 that Italy had joined the Allies, leaving the Tripartite arrangement; the Germans would have recognised this historical irony. The diplomatic pressure continued, the Polish diplomat Wieniawa informing Ciano that he thought war inevitable; once again Ciano responded that Poland had a choice between Russia and Germany. The American ambassador followed, complaining about Mussolini's claim that America was run by Jews, but unlike the Polish ambassador the American added a veiled threat: that as Americans had originated in Europe they would not stand aloof in a European war.

BERLIN

When Ciano arrived in Berlin on 21 May he was met with the warm reception he had anticipated, which boosted his ego. There was, however, some gullibility in this response, as he would have known that Goebbels could rustle up an adoring or hostile crowd at the drop of a hat. Hitler presented Ciano with a new Nazi award, the Knight's Order of the German Eagle, a medal made from solid gold. In return for these staged diplomatic niceties, Ciano, on behalf of the Italian monarchy, presented Ribbentrop with the Collar of the Annunciation, one of Italy's most revered awards.* Göring was infuriated because he believed that as he had done all the work with the Italians that award should have been added to his own collection. In time Ciano's choice of recipient would cause him more problems, but that evening he visited Salon Kitty.

Ciano, testing the waters with Ribbentrop, spoke of the possible conflict in Croatia, seeking independence, and claimed that Italy could not be indifferent to this situation, which Ribbentrop, all too keen for the signing, could do nothing else but agree to. The Tripartite Agreement was formalised on 22 May 1939, and this Pact of Steel soon became the Tripartite Pact, signed on 27 September 1940.

The planning of the treaty had been organised by the Germans and it was astonishing that Ciano as foreign minister appeared to take little interest in the drafting, not even scrutinising the final documents. This was a diplomatic weakness with long-term ramifications. Amongst the more pertinent details were the first two articles in which both countries would consult one another on any points of mutual interest, followed by the critical clause that there would be automatic reciprocal assistance if either side were embroiled in any conflict. The Germans would never adhere to consulting the Italians, as they had already demonstrated, and Hitler had ordered the Polish plan to remain secret; Attolico had heard the rumours, but Ciano failed to listen to his ambassador. All Hitler wanted was the pact signed before the Polish enterprise started, with Ciano meeting Hitler, whom he thought looked tired,

Back in Italy, Ciano could tell by public reaction that the recently signed pact was more popular in Germany than in Italy. He wrote that 'we must recognise that the hatred for France has not yet been successful in arousing love for Germany'.[184] Many thinking Italians wondered whether this alliance would lead them into a major conflict.

Victor Emmanuel sent his congratulations to Ciano and suggested to Mussolini that Ciano should be made a marquis, to which Mussolini objected, as indeed he was to do later when the king proposed that Ciano should have the Collar of the

---

* Only about twenty 'Collars' were available, and on the death of the holders were returned to the crown.

Annunciation. Mussolini and the king would have regarded this pact with Nazi Germany as some form of security, but more probably felt a sense of nationalistic pride in their relationship with their powerful neighbour; it would be the undoing of the leaders, both royal and political, within a few years.

BULLY BOY OF THE BALKANS

Energised by a sense of power, Mussolini and Ciano were turning their avaricious attention towards Croatia, where Vladimir Maček, Ciano's friendly Croatian politician, was making noises about having the Croats' own republic. On meeting Percy Loraine,

King Victor Emmanuel III, 1915
(Library of Congress)

Mussolini attacked him, with Ciano observing that Loraine 'argued with a certain professional ability'; when Mussolini suggested that there could have been an agreement between Poland and Germany had the British not interfered, Loraine was furious, and Ciano noted the session ended in an icy atmosphere, which was hardly surprising. Loraine later told Churchill's secretary that he found Ciano 'likable, though conceited, and very quick. He also genuinely believed Ciano was now disgusted with the Axis' but noted that Italy remained fascist.[185] Loraine always held the view that although the king of Italy and Ciano were favourable towards the British, Mussolini was not, and he was generally correct.[186]

Ciano's sense of self-importance was inflating yet further, revealed by a telegram he sent to Sofia warning the Bulgarians that they ought to position themselves alongside the Axis, because 'Italy has now assumed a role of first-class importance in the Balkans', and that they must tighten their bonds with the Axis, and if they needed arms Italy and Germany would supply them.[187] This singular assertion of Italy's supposed supremacy portrays not just a sense of arrogance but also a hint that Ciano was expecting war. Although Ciano had shown some signs of concern over the Pact of Steel and where it might lead, he was still behaving like the bully boy of the Balkans.

Mussolini had moments of doubt about the speed of events and, through his General Ugo Cavallero, delivered a message to Hitler that Italy was not prepared for a war before 1943. There was no response. Ciano was suddenly concerned that Germany would force Italy by the recent treaty into war, but Mussolini believed that the Danzig corridor issues would be resolved in the same way as the issues at the Munich conference.

During June Ciano's diary gives the impression that he had a relaxing month, on seven days simply writing 'nothing new'; he was undoubtedly back on the beach or in his golf club. The month started with Mussolini petulantly refusing to review the returning legionnaires from Spain, because they had landed in Naples and the king would be present. The king had been angry when Costanzo Ciano announced that Mussolini was to be raised to Primo Maresciallo dell'Impero (First Marshal of the Empire), a post without precedent and with semi-regal implications. This heated relationship prompted Ciano and Starace to discuss possibilities about a Fascist Republic. When on 3 June the king asked to see the new constitution for Albania, in Ciano's language the king was 'sarcastic' about the new flag, observing there was no 'heraldic symbol'. Ciano responded by pointing out that it had the 'blue Savoyard sash' and the 'crown of Scanderbeg'.[188] Mussolini was furious, and Ciano recorded him stating that he was 'sick and tired of dragging behind him "empty baggage cars, which very often have their brakes on," that the king is a bitter, untrustworthy little man, who at this time is concerned with embroidery on the flag'.[189] Mussolini hated the monarchy, and talked about 'liquidating them', but the influence of Church and monarchy were too entrenched in Italy for Mussolini to provoke drastic changes.

During June Ciano had increased contact with the Spanish Serrano Suñer, to whom von Mackensen took offence for not praising Germany sufficiently for its contribution in the Spanish conflict.* Serrano Suñer was, like Franco, staunchly Catholic; the Church had supported Franco during the war, and Serrano Suñer was suspicious of the Nazis and their attitude towards the Christian faith. Goebbels had no time for Serrano Suñer, whom he called 'a Jesuit' and the real 'fly in the ointment'.[190] Ciano described Serrano Suñer as a 'slender sickly man' (in fact he survived until 2003) who explained that Spain was 'at the end of her tether' and could not as yet afford a major war, but still wanted Gibraltar back, and Portugal removed from the British sphere of influence.

Meanwhile, the British confirmed that they still upheld the 16 April agreement, but Mussolini was negative and used Hitler's pretext that the 'others' were just trying to 'encircle the Axis'. The Slovenes had requested whether they could print a local newspaper in their own language, which again drew forth a typically cynical comment from Ciano, writing 'if we want to carry out our policy … we must start by giving them the feeling that we are being intelligently liberal. We shall think of tightening the reins later'.[191] Consumed in his ever-growing self-importance, Ciano was behaving like a leading politician, dictating what should happen.

---

* Serrano Suñer, the so called *cuñadísimo* (supreme brother-in-law) would soon become a dominant figure, and Franco and Serrano Suñer forged the Caudillo's National-Syndicalist State. See Moradiellos Enrique, *Franco, Anatomy of a Dictator* (London: I B Tauris, 2018) p.41.

On 26 June he heard that his father Costanzo had, at age 62, died unexpectedly from a heart attack, possibly induced by his luxurious lifestyle. Ciano was shattered, devoting many diary pages addressed directly to his 'dad' as if they were having a personal conversation from beyond the grave. This is a sharp reminder of the personal nature of the diary, and there is a hint that like as with many others on the loss of a family member there was that tinge of guilt. The king arrived to express his grief, as did Mussolini, who met him on the stairs. Mussolini gave Ciano a copy of a letter he had once addressed to Costanzo, asking him to succeed Mussolini if he suddenly died. From 26 June until 3 July Ciano made no entries; the death of his father had eliminated all other issues.

More pertinently, when Ciano stabilised after the death of his father, he soon picked up the rumour that Hitler was preparing to take over the Danzig corridor.[*] The gossip about this proposed action was rife, and Ciano and Mussolini were continually unhappy that Hitler had not kept them informed, despite the agreement in the Pact of Steel. The Italian Ambassador Attolico was one of the better diplomats, highly experienced, anti-Nazi, and had given them due warning of Hitler's intentions, but Ciano had ignored him, dismissing him as suffering from war panic. On 2 July Ciano wrote to Attolico asking for information, instructing him that 'you must now discuss it with Ribbentrop himself, and he must inform us how they regard the situation'.[192] Ribbentrop would ignore these demands because the Nazi regime had no intention of informing the Italians. As mentioned above, Attolico was a veteran diplomat, referring to the Nazis 'as dangerous clowns who know nothing of the world … and in Italy there were no longer men with a sense of responsibility'.[193] Later in the month Ciano called his brother-in-law Massimo Magistrati, working in Berlin, who thought that the sense of panic was created more by Attolico's 'endemic sense of fear'. Attolico stuck to his guns – observing, as any good diplomat should, the build-up of forces – and suggested Poland would be attacked on about 15 August. It was a month of anxiety for Ciano, and when on 4 July he had heard nothing from Berlin he naïvely wrote that this 'confirms the fact that nothing dramatic is in the offing'.[194]

On the general diplomatic front Ciano noted that many were packing up their bags for the summer holidays, especially as the Danzig storm had 'blown over', or so he thought. He saw the Greek Minister Metaxas and warned him about the consequences of accepting the British guarantee, which he warned 'placed his country in the somewhat unenviable position of becoming a semi-protectorate'.[195] The self-assurance of this threat was typical of Ciano's attitude and youth. The

---

[*] The Danzig corridor had been the result of the post-Great War agreements to establish Polish independence with access to the Baltic Sea, but Danzig (now Gdańsk) was a free city, separate from Poland and Germany – and an aggravation to Hitler.

British Ambassador Loraine demanded an interview with Mussolini to raise the issue of Danzig, and Villani the Hungarian brought two letters from Teleki, the first about Hungary's adherence to the Axis, but the second raising reservations about Poland. Diplomats may have been packing summer holiday bags, but the world was on edge.

CIANO IN SPAIN

On 9 July Ciano set sail for a visit to Spain, still feeling guilty about his father, whom he felt he had treated somewhat arrogantly. He spent time with Franco, noting that the Generalissimo always changed conversation from politics to military questions, and that he affirmed a 'strong' neutrality with Italy; but Ciano wondered whether Franco regarded Germany in the same light. Franco pointed out that 'Spain must take sides in the interest of its own future existence'.[196] How far Ciano took on board the fact that Franco had no intention of joining in a European war is difficult to fathom. It was agreed that Spain needed to accelerate its armaments programme, (as did Italy), construct four new battleships, and prepare defence lines across the Pyrenees. Franco, as a totalitarian leader, always supported his fellow dictators, believing that the Germans would win, but he refused to participate. He remained wary of British blockades. Spain was now seriously diminished militarily and economically, and Franco remained stubbornly neutral despite a later visit by Hitler; Franco only turned towards the Allies once he was totally convinced that they were winning.

Ciano had already noted in his diary that Mussolini was happy for Italians fighting for the republic to be executed. However, once Ciano saw what was actually happening, he was shocked. He recorded that some 200,000 Italians were under arrest, and that many would be shot, while others were forced labourers. The number being executed stunned him. 'In Madrid alone some 200 to 250 a day, in Barcelona 50; in Seville, a town which was never in the hands of the Reds, 80.'[197] He put it down to 'Spanish mentality', but the figures shook him. He was right to be perplexed about the barbarity, as Franco would spend hours signing death warrants, and this persisted until after World War II concluded. Many of Franco's colleagues criticised him for this, and when the British Ambassador Samuel Hoare 'met Franco for his final interview, he was blunt and criticised Franco for the continuous executions still taking place. Franco promised reform but remained his usual unperturbed self'.[198] Even as late as 1963 with the trial and execution of a Grimau García, who had been a senior communist, facing charges based on 'Civil War crimes ... despite pleas from Khrushchev, Willy Brandt, Harold Wilson and Queen Elizabeth II he was convicted. He was also badly tortured'.[199] Ciano may have romanticised war, especially in his golf club, but it was a vastly different matter when he witnessed the brutality. While he was in Spain two appeals were made directly to him, and Franco at least upheld those.

It must have been something of a relief for Ciano when he returned to Italy – only to be instructed by Mussolini to present an ultimatum to the Papal Nuncio for the *L'Osservatore Romano* (the daily newspaper of the Vatican City State) to stop its subtle attacks on the Axis or be prepared for its circulation to be prohibited; at least there was no threat of execution. Mussolini, having signed the Pact of Steel, was becoming concerned about being dragged into the German–Polish conflict, and he was calling for a conference at proposed meeting with Hitler at the Brenner, which Ciano thought unlikely; Ribbentrop confirmed he was correct.

Ciano spent more time on his father in his diary than he did on his wife Edda. He had tried to reach his family holidaying on Capri after his return from Spain, but the rough seas stopped him. As ever, he and Edda were living their own lives with their own lovers and interests, but it has been suggested that she was a force to be reckoned with in terms of influence over her father. The American Ambassador William Bullitt in Paris cabled a state department message which explained that 'Mussolini's daughter has the greatest influence over him as well as Ciano, and the influence is far from the good'.[200] Bullitt was not always correct in his various opinions, and he was wrong about Edda, with Ciano worried about her statements and public image.

Rumours of German plans

Despite Attolico's warnings from Berlin, Mussolini was more concerned about the news on 1 August that the British had sent Indian troops to Egypt. He ordered Ciano to confront Loraine with this breach of agreement of keeping one another informed, only to find that the Italian military attaché in London had in fact already been notified. More concerning was the lack of information from Berlin, because all Ciano heard was rumour. As noted earlier, Ciano considered Attolico to be a scared man but was now questioning whether his views on the man were correct. Attolico always sent his messages by hand to Ciano but there were indications that the Germans knew their contents, which meant they were able to access his desk or Ciano had informed von Mackensen, as was his habit, for a time.[201] Ciano wrote in his diary that 'Attolico's insistence makes me wonder, either this ambassador has lost his head, or he sees and knows something which has completely escaped us.'[202] His brother-in-law had not helped by stating that the Germans were not up to anything, implying their ambassador was wrong. Had he been correct, he might have hoped, with Mussolini's influence, to take Attolico's place. The disturbing news for Ciano came when General Mario Roatta, the Italian military attaché in Berlin, sent messages about German troops massing on the Polish borders. It was at this stage of events that Ciano heard that the king wanted to bestow the Collar of the Annunciation on him. Mussolini had initially objected, Edda may have intervened, but it was agreed that Ciano would officially hear while on a planned trip to Albania, the conquest which had apparently earned him the honour.

CIANO IN SALZBURG

By 9 August 1939 the Japanese were making up their minds whether or not to join the Pact of Steel, and Mussolini agreed that Ciano should meet Ribbentrop at Salzburg to try and ascertain the validity of the rumours appertaining to Danzig. It is easy to detect from Ciano's diary that Mussolini simply could not work out where he stood on this matter. As Bosworth wrote in his biography of Mussolini, 'certainly at this time of extreme crisis, the decision-making process, or lack of it, under charismatic rule was plain'.[203] In August it was mere speculation, because the Germans were not sharing their plans and Mussolini was frequently changing his mind. Later Ciano would describe it as Mussolini's 'see-sawing state of mind', but in August the main issue for the Italians was simply trying to discover their Axis partner's intentions, hence the meeting in Salzburg. Mussolini informed Ciano that he had to try and delay any war, and to 'tell' the Germans to avoid a Polish conflict 'since it would be impossible to localise it'. Ciano was in full agreement.

In his diplomatic report to Mussolini on the Salzburg meeting, Ciano wrote 'I cannot say he produced any new facts', and Ribbentrop had started with two assertions which he could not counter. The first was that any conflict over Danzig would not become a general war because 'Europe will be an impassive spectator of the merciless destruction of Poland by Germany', and secondly Britain and France did not have the military capacity to intervene.[204] It would be, Ribbentrop claimed, a 'totalitarian victory', undoubtedly trying to convince Ciano that Italy would share the honours.

Ribbentrop, as always, gave a sweeping survey of his version of the European chessboard. He pointed out that Russia would not intervene, not least because the Anglo-French talks in Moscow had failed. Britain and France were too weak, Belgium and the Netherlands would stay neutral for safety reasons, Turkey could make no concrete contribution, Yugoslavia was weak (of which Italy should take advantage), Romania would continue its 'balancing trick', and the USA would remain isolationist. Ribbentrop was not far off the mark in 1939, but wars never go the way they are planned, and he had overlooked the significance of the English Channel and the potential power of America – and of course he could not have foretold the effect of Hitler's making an enemy of Soviet Russia.

In his diary Ciano recorded that Ribbentrop's 'conscience bothered him' (which was extremely unlikely), that the 'conversations were tense' and the 'atmosphere icy', and that they 'were distrustful of one another'.[205] The Germans entertained the Italian party in a restaurant called the Weisse Rössl; Ciano sat opposite Ribbentrop and beside his host's wife, but the meal was held in total silence, which was not only embarrassing but intimated the disagreement more than the arguments had managed.[206] The coldness of the evening meal was evident, and 'even spread to their secretaries'.[207] Although Ciano had been happy to invade Albania, the German action proposed against Poland concerned him because of its possible consequences, and Giuseppe Bottai* in his diary later claimed that it was at this juncture that Ciano turned against the Axis. Bottai may well have been correct.[208]

The next day, 12 August, Ciano met Hitler, whom he found cordial. Hitler listened to Ciano's explanation of the problem and the military resolution, as he perceived it, causing him to write that Hitler 'exhibits a truly profound military knowledge'. However, it was noted that Ciano was in fine debating form, and he countered Hitler's arguments over Poland being a local affair, even poking fun at the flower arrangement (which Dollmann believed was the effort of Hitler's girlfriend, Eva Braun).[209] Ciano had another meeting with Hitler which 'was more concise', but when he explained that Italy was not yet ready or prepared for a major war, Ribbentrop rudely told him, 'We don't need you,' to which Ciano promptly replied, 'The future will show.'[210] Paul Schmidt reminisced that 'Ciano stood up to Hitler very energetically, that war in Poland would not be confined to that country … and he could not have been more explicit.'[211] The next day Schmidt observed that Ciano made no more effort, and 'folded up like a jack-knife'.[212] It was probably not a change of attitude, as Schmidt thought, but an indication that Ciano had recognised that nothing could be done, realising that Hitler was going to strike, and as far as the Germans were concerned about Italy, it was simply 'the number of divisions that the enemy will be obliged to keep facing us, thus easing up the situation on the German war fronts'.[213] On a slightly more curious level Eva Braun was watching Ciano from the window and photographed him. Ciano saw her and asked who she was, but Ribbentrop gave no direct answer and her window was closed by a guard.[214]

When he returned to Rome, he wrote that he was 'completely disgusted with the Germans, as leaders, with the way they do things'.[215] This outburst signified a critical turning point in Ciano's thinking. It might be tempting to raise the issue at this stage of a revamped diary, but there are too many pieces of other information to doubt the validity of what he was writing, though there is always

---

* Bottai was a member of the Chamber of Deputies, and a firm supporter of Italian fascism – but he became deeply concerned as the war turned against the Italians.

the possibility that he may have 'tweaked it in places'. He had gone to Salzburg somewhat jauntily, arriving in a militia general's uniform, hoping the Danzig issue could be resolved by another Munich conference. When he was asked by a journalist if there would be a war he replied, 'Well, if I manage to see the "the little moustache" I will remove the idea from his head'.[216] If this were true it exhibited overconfidence, and was a potential *faux pas* had it been overheard in the wrong circles. He also noted that the Italian people would shudder when they eventually heard of Germany's attack on Poland. He informed Mussolini of the meeting and showed him documents which proved the German 'bad faith', and he instructed Starace to ensure that Mussolini was aware of public opinion.

Mussolini was still muddled about the position he should take, and by mid-August was sharing with Ciano that he was thinking of breaking with Germany, but not too rapidly. They had to be careful; he did not want 'to miss out on any of the spoils' but did want to make time to see 'how the democracies would react'. It was this line of Mussolini's thinking which probably caught the attention of one of his many biographers who wrote that 'even greed was now held in check. Only sheer terror of the Nazis could justify the survival of the Axis'.[217] Mussolini and Ciano had a six-hour discussion in which Ciano claimed he was frank with the Duce, telling him that Italy's economic and military situation, meant they could not entertain war.

There were more conferences, and Ciano found that Mussolini was always 'shifting his attitude', because he was worried that Hitler's rage might take his focus off Poland 'to square accounts with Italy'.[218] The day before Mussolini met with Ciano and Attolico, the latter had been instructed to tell Ribbentrop that 'Italy will march with Germany'. Ciano met Percy Loraine, who lucidly informed Ciano that Europe would take no further *Diktats* from Hitler, and he expressed his concern that 'for the first time in history' Britain and Italy might be at war against one another.

Ciano took a break on 19 August to travel to Tirana, where he had anticipated hearing that he had been honoured with the Collar of the Annunciation, but he had barely been there a day when Anfuso phoned and warned him he was needed back in Rome. It transpired that Mussolini had changed his mind yet again, and he wanted to support Germany whatever the cost. Ciano found himself in conference with Mussolini and Attolico, hearing Mussolini explain that he did not want the world press calling Italians the 'cowards' who 'pull back at the spectre of war'.

This was a significant moment insofar as it marked the point in Ciano's life when his relationship with Mussolini began its downward spiral. Ciano boldly suggested to Mussolini that he 'rip up the pact. Throw it in Hitler's face and

Europe will recognise in you the natural leader of the anti-German crusade'.[219] For a moment this impressed Mussolini, who asked Ciano to arrange a meeting at the Brenner. Ribbentrop, as Ciano had suspected, could not make it, but suggested Innsbruck instead. Mussolini asked Ciano about 'Ribbentrop's tone', appearing worried about German reactions. Ciano then heard of what he called a *coup de théâtre*, the Ribbentrop–Molotov Pact, thinking the Germans 'had struck a master blow'. Ciano was instructed by Mussolini to see Loraine to confirm that the Duce wanted peace and for him to lead the necessary conference. According to Ciano, Loraine nearly fainted and had 'to rest in the toilet' to recover; understandably, for the British ambassador this news offered some hope.

Back with Mussolini, Ciano discovered that Hitler had sent a veiled message which hinted that action was about to start. Mussolini now tried another ploy, informing the Germans that they could not join with them until their Axis partner supplied them with the necessary materials. The initial German reaction was somewhat cold, but soon came a demand to hear about Italy's shopping list, which Attolico swiftly built up to ridiculous proportions. Hitler's response was that he simply wanted Italy to remain friendly and for Mussolini to keep Italy's neutrality out of the headlines until the last moment.

WORLD WAR II

On the last day of August, the Italians, still hoping for a conference with the British and French, heard the news that Germany was invading Poland. This was the beginning of the conflict which would become global, and in which Italy, now tied to Nazi Germany, would be submerged in a catastrophic disaster. Mussolini had looked to Italy regaining the Roman Empire, and Ciano had signed the Pact of Steel. Had Italy managed to remain neutral, as Spain did, Mussolini might have died in his bed (as Franco managed to do, in 1975), and Ciano would not have been executed. The two Italians both showed a high degree of ineptitude when it came to international relationships – Ciano was still inexperienced – and they would regret the turn of events. Ciano had yet to see the Damascus light, but he was beginning to see a little more clearly than Mussolini that this conflict could be disastrous.

On 1 September Ciano recorded Mussolini as appearing calm, the Duce having decided that Italy would stay neutral. Mussolini had ordered a blackout and restaurants closed, but the news from Anfuso was that the British and French had cut telephone links, creating a sense of panic. The lines were soon restored, as Ciano connected with the British and French to indicate that that the Italians were staying neutral. In the afternoon there was a Council of Ministers when Mussolini spoke briefly, and Ciano gave an anti-German speech which according to him was well received. Mussolini was on tenterhooks as to where he stood in relation to all that was happening, and Ciano appeared to have become anti-German, wanting to avoid a major war. There seems little question that Mussolini constantly vacillated as to where he stood. One biographer wrote that 'Mussolini liked to portray himself as a man of decision and iron will. In reality he was mercurial to an almost pathological degree, making decisions one minute that could be overturned half an hour later, then revived before the day was out.'[220] Mussolini was probably dealing with personal frustration, because he considered himself important and the leader of the Axis, an illusion now wrecked.

Most of the Italian population seemed happy for their country not to be embroiled in a major war, and some older fascists who had hitherto regarded Ciano as a mere whippersnapper, holding power because of family connections, started to move in his direction. Bottai called on Ciano, who explained he had broken with Ribbentrop in Salzburg, and that the Pact of Steel had been signed on the understanding that there would be no war for three to four years; it was unusual for Ciano and Bottai to be so close.[221] Dino Grandi also started to appreciate Ciano, and a few other leaders such as Farinacci still persisted in praising their Axis partner, but most were anxious about the potential consequences of going to war.

Ciano and Mussolini were constantly made aware of their lack of military preparation, and on 5 September Pariani again 'painted a dark picture' of Italy's military. A fortnight later Graziani gave an account of potential front-line forces, which amounted to only 10 divisions, with 35 others which were 'patchy' and not fully manned. In Ciano's opinion the air force habitually gave false estimates, and the navy's chief of staff, Admiral Domenico Cavagnari, pointed out that the British and French fleets combined outnumbered the Italians by six to one. Finally, Raffaello Riccardi, the minister of exchange and foreign currency, informed his leaders that Italy was in a desperate financial situation. It was little wonder that Mussolini decided to stay neutral, even though he was notorious for ignoring economic concerns. As Ciano noted at the end of the first week 'the Duce still has intermittent belligerent flashes'.

On 3 September they heard that Britain and France had declared war, and Ciano questioned how the democracies could win against German military might, while Mussolini thought the clash would not happen and the French would never fight. Mussolini was proud of his new relationship with the all-powerful Germany, but still hoping for a conference which he might personally lead, to establish peace. This was no mere moral stand, however, because he was already 'dreaming of heroic undertakings' against Yugoslavia, which he thought would bring him access to Romanian oil. Ciano, now indicating concern about the future, tried to hold his master in check, writing that he must do so, 'otherwise it will mean the ruin of the country, the ruin of fascism and the ruin of the Duce himself'. Having convinced the Western democracies that Italy was not going to fight, Ciano adopted his bullyboy pose again to assert himself once more while they were eating out of his hands for the sake of peace; he demanded from Françoise-Poncet that the anti-Italian measures in Tunis, Djibouti, and Oran had to stop, and the French ambassador promptly replied that he would investigate the problem. Ciano was pleased when Loraine apologised for a damaging article written by David Lloyd George, and Ciano then informed Loraine that Italy would not take Britain by surprise but added the warning that 'he had to be careful not to dictate to us'. Ciano was feeling on secure ground again, sounding pompous once more, but he still had to convince Mussolini that he was not missing 'heroic moments' with the Germans.

Meanwhile the Wehrmacht had already reached as far as Warsaw, but Ciano realised that even with Poland occupied there could still be a major European war, and wrote that 'I do not believe that Hitler can have the wisdom to be moderate in victory'.[222] When Hitler later hinted at peace, the peace-loving but resilient Chamberlain decided Hitler was no gentleman and could not be trusted, and remained determined to fight. Loraine confirmed this attitude, causing Ciano to note that the 'English have taken up the sword and are not likely to sheathe it to their dishonour'. Ciano detected cracks in the Anglo-French relationship (an astute observation, as the discord would become apparent during the Phoney War). Ciano also heard that the Hungarians were nervous. Mussolini suddenly condemned German conduct, but swiftly added that Italy had to be cautious. Ciano agreed with him and added 'if Germany wins before Christmas, well and good, otherwise she will lose the war'.[223] This and other statements tended to indicate that Ciano was not thinking on moral grounds but purely about safety; peace was necessary only because Italy was not ready.

Attolico shared with Ciano that he was pleased that the Duce appeared moderate, and he had noted the change in 'Mussolini's psychology' during the month. It was not all milk and honey, though, because the German economic agent in Italy, Karl Clodius, brought the message that the German leaders had asked if the Italians would postpone the expatriation of the Germans in the Alto Adige until the war was over. Ciano was immediately suspicious of German intentions: the Alto Adige had been Italianised, and even though 75 per cent of the population was German, 95 per cent of public posts were held by Italians.[224] It did not take too much imagination to wonder what Hitler might be planning.

It was an impossible task for the Italians to have any real idea of Hitler's next step. On 14 September Magistrati in Berlin had a conversation with Göring, who thought it wise that Italy should remain neutral, but then dropped a hint that Russia might intervene. The news had come through that the Russians had entered Poland, with the sudden realisation that the well-known non-aggression Molotov–Ribbentrop Pact, signed in August, had included a clandestine protocol. Despite the Pact of Steel the Italians had had no idea of this. Ciano was furious and told Mussolini that it was 'a monstrous union against the letter and spirit of the Pact. It is anti-Rome as well as anti-Catholic'.

Mussolini gave a speech in Bologna on neutrality, and Ciano told him how well it had been received and that the country was right behind him. Ciano had to keep encouraging him because he knew that 'the Duce is in favour of peace only, but the position as a neutral is not to his liking', adding that he could not contradict Mussolini because it would only make matters worse.[225] Mussolini's stand was not helped when Hitler gave a speech at Danzig in which he mentioned Mussolini twice, which flattered him; this was probably Hitler's intention. It was no surprise that just a week later the Germans were asking for Italian help in naval matters such as providing U-boat stations, keeping an eye on British and French naval movements, and giving the Germans some submarines. In terms of Italy's future, Ciano recognised that this last request was potentially dangerous, and claimed in his diary that he and Admiral Cavagnari set out to sabotage this plan. Ciano was determined to try and hold Mussolini back from succumbing to German influence, and even persuaded him to reappoint an ambassador in London, suggesting Giuseppe Bastianini, the Italian undersecretary for foreign affairs, whom he described as 'no eagle but trustworthy' and who, more to the point, was on the side of 'non-intervention'.

All Europe appeared unsettled, and Mussolini, who was considering creating a bloc of Danubian and Balkan countries, decided that Croatia was working up towards a crisis, and after hearing the news that the Romanian prime minister had been killed by the banned 'Iron Guard', suggested that the Italian plan should be put into action. More unsettling at the end of the month was an unexpectedly polite phone call from Ribbentrop asking for three meetings, one between Hitler and Mussolini in Munich, then Ciano to go to Berlin to meet Hitler, and finally a meeting with Ribbentrop at the Brenner. This had no appeal for Ciano, but Germany called. He wrote at the end of the month 'I will fight like a lion to preserve peace for the Italian people'.

Ciano with Hitler

In the first two days of October Ciano found himself, somewhat unwillingly, having to listen to Hitler and then meet Ribbentrop. He found Hitler 'tranquil and relaxed', very sure of himself, as the victory in Poland had filled him with confidence. Hitler explained to Ciano that he was certain of victory in the West, and he wanted Italy to be more active in their alliance. Ciano, trying to ignore the request, noticed this confidence, writing that Hitler was 'either hallucinating or he really is a genius'.[226] Hitler was exuberant about Poland and, according to Paul Schmidt, would not stop talking about his success, and said he could tell from the expression on Ciano's face that he was bored, reminding him of a popular song with the words 'we don't want to have all the details'.[227] Hitler informed Ciano he would make a peace offer to the Allies and because of his U-boats was not worried about the USA.

Ciano dined with Ribbentrop, regarding him as 'Hitler's amplified echo' and not enjoying the moment. Ciano could hardly face Ribbentrop and tended to address Paul Schmidt, who later wrote that 'I came to know and have a regard for this man [Ciano] who, despite his frequently arrogant and somewhat uncivilised behaviour on official occasions, perceived the trend of events with greater clarity, and did not allow himself to be blinded by Hitler and Ribbentrop's fine words'.[228] Ciano was becoming more astute and beginning to develop his own views, which did not always reflect those of Mussolini. On the way back to Italy he spoke on the train with a journalist, revealing his thinking not only about Hitler but on Mussolini, and with 'corrosive irony'. The journalist noted that when they arrived at a platform there was a crowd gathered, so Ciano jumped up to smarten himself, made sure he looked stern on presenting himself, and returned with the words 'the Italians adore me'.[229] His international outlook may have become a little more discerning, but his domestic persona still remained top of his priority list.

Back in Rome Ciano discovered that Mussolini was considering changing elements within his government, but was still vacillating between war and peace. There was another curious element in Mussolini's mixed thinking, namely let the 'giant European powers' fight, and even suggesting that Ciano should 'throw some kerosene on the flames'.[230] Mussolini's infantile wish was that as head of Italy he would be the last one standing. They incessantly discussed the German situation; Ciano described Ribbentrop as a parvenu or an ex-champagne salesman who had found his way to his position, but opined that Hitler was a worker and 'preferred victories without spilling blood'. Quite how Ciano came to this conclusion about Hitler is beyond explanation, especially when he had heard from Attolico of the barbarities being committed in Poland. He and Mussolini read Hitler's speech where he had dropped hints about peace, which drew Mussolini to the conclusion that the war was over; he failed to understand that Britain and France had declared war and were making a principled stand against Hitler's belligerence. Ciano, however, was aware of this and did not agree with his Duce.

The next day Ciano noted that Mussolini 'would like to do something to get into the game … he feels left out, and this pains him'.[231] The expression of playing a game, often used by Ciano, tends to underline his immature approach; the fact that war brings death and destruction appears to have been missing from his equations. Françoise-Poncet met Ciano and told him that the war could not be stopped by mere overtures. Ciano heard that Bernard Shaw and Lloyd George wanted peace, that Daladier had given an 'uncompromising speech', and that Chamberlain's reply dashed hopes of peace for even 'the most convinced pacifists'.

Mussolini shared his personal feelings with Ciano, saying that what worried him most was that while for years the Italians had heard his bellicose speeches they would now see him seeking peace; it must in fact have been a relief for most people. Mussolini's vacillations caused his critics to speculate that he had syphilis, which affected his mind. There was further tension in the Alto Adige, where the Germans were being difficult, and news of trouble in Croatia, where Mussolini was considering the possibility of action. Ciano was less certain about that, because he knew it would unsettle the French and the British.

Meanwhile, Mussolini had been studying the Russian situation and seeking a way to come to terms with Stalin's unexpected pact with Germany. He decided the best way was to explain to the public that Bolshevism was dead, and the Russian state had become a form of Slavic fascism. He was unwittingly close to the truth, because of course the so-called communist Stalin was already a dictator. Ciano tried to dissuade Mussolini, because the Italians, in Ciano's language, 'would not swallow this'. Ciano had asked his Ambassador Augusto Rosso in Russia to weigh up Stalin's foreign policy, and received some sound if unwelcome advice: Rosso noted that 'for the first time in three years at this post, he had been asked some intelligent questions'.[232] Rosso and many others had recognised that Ciano was inexperienced, still the playboy infatuated by himself, but the reality of late 1939 began to instil a degree of maturity in him. When the French and British signed a treaty with Turkey, Ciano was less concerned than he would once have been, because he saw it as a moment when Hitler had 'lost a point'.

Ciano's mind became consumed with his sister Maria who during October became ill, and it was clear that she was in a serious condition, prompting Ciano to send an arrow prayer, 'may the Virgin Mary accomplish the miracle'. Maria was suffering from anorexia with the additional problem of tuberculosis, which in those days was often fatal. Hitler sent his good wishes for Maria, who did not suspect her own fate, being conscious most of the time. On 22 October, however, she died, and once again Ciano was beset by deep grief, writing intense lines of his personal feelings, 'she was my link with the past … two colts who fed from the same manger, and melancholy dominates my spirit'. He went once again to the Purificazione cemetery in Livorno, and laid her to rest with 'my unforgettable father'.

Despite his public demeanour he obviously loved his family. There was a sensitivity in his words which reveal something of the inner man. He found the Duce paternal, but more disturbingly he also heard that Mussolini had written a personal letter to Hitler. In this missive Mussolini had assured the German dictator that Italy stood by Germany in economic terms and in moral backing, and later probably in a military role. Ciano could not see the point of the letter, but Mussolini was having another pro-German bout, informing Ciano 'that the Axis and the Alliance with Germany still exist and are fully operative'.[233] Ciano was preparing an important speech for 16 December, in which he wanted to widen the breach, but Mussolini was insisting that he give out a pro-German line. Ciano noted that Mussolini was 'the most dissatisfied and restless person among us all'. Ciano, realising the Nazi danger, had hoped that Italy would stay neutral, and that Mussolini would agree with him, but Mussolini reminded Ciano that it was *he* who was the Duce. Deep in Berlin, Goebbels wrote in his diary 'yesterday: Count Ciano is against us. But the Duce has intervened in our favour and given Ciano a sharp rebuke'.[234] This was the beginning of a long and difficult road.

By November 1939, after two months of inactivity on the Western Front, the war was becoming known as the Phoney War. The British were active at sea but had sent only a small expeditionary force (the BEF) to France, where according to the British General Brooke, another diarist, relations with the French military, who were in command, were never easy. The sense of stalemate would last until May 1940, but there were rumours and counter-rumours of an impending German attack. For Ciano and others in Italy it seemed as if the frenetic activity of September 1939 had calmed down.

On 2 November Ciano visited the graves of his father and sister at Livorno, and it may just be speculation, but these personal losses may have made him more reflective. While they did not change his lifestyle, he was a little more mature in political judgements, yet he remained subservient to his father-in-law. Mussolini had established his new government, and Ciano noted in his diary that some quietly called it the Ciano Cabinet. Goebbels in his diaries made several short references to Ciano, addressing him as Count when happy with him, otherwise simply Ciano. Later in the month Goebbels noted in his diary that 'Ciano is the strongman, even more so than before … politics is a dirty business'.[235] Goebbels and other German observers often blamed Ciano for not entering the war.

Ciano and Mussolini were annoyed to hear that the 'warlike' and belligerent Ribbentrop had reportedly suggested that the British had entered the war because they had known that Italy would remain neutral. Ciano talked with Badoglio, who was pessimistic about the state of the armed forces and preferred neutrality, and Ciano gathered that Badoglio would rather fight the Germans than fight alongside them. Various heads of minor states, hoping for peace, offered themselves as mediators, fearing they would be dragged into a conflict reminiscent of the Great War. France and Britain rejected all these overtures, and by 12 November Daladier and Chamberlain had agreed to reject all offers of peace, announcing this four days later. Apart from seeking peace the smaller countries were understandably regarded as trying to appease the Germans with their goodwill offers, mainly because of their fear of an invasion. Ciano heard all this information and realised that a peaceful outcome was rapidly becoming impossible.

When he heard of the 8 November attempt on Hitler's life in the Munich Bürgerbräukeller and considered the various rumours, he thought it might have been a master-plot to create anti-British feeling, or a family Nazi brawl. He may have been right on all counts, as the evidence appears to indicate that even Hitler, who had left the meeting unusually early, seemed to know what was happening. Shreds of evidence have been gathered, but no reliable confirmation, and it remains a curious area of interest. It also happened at the same time as the Venlo incident, where Ciano believed the misleading news that the chief of the 'English Secret Services had been captured'.*

After the November ceremony to commemorate Italy's 1918 victory, Ciano confided to Bottai, along with Alessandro Pavolini and Ettore Muti, his fellow fascist chiefs, that he profoundly hoped that Britain and not Nazi Germany would win the war. Britain, he brightly explained, 'deserved victory because it stood for the hegemony of golf, whisky and comfort'.[236] It is easy to detect a sense of levity here, but in fact the golf clubs, hunts, beaches and other social gatherings were often used for significant discussions. Ciano wondered why the Allies did not make an issue of Alto Adige, where the Germans were now suggesting a plebiscite with obvious intentions of driving a wedge between Italy and Germany, but he failed to understand that as far as the Allies were concerned Alto Adige was a lost pawn on the chessboard.

As Ciano reflected on the news that Germany had ignored the pleas for peace by the Low Countries, he demonstrated his inexperienced views, writing that 'Hitler and Ribbentrop have always specifically excluded an attack on the neutrals for moral and technical reasons', but with the change in his views adding 'but considering what has happened before would lead one to think that anything is possible'.[237] What probably staggers the 21st-century reader more than anything

---

*   The British secret services had blundered. A Captain Sigismund Payne Best, a British army intelligence officer, believed he could meet a German general resisting Hitler. He joined with a Major Stevens, supposedly a passport control officer, and the Dutch loaned a Lieutenant Dirk Klop to attend a meeting on the Dutch–German border town of Venlo. They were supposed to meet on Wednesday 8 November, but the Germans swept across the border and captured Best and Stevens who, far from being Secret Service chiefs, were only agents.

else is the use of the word 'moral' relating to Hitler and Ribbentrop. Ciano had heard from the Prince of Piedmont that Italian troops were fraternising at the border with French troops; this seemed of little concern to Ciano, who took himself hunting on the Medici estate in Turin.

As noted, the British were waging war at sea, and this included blockading merchant ships whose cargoes included commercially essential coal supplies going from Germany to Italy. The French ambassador assured Ciano that he would intervene to stop this blockade. Later, when the British Ambassador Percy Loraine returned, Ciano discussed the issue with him, warning that it would be calamitous to break their current relationship. He detected from Loraine that the British were becoming more intransigent.

Near the end of the month Ciano completed his December speech, which he hoped would end or at least undermine Italian relations with Germany, and Mussolini appeared to accept the contents. There followed the news that the Russians had launched their attack against Finland, an ominous reminder that beyond the appointment of a new president of chamber and the humdrum existence of the Phoney War, life in Europe was on the edge of a precipice.

German Pressure

December started with Ciano's office being 'showered' with cables from Ribbentrop, demanding that von Mackensen, wishing to bypass Ciano, should have an audience with the Duce. This meeting soon happened, with Ciano cynically commenting that 'when the Duce speaks with Germans he can't help adopting a warlike attitude'.[238] Ribbentrop wanted Italy in the war immediately; meanwhile Ciano was pleased that Mussolini reaffirmed the anti-Bolshevik policy and said he was indignant about the Soviet attack on Finland. Nevertheless, Ciano was concerned about Mussolini's state of mind and hoped that nothing would be said to cause an incident with London. Ciano knew that Mussolini was restless, writing that 'out of this great struggle and in one way or another he [Mussolini] would like to find a way to fit into it'.[239] To Ciano's consternation, he gathered that Mussolini was thinking of sending Hitler a letter asking whether he would like Mussolini to find a diplomatic solution, but if not, Italy would join in the fray in 1942. Ciano could not see the sense in sending such a potentially risky letter.

Italian students were protesting on the streets about the attack on Finland, and a report arrived from an Italian professor, Grande Ufficiale Volpato, living in Posen,* giving details of Nazi atrocities in Poland. It must have been a graphic report, as it infuriated Mussolini, who instructed Ciano to make sure the French and American press saw a copy, because the 'world had to know'; it can only

---

*   Now Poznań.

be hoped that Volpato's name was removed. Starace turned up to warn Ciano that he had heard that the Germans were preparing a press release inferring that Ciano and Mussolini were having collisions with one another. The Germans were probably correct, but in fact Mussolini was not yet aware and Ciano, being cunning, ignored Starace, hoping to keep Mussolini in the dark.

The Germans persisted in their pressure, and a German politician, Dr Robert Ley,* arrived ostensibly for a holiday but was soon in Mussolini's office. He took Mussolini into his confidence and according to Ciano dropped four major hints: first, the Germans would attack the Netherlands because the Dutch were not neutral; secondly, Russia had been given a free hand in Sweden; thirdly, he foresaw a conflict with Russia in a few years; and finally Hitler's only policy was to continue the war. Ley was emphasising Hitler's aggressive intentions, asserting that no diplomatic solution was needed, that the Russians were dangerous and that the German alliance with Stalin was only temporary, thereby implying that Mussolini's hatred of Bolshevism was shared by Hitler. At least it was some form of communication. Attolico had returned from Berlin with no news or information, because the Germans were a closed shop to Italy and everyone else. The only good news was that the French ambassador arrived to tell Ciano that the Allies would not interfere with the coal ships; he seemed, however, to have made a mistake in using the word 'Allies', because the British continued the blockade.

Ciano gave a report to the Chamber, pleasing Mussolini, and although Ciano stated that it was supposed to be a closed session and 'watertight,' he knew his words would soon percolate through the system. Once again Balbo was annoying Mussolini because he was constantly attacking the communists, which once Mussolini would have appreciated, but he was now more concerned that this might upset the Germans. Ciano suspected that the Russian–German pact was not as strong as some believed – and it turned out, of course, that he was right in this perception. Mussolini was yet again shifting his position, and he insisted that his tone towards the Russians should at least be civil, as he was still entertaining hopes of Italy taking Corsica and Tunisia from the French. Mussolini was swinging like a pendulum and was childishly pleased to hear of a British press article suggesting that the Italians would fight with the Germans 'out of a sense of loyalty'. Ciano once again wrote in his diary that he was concerned about the Duce's state of mind. In today's world the expression 'U-turn' would be hitting the headlines – but the Duce's behaviour, recorded by Ciano and noted elsewhere, was generally contained within confined circles. Ciano recorded that Mussolini was feeling humiliated and angry over the continuing British blockade, which he

---

* Ley, the Labour front minister from 1933 to 1945, would commit suicide during the Nuremberg Trial.

took as a personal insult, but as Ciano and others knew, the lack of preparation by the military meant there was nothing they could do, and, as he added, 'there was no way out.'

When Mussolini had offered economic support to Germany, the fact was that Italy needed German support more than vice versa, but the Italians were successfully mining titanium and the Germans were demanding it. A certain amount was offered but von Mackensen made it clear they wanted more, prompting Ciano to refer surreptitiously to them as 'bullies and robbers'. However, Ciano was more concerned about his major speech to the Chamber, after which he proudly wrote that 'my speech was very successful, even if everybody did not understand the subtle anti-German poison permeating it'.[240] It was obviously a typical political speech, inundated with innuendo which could be read several ways. Goebbels had earlier in the month written in his diary that 'Ciano is the worst enemy … and is the strongman' but following this speech he wrote that 'Count Ciano has made a speech. Positive for us, along the lines of recent Italian statements. A few minor niggles, but not significant, with a strong denunciation of Versailles'.[241] Goebbels had lacked the perception to understand Ciano's subtle if not obscure expressions, but the British ambassador had not, and was pleased with the content. Ciano, meanwhile, was curious as to why the French ambassador thought Ciano had made too much of the German relationship. Ciano had mentioned the Pact of Steel and that the Germans had kept them out of the picture, and they were not ready for war. Unlike Goebbels, Ribbentrop was furious, but the speech appeared to make no impression on Hitler. Ciano felt it had been more successful abroad than at home, as being a typical political address it could have several interpretations.

On 21 December Himmler was in Rome. When they met, Ciano attempted to extract more information from him about German plans but was unsuccessful, writing in his diary that 'the Germans now distrust me, and the information was not forthcoming'.[242] Ciano was concerned that Himmler had spent two hours with Mussolini and left his offices looking satisfied. The Duce told Ciano that he had reaffirmed his anti-Bolshevist policy only to discover that Himmler agreed with him, and that he had told Himmler that he 'would not allow a German defeat to take place.'

Ciano saw Loraine, again raising the problem of the coal blockade, and warning him that an incident provoked by this action could destroy all their good work. The Romanians had sent their Foreign Minister Victor Antonescu on a fact-finding mission, and a few days later he passed on to Ciano some information gleaned from an intercepted French message in which three vital points were of interest: it was essential to keep Italy on the British side; it was suspected that Italy wanted to move into the Balkans; and finally that the British would not object so long as Italy stayed on their side. This was useful information, because only a few days earlier Mussolini had been pondering whether to make the anticipated move towards Croatia, and in line with this information Loraine informed Ciano at the end of the month that the British were taking a more sympathetic approach to the coal blockade.

Just before Christmas Ciano received information on a lecture given by the German deputy mayor of Prague, a Dr Pfitzner, in which he made a direct reference to Germany's intentions to take control of the Alto Adige and Trieste. As a result of this bombshell, Ciano called in von Mackensen, who had to endure Ciano's attack and who, according to Ciano, 'trembled'. The Germans were alarmed, and a few days later von Mackensen was recalled to Berlin for discussions. Ciano, meanwhile, was pleased that the Prague incident had made Mussolini more distrustful of the Germans. Mussolini instructed him to let the Belgians and Dutch know that the Germans were about to attack at any moment. (This move has often been interpreted as a sign of goodwill on the part of the Italians, but in fact it was more a bitter recriminatory attack by Mussolini for the Prague blunder.) Ciano's telegram was intercepted by the Germans, who interpreted it as a betrayal by Ciano (who had in fact been acting on Mussolini's orders).

These fluctuations by Mussolini concerned not just Ciano but others within the governing circle. Arturo Bocchini, chief of police, pointed out to Ciano that all the staff were too aware of Mussolini's restless moods, and he informed Ciano 'that the Duce should take an intensive anti-syphilitic cure, because Bocchini claims that the psychic condition of Mussolini is due to a recurrence of this old illness'.[243] The mood swings were well known to Ciano, and Mussolini was clearly politically unstable.

SUMMATION OF 1939

The belligerently inclined Mussolini wished to be at war when Italy could not afford it, his schoolboy sense of loyalty clashing with his fear of Hitler, and his deep sense of wanting to be regarded as the leader who restored the Roman Empire. History would condemn this as his pipedream, but to Mussolini, frustrated by events which changed daily, it was a major factor.

At the end of the year Ciano was anxious that once again Mussolini was suffering another wave of pro-Germanism, having told Ciano that he was thinking of writing to Hitler to tell him that the Italians were busy rearming. Ciano recorded his concern about this, wondering what Mussolini was preparing for, and noting that 'we cannot talk of war because of our state of unpreparedness'.

As the year 1939 ended, Ciano noted in his final comments that the year had been cruel to him in his personal life but generous in his political career. Politically,

Goebbels had described Ciano as 'the strong man', and most recognised that he was more powerful than he had ever been before, but the Germans were growing suspicious about his attitudes. He believed (correctly, as it turned out) that the new year would hold many surprises, concluding that as 'this absurd and inexplicable war is understood by no one, we can perhaps, find the key to its end'.[244]

During 1939 the Germans had felt the Italians had let them down but still needed them to join the conflict. The British and French, of course, were doing their best to ensure this would never happen. In Number 10 Downing Street, Sir Jock Colville, as a recently appointed high-ranking private secretary, was (illegally) keeping his own private diary of events.* He concluded, having heard of Ciano's speech and watching events unfold, that 'the Italians are openly disgusted and frightened, and clearly Ciano is now in the Allied camp. He even gives Loraine information, which is obviously to the detriment of Germany, and he is a restraining influence on his father-in-law, who hates democracies and cannot forgive or forget sanctions.'[245] Colville's astute observations were written from a distance and based on diplomatic notes and rumours. The Italians had been horrified by some Nazi behaviour. There was an incipient fear of the German strength and Ciano was steering away from the Nazi affiliation – but as to how far Ciano could influence or restrain his father-in-law could only be speculated. The year 1939 had witnessed the beginning of World War II, but Italy remained uncertain as to how to respond.

---

* Senior civil servants were not allowed to keep diaries of their professional lives; many, however, did.

6

1940 – THE CRITICAL YEAR

Mussolini declares war, June 1940
(ilgiornale.iy, unknown author)

VACILLATIONS

1940 was a dramatic year for Europe, with serious ramifications in Italy, led by the ever-wavering Mussolini. Ciano was of course constantly confused as to where his master stood. New Year's Day set the tone, with Ciano noting that Mussolini was chiding the democracies and that 'keen pro-German feelings were awakening in the Duce'.[246] The dilemma as to whether to fight alongside Germany or remain neutral still dominated Mussolini. Graziani revealed that he was an interventionist and pro-German, and denounced Badoglio, causing Ciano to note that Graziani had to be monitored. The next day Ciano favoured Badoglio by accepting his son as a diplomat even though, according to Ciano, 'he was no ace'. Mussolini was pontificating about the state of the world, outlining the popular views that 'Italians have no liking for Germany, are indifferent towards France, [and] hate Great Britain and Russia', and Ciano in his subservient position had to accept his master's opinions, writing in his diary 'only after many reservations'.[247] Mussolini tried to simplify complex situations, and it was hardly surprising that he suffered the symptoms of a stomach ulcer. Later in the month he 'ranted' about the Italian population when he heard they were grumbling about lack of food, and accused the Count of Turin of hoarding soap for his 35,000 whores, suggesting that the Italians were 'a race asleep' and that 18 years of his rule had not changed them.

When Mussolini heard that the Hungarian Foreign Minister Count Istvàn Czaky had informed Ciano that Hungary had no intentions in the Balkans, Mussolini was furious that they had even considered this possibility. Goebbels had noted in his diary that 'Count Ciano meets Czaky in Venice, undoubtedly curious as to what machinations the Hungarians and Italians were cooking up over the Balkans'.[248]

Tensions were constantly simmering, with Badoglio claiming it would be impossible to prepare defences for the coming year because of the lack of resources; Ciano felt it was critical to put the brakes on Graziani's ambitions. Attolico reported from Berlin that he had the distinct feeling that the Germans were under the impression that the Italians would soon be joining the war, causing Ciano to note that this was because Mussolini had been left alone with Himmler. Mussolini informed Ciano that he anticipated joining the war in 1941, later suggesting it could be late 1940.

The hesitation was driven by economic and military factors, those wishing to remain neutral always raising these problems. When the Germans protested at Italy manufacturing aircraft for the French, Riccardi promptly claimed that such sales were essential – otherwise, with the lire already drastically devalued, Italy's foreign exchange would empty. On 20 January the Council of Ministers discussed economics which Ciano described as 'characterised by a phantasmagorical display of billions which we do not have'.[249] Mussolini's response was, as usual, claiming that states only fell because of military defeats, but 'never because of economic reasons'. It was one of his habitual sweeping proclamations, intended to be taken as true simply because he had spoken. Mussolini held forth that Italy could not stay neutral, and that France and Britain were the enemies. The British were still blocking German coal supplies to Italy, but Mussolini believed Italy could work with alternative fuels, having been misled, according to Ciano, by 'so-called experts'. Mussolini had also halted Italian aircraft production for the British, reneging on orders previously signed, and Italy's foreign exchange was well below the danger level.

Ciano had hoped to stop the coal blockade diplomatically, but despite a courteous letter from Halifax, Loraine informed Ciano that the blockade would continue. Both François-Poncet and Loraine were constantly in and out of Ciano's offices, questioning what Mussolini intended to do, detecting his 'warmongering' (and they were generally correct). Ciano tried to avoid the issue, writing that he could not deny it, and that Loraine 'does not listen to me, nor can I proceed on this line with an intelligent and candid man like Percy Loraine'.[250] There is just a hint that Ciano respected the professionalism of the British ambassador and possibly even admired him.

There was news of problems with the Serbs, prompting Mussolini to think again of turning Croatia into an independent kingdom, with Ciano warning Mussolini that London and Paris should be notified – only to be 'brushed aside' and told that Italy would never join with Britain and France. Although Mussolini often became hostile towards Germany, on the grounds that 'they should listen to me', it was becoming obvious he was now turning towards the Nazis. Ciano had to follow his lead, as Welles observed: 'Count Ciano was wholly subservient to Mussolini', and although Ciano did not lack courage 'yet I have seen him quail at an interview with Mussolini when the dictator showed irritation'.[251]

There were further confrontations with the British over commercial negotiations regarding weapons, causing disquiet among financial experts such as Riccardi, not least because the British deals amounted to £20 million in arms alone.[252] There was growing concern over lack of food, and General Giacomo Carboni, back from Germany, informed Ciano that the German people, too, were lacking food, and were not enthusiastic at the prospect of more war. Ciano heard from the Prince of Hesse that Göring was incensed with Italy, but Ciano thought it was more to do with him not receiving the Collar of the Annunciation. Ciano was doing his best at this double-edged balancing act of not annoying the all-powerful Germans while desperately trying to persuade the Duce to remain neutral. Hesse asked if Mussolini would meet Hitler at the Brenner, and Mussolini swiftly accepted.

It was ever more evident to Ciano and others that Mussolini was veering towards the Nazi regime, with Mussolini telling Ciano that 'governments are like people and must follow a line of morality and honour'.[253] The use of the word 'honour' in Mussolini's context belonged more to the playground, and the word 'morality' had no ethical bearing for Mussolini, who was now informing Ciano that the Italian people must be disciplined and kept in uniform from morning to night. When Ciano informed Percy Loraine about Mussolini's views, and that they might change again in six months, the British ambassador replied, 'By that time Europe will be reshaped for ten generations to come.'[254]

Despite Mussolini's posture Riccardi made a 'brave speech' on the economic ramifications, which infuriated Mussolini, as he had promised 3,500 tons of copper to Germany, which Ciano claimed 'was extorted from Italian homes', and from churches. Ciano pleaded with Mussolini not to take the Church's sacred objects, only to be met with the reply that 'they do not need copper but faith'. The British–Italian relationship was deteriorating, so Loraine was astonished to hear that Ciano praised the Royal Navy over the *Altmark* attack, comparing it to the days of Francis Drake.*

On 16 February Welles, 'the personal agent of the American President Roosevelt who was on a peace mission', arrived.[255] Welles and Roosevelt hoped for peace, with Welles on a fact-finding mission. He met Ciano, who showed him his diary and obviously liked his visitor, describing him as dignified and courteous. He wrote that 'I gave a normal simple tone to the conversation, and this impressed him, because he was not expecting it'.[256] The play-actor side of Ciano surfaced, as he was known for his arrogant bearing in addressing visitors from 'minor' countries, which would not have impressed a senior figure from America.

On the other hand, he described in his diplomatic notes that this meeting with Mussolini was 'icy'. It started happily with Welles offering US$2 million for the proposed Italian Trade Fair while suggesting commercial negotiations. Welles was 'smoothing the way' towards questions about economic peace by exchanging views between neutral countries, with the possibility of helping the belligerents talk their way through the issues. Mussolini's reply referred to Hitler's speech, endorsing the German dictator's belief that the Germans deserved *lebensraum* in central Europe, and Germany should have its colonies returned. He told Welles that the Mediterranean Sea was a prison, explaining to him that when he arrived his ship had to pass the British checkpoint of Gibraltar. Welles admired Ciano to a degree, claiming, 'he was the only one who made it clear to me, without subterfuge and without hesitation, that he opposed the war'.[257]

Welles recognised his efforts were futile, noting 'one man, one man only, the dictator Benito Mussolini, made the decisions which plunged Italy into the holocaust and brought about the tragedy'.[258] It was during this month that it was becoming clear the direction that Mussolini might take. After Ciano had been away at the end of the month, he returned to discover that Mussolini had written

---

* The Royal Navy had captured the *Altmark* in Jøssingfjord, to release British prisoners. The successful action was achieved by Captain Philip Vian (HMS *Cossack*), giving a slight glimmer of hope to some in the fog of Europe.

an editorial for the *Giornale d'Italia* responding to an article in the British *Daily Herald* clearly indicating that Italy was willing to join Germany and even Russia if there were any intention of the totalitarian systems being threatened. Ciano noted that 'this made quite an impression, none of it favourable'.[259]

As Europe approached the dangers of a major conflict and Mussolini leaned closer to Germany's direction, Ciano continued his personal life as a playboy. The Duchess of Sermonera described one of his dinner parties, with Edda away, in which the drink and food flowed in a somewhat ostentatious way, followed by gambling and Ciano flirting with all the adoring women.[260] As Mussolini led Italy towards an uncertain destiny Ciano remained a point of gossip rather than a potential political force.

During March Mussolini became more pro-German, prompted by his anger towards the British over coal supplies. Italy normally required 12 million tons of coal annually, indispensable for military material, the reduction in supply causing Mussolini to explode that 'without coal there are no guns'.[261] Ciano warned Sir Noel Charles, standing in for Loraine, that the British were in danger of pushing Mussolini into Hitler's arms. Mussolini told Ciano that 'within a short time the guns will fire off by themselves', and 'I shall become the laughingstock of Europe'.

In early March General Marras (military attaché in Berlin) and Ciano had an interview with Mussolini, explaining that the Germans were sceptical about the Italians, and frequently referring to their treachery in the Great War, which shocked the Duce. This launched Mussolini into his projected policy of the *Guerra parallela*, the Parallel War. Mussolini, frustrated by the British control over the Mediterranean, toyed with the projected image of Italy controlling the sea from North Africa to the Balkans and acting as Germany's southern wing, becoming more buoyant about potential Italian success.

The next day Ciano met the king, who confided to Ciano that he knew he was in Germany's 'Black Book'. Ciano promptly replied, 'Yes, Your Majesty. At the top. And if you allow me to be bold enough to say so, I am in it immediately after you,' which the king considered to be an honourable situation.[262] Two weeks later, on the golf course, the king made an indirect approach through a member of the royal household, a Count Alberto Acquarone, informing Ciano that the king was aware of the unrest in the country and wondering whether he 'ought to intervene'. Mussolini's biographer Bosworth wondered whether Ciano had deduced from this conversation whether the king was contemplating replacing Mussolini, with Ciano as the possible candidate.[263] In these uncertain times anything was possible, and the French and British ambassadors were constantly meeting Ciano at the golf club, trying to ascertain Mussolini's latest position.

There is no doubt that Mussolini was aware that Ciano disagreed with him, though it is doubtful that Ciano ever challenged him directly. Ciano had sufficient enemies for them to 'spill the beans', with his golf club and beach visits being well known as rumour circuits where Mussolini's flunkies would have been listening. Early in the month Mussolini suddenly challenged Ciano, and told him 'to get it into his head that England will be defeated'. Ciano was clearly upset by this reproach, noting in his diary that 'I only serve him and my country'; he must have felt that 'Mussolini and Italy's interests' were in conflict.

Renewed German pressure

Following this brief *contretemps* Ciano heard that Ribbentrop had announced he was arriving to meet the Duce and the Pope. Ciano found this demand arrogant – a view of Ribbentrop shared by many, even in Germany. He arrived on 10 March, and Ciano was pleased to note that although a small crowd had been rustled up Ribbentrop received a 'cool reception'. As they drove away Ribbentrop told Ciano that the improving weather would soon lead to the defeat of France and the English would become prisoners on the continent. He also told Ciano that the conflict would be a military victory and Italy would stand alongside Germany. In this brief journey Ribbentrop encapsulated the purpose of his mission, which was a two-day meeting with the Duce, the second day to be taken up with Mussolini's answers and views.

In the first session Ribbentrop explained to Mussolini that Clodius would assist with the coal problems by using railways; Hitler knew that peace with Britain and France was impossible; American ambassadors could not be trusted; and the American people were against the war, with their demands for isolationism. Ribbentrop moved on to the delicate subject of Soviet Russia, assuring Mussolini that Stalin had renounced any idea of a world revolution, and after the departure of Litvinov (the Jewish foreign minister) all Jews had been dismissed from important positions. This was an exaggeration; in fact Stalin only shut down Comintern a few years later, to please the Allies whose economic support he needed. Ribbentrop claimed that 'Russia – and this is known with complete certainty in Germany – was dragged into the Finnish War.'[264] Few people would have believed Ribbentrop's version of the Russo-Finnish war. He explained to Mussolini that the Axis had to move rapidly while Hitler and Mussolini were in good health, as the Bürgerbräukeller bomb had been a warning that anything could happen. He then offered Mussolini some documents 'proving' atrocities committed by the Polish, causing Mussolini to note that 'in that case, events have justified the Führer'.[265] Ribbentrop explained how Russia was sending tons of cereals to Germany, that the German army was confident, having 'perfectly' trained divisions, and the Maginot Line was no problem as they had 'special weapons'. Ribbentrop was trying to propel Mussolini into the conflict, and his persuasive efforts were recorded by Ciano, making it no surprise that his diary was later used by Ribbentrop's prosecutors at Nuremberg.

Mussolini gave his replies the next day, questioning Ribbentrop on his Papal visit, claiming that there was no hope of friendship with the Church, and affirming that he was firmly anti-communist.[266] He modified it by telling Ribbentrop that Ciano in his December speech had made no reference to Russia or Finland, but he did not want Russia entering Romania with designs on the Balkans. Mussolini claimed that his naval fleet was growing, as was the air force, and he had two million men in the army, of which half were 'perfectly' trained. This was a gross exaggeration: the air force, according to a German military observer, was seriously out of date, even as late as '1941 biplane fighters went into action with a top speed of no more than 170 mph', and the army officers lived 'in a world of their own, having only the slightest contact with their men' who resented their appalling rations compared to those of the officers.[267]

If Mussolini was adept at exaggeration, he further spoke to Ribbentrop about his concept of the parallel war, and that he could supply food to Germany but with the vital 'vitamin C'. On reading Ciano's diplomatic papers, it was evident that Mussolini was trying to please the Nazi diplomat, also explaining that Italian troops were occupying the British in Africa. Ribbentrop immediately asked the leading question as to how many were on the French frontier. Mussolini replied that there were between 10 and 12 divisions. The unabashed Ribbentrop said that his experts thought it was lower, but quickly moved on to tell Mussolini that Hitler would like to meet him at the Brenner. Ciano was dismayed when Mussolini promptly accepted the offer.

Mussolini ensured that Ribbentrop understood that Italy would choose the moment it entered the war, but Ciano gathered the impression that the Duce was worried that he had 'gone too far'. In his diary Ciano wrote on 12 March that the Duce was fascinated by Hitler, 'a fascination which involves something deeply rooted in his nature'.[268] The next day Ribbentrop returned offering 18 March as the Brenner meeting, making Mussolini angry, saying 'these Germans give you no time to breathe'. On 16 March Sumner Welles returned, telling Ciano that Berlin held the firm opinion that Britain and France intended to destroy the Reich, and he questioned Ciano about Mussolini's long-term plans. What Wells, Mussolini, the British and the French did not know, however, was that on 1 March Hitler had given orders to prepare an attack on Denmark and Norway, which would take place on 9 April. Welles later recorded that Ciano had 'reminded me that Mussolini was definitely pro-German', and had predicted that Germany would soon turn against Russia.[269] Ciano was sure that Mussolini intended to keep solidarity with Germany, noting that it was 'easy to push Mussolini on an undertaking, but difficult to pull him back'.

The German ambassador called on Ciano, embarrassed that Hitler had demanded that he speak alone with Mussolini at the projected meeting. They arrived at a snow-covered Brenner, and Ciano recorded Hitler as cordial and not agitated. Before the two leaders met there had been a conversation between them and their foreign ministers in which Hitler had given a general historical survey and addressed their military strength, while Ciano, on Mussolini's instructions, had advised against an immediate conflict. As far as Ciano could tell the private meeting was a typically long monologue, with Hitler explaining that he only needed to put Mussolini in the picture, that his forces were prepared, and he was not asking anything of Mussolini apart from understanding they would defeat the Western powers.[270] One thing Mussolini gleaned from the various meetings was that 'Germany's flirtation with the USSR had its limits ... and the Führer went on regarding Mussolini and Italy as his real friends'.[271] This was music to Mussolini's ears.

In Italy Mussolini had some political support, causing Ciano to write that 'people who hold positions they do not want to lose' soon become lackeys; a valid criticism which some have justifiably aimed at Ciano. Bottai and Grandi opposed Mussolini, which would have been impossible in Germany. One of Ciano's social golfing friends was the Hungarian Count Pal Teleki, who was concerned about the direction in which Italy appeared to be turning. He told Ciano that 95 per cent of Hungarians hated the Germans, and asked Ciano whether he played bridge. When the astonished Ciano asked why, Teleki answered, 'For the days when we are together in Dachau concentration camp.' Ciano thought that this response merely revealed Teleki's state of mind, but it turned out to be uncomfortably true, with Teleki committing suicide in 1941 and Ciano being executed in 1944.

Near the end of March Ciano heard a rumour that Mussolini was considering firing him. Unsurprisingly he was concerned, writing that 'everything I have done was done for the sole purpose of serving my country and the Duce'. He further noted that 'the Duce will do whatever he wishes, *Dominus dedit, Dominis abstulit*' (the Lord gives, and the Lord takes away).[272] He was warned by a Monsignor Francesco Borgonini Duca to take care, because it was not only the Germans who would prefer him dead but also some Italians. He replied that he was not worried, because the Italians 'love me because they know the work I am doing'.[273] He was wrong. He may have had courage, but his opposition to joining the German war had made him enemies in Germany and was putting him on the wrong side of the all-powerful Duce – and in Italy itself he was far from popular.

The month of April was not a good time for Ciano, not just because he was ill for a week or because hostilities had started in Scandinavia, but because he realised that Hitler did not trust him, and Mussolini was becoming seriously irritable. The month started with Hitler's report on the Brenner meeting, but Ciano heard that 'Hitler raised objections about furnishing me with a copy'.[274] Attolico had warned Ciano that Ribbentrop hated him – the feeling was mutual – but the inference of Hitler's distrust may have been alarming. Ciano perceived that Mussolini was agitated, demanding 'full speed ahead' as the two Western allies threatened to tighten the blockade, telling the Council that 'he favoured going to war', and not to prostitute themselves to the democracies because it 'would demote us as a great power' – still reflecting his dream of a new Roman Empire.

THE GERMAN ATTACK ON DENMARK AND NORWAY

At 2 a.m. on 9 April Ciano was awakened by a call from the German embassy informing him of the Nazi attack upon Denmark and Norway. Denmark had had little choice but to succumb quickly, but there was fighting in Norway involving the Western powers. (Ultimately, as is well known now, the Germans were successful.) Ciano warned von Mackensen that this would cause a severe reaction from the neutrals, especially the USA, but Mussolini's response was simply 'I approve Hitler's actions whole heartedly. It is a gesture that can have incalculable results, and this is the way to win wars'.[275] Mussolini had long been concerned about German ambitions, as had many Italians, and this action by Hitler in the northern climes may have come as something of a psychological respite. Even in France many hoped that the Scandinavian invasion intimated that the war would be fought away from French soil. Mussolini naïvely expressed the opinion that the main conflict could now be avoided, and on 22 April he announced that Italy would not enter the conflict until spring 1941.

The Italian king was disturbed by the events, Mussolini informing Ciano that all the king wanted was for Italy to 'pick up the broken dishes', with Ciano prophetically noting in his diary that 'I hope that they will not break them over our heads before that'.[276] As the battle in Norway unfolded Ciano had to take to his bed for just over a week with a sudden attack of the flu. As he returned to the scene on 21 April, he was alerted to a rumour that he had been suffering from a 'diplomatic illness' induced by his failure to stop war. The rumours that he was being forced to resign spread like wildfire. It has been claimed that Mussolini put in front of Ciano a magazine account of the death of Ernst Röhm in the infamous Night of the Long Knives, implying what could happen to others who opposed a totalitarian leader. Mussolini made Ciano read the article in full, and according to the historians Moseley and Susmel, Ciano was 'frightened'.[277]

The diplomat Giuseppe Renzetti contacted Ciano, expressing concern over

Göring's attitudes, and Ciano decided that this was caused by Göring's aggravation at not receiving the Collar of the Annunciation. Ciano approached Mussolini, who was reluctant to ask the even more reluctant king to award the collar to Göring, whom Ciano described as the 'tender Hermann', to appease him. Mussolini, who was suffering a serious bout of hatred towards the monarchy, assured Ciano that the king 'would accept' the idea.

The French Prime Minister Reynaud annoyed his own ambassador by conveying a sealed message to Mussolini, a plea for them to meet before their nations 'crossed swords'. Mussolini refused. To cap this flurry of diplomatic issues, von Mackensen returned from Berlin with the request that Attolico be replaced as ambassador by one of Hitler's two suggested candidates, namely Franco Farinacci (son of Roberto) and Dino Alfieri. Ciano preferred the latter choice and the next day Mussolini confirmed his decision. Ciano ensured that Attolico should be appointed to the Holy See, showing the Germans that although they might ask for a change of personnel, they could not 'liquidate' them. In the early stages Ciano had been critical of Attolico, but as Ciano emerged from his inexperience he had started to understand Attolico's skills. Attolico, on hearing of his transfer to the Holy See, was pleased, telling Ciano that it was 'like going from the Devil to Holy Water'.[278]

Ciano noted that Mussolini was becoming more infatuated with the prospect of war; he had written to Hitler advising him to 'hang onto Narvik', which must have brought a cynical smirk to Hitler's face. He responded with a letter outlining the German success in Norway, causing Ciano to note 'these letters are, in general, of meagre importance, but Hitler is a good psychologist, and he knows that these messages go straight to Mussolini's heart'.[279]

During May it was clear that Mussolini was standing precariously on a precipice of his own creation. Roosevelt wrote a letter to Mussolini warning him not to enter the war; Ciano noted that the letter was 'dressed in polite phrases', but the meaning was clear. Mussolini, according to Ciano and confirmed by other sources, did not react well, and 'wrote a cutting and hostile answer'.[280] Roosevelt wrote again a fortnight later with a more conciliatory message referring to the Gospel of Christ, which of course meant nothing to Mussolini. The American Ambassador Phillips told Ciano to inform Mussolini that Roosevelt did not want the war in the Mediterranean, and cunningly suggested that as a neutral Mussolini could be part of the peace negotiations. In response to this, Ciano had to explain Mussolini's views and temperament.

At this juncture the Americans had only a small army and were not prepared for conflict, but warning bells had sounded, and they were making rapid preparations. Mussolini fell into the same trap as the Nazis; while perceiving that the Americans were good at producing kitchenware, he failed to foresee the industrial power which when turned to military hardware would make Italy's efforts look more like those of a local town.

For most of this month Mussolini's belligerence grew exponentially, and by the end of May he was announcing precise dates for Italy's intervention on the side of Germany. On 2 May Mussolini sent Hitler a message that the Italian people are 'unanimously opposed to the Allies', causing Ciano to wonder how he gleaned such information.[281] There were no Gallup Polls, and Italy was being driven by Mussolini's impulses.

It was a time of rumour, of uncertainty and of fear. Hitler had sent a message to Mussolini which claimed that speed was essential 'because of the hidden threats of American intervention' – not that, as far as we can tell, he believed this but was simply stimulating his Axis partner. In the meantime the placation of Göring over the Collar of the Annunciation continued to rumble on. Mussolini had eventually persuaded the king to grant Göring the award, telling him it was 'a lemon he had to swallow', but the king was unhappy about the traditional congratulatory letter, which Göring insisted he needed. In the turmoil of the major world events taking place it seemed as trivial as Alice in Wonderland. It was a matter of pandering to Göring, who had refused to attend meetings because of this disappointment, but Mussolini was desperate for German aid, and once the offended Göring had been granted the award he re-established cordial relationships with the Italian leaders.[282]

THE BATTLE FOR FRANCE

Percy Loraine had returned from London and he, François-Poncet and the American ambassador, working together, were constantly in contact with Ciano, trying to fathom out Mussolini's next step. Ciano continued to feed von Mackensen with documents stolen from the British embassy, which had been infiltrated by one of the Italian agents. Ciano attended what he described as a thoroughly boring meal at the German embassy, but was warned to expect a visitor in the early hours of the following morning, 10 May. This happened as predicted, and the visitor, accompanied by von Mackensen, met Mussolini, who was waiting in anticipation, and read the message announcing the 9 May German opening of the Western Front against the Allies. Mussolini told the German ambassador that he was convinced that 'France and England were preparing to attack Germany through Belgium and Holland, and he approved of Hitler's actions wholeheartedly'.[283] When Ciano suggested caution with the words 'we should wait and see', he was met with a brusque response; his remark had annoyed the Duce. Edda later in the day encouraged her father to step away from neutrality, telling him that it

111

was dishonourable for Italy to remain neutral; this was the button to press for Mussolini. Edda later spoke to Ciano, telling him Italian intervention was essential as she was preparing to leave for Florence for a music festival, causing Ciano to note 'I think she does well to go to the Florentine music festival, where she can more profitably busy herself with music'.[284]

Despite ignoring Ciano, Mussolini took his advice for the moment and responded to Hitler by letter. The Western ambassadors were soon at Ciano's door, believing that he stood with them, but then realised he was under the thumb of Mussolini. It fell to Ciano to explain to the Nazi regime what the Italians meant by 'non-belligerent' status, explaining it was not strictly a neutral term but implied no action in the West.[285] It was a confusing expression, and undoubtedly raised Nazi cynicism even further.

The news that Churchill had taken over from Chamberlain was met 'with indifference' in Italy; some local fascists had a street brawl, with an English official taking down anti-British posters, and the Pope called for peace, which incensed Mussolini. He called the Church a cancer, with which Ciano privately disagreed, writing that although Italians may scorn the Church at times they are religious at heart, and 'in times of peril they draw closer to the altars'.[286] The Pope informed some of his advisers that he was ready to be deported to a concentration camp, while Mussolini remained convinced of a German victory.

Hitler wrote to Mussolini outlining the progress of military events, which by 14 May were already looking promising for the Germans, and still trying to induce Mussolini to join the battle. Ciano appeared to accept that the Germans were winning, but added that it was 'too soon to count our eggs'.[287] Mussolini, in his desperate desire to be the military leader, was tussling with the constitutional problem that technically the king headed the military. He was frantic to take over, and he told Ciano that after the war the monarchy should be banished.

When Ciano heard that the Maginot Line had been breached, he could hardly accept it as true, but the next day he heard of the Germans' overwhelming success in breaking through to Sedan and into France. Ciano was facing a series of events he had thought would never happen, and he noted that 'the Italian public opinion (I mean honest opinion, not the clownish politicians who have become exaggeratedly pro-German) reacts in a strange way to the news: admiration for the Germans, a wishful belief in the rapid conclusion of war, and, above all, a great concern about the future'.[288] His estimation of public feeling sounded more plausible than that of Mussolini, but also tended to reflect his own thoughts.

The French and British were aware that military developments were precarious. They were anxious to keep Italy neutral, culminating in Winston Churchill's letter of 16 May 1940 urging that 'the joint heirs of Latin and Christian civilisation must not be ranged against one another in mortal strife'.[289] It meant nothing to Mussolini, who according to Ciano was 'needlessly harsh in tone' in his reply – which, when Ciano gave it to Percy Loraine, was received without comment. The British ambassador warned Ciano that it would not be in Italy's interests to see France crushed. Mussolini instructed Ciano to establish contact with his *bête noire*, Ribbentrop, to 'draw up a report on what our share should be at the end of the war'.[290] Their arrogant avaricious greed is unbelievable.

Ciano paid a visit to Albania, where he claimed he was well received and the crowds seemed excited to see him. He reported, 'Cheers for Duce! Ciano! Which Bottai maliciously thought he heard [as] Duce Ciano!'[291] On his return a few days later he found Mussolini in an argument with the king as to who should be the acknowledged military leader; the king later resolved this by announcing the newly constructed high command at the Palazzo Venezia, making Mussolini the happiest Ciano had seen him for a long time; ominously, however, Mussolini was also trying to find a date for 'Italy's intervention'.

François-Poncet, understandably distraught as his country was collapsing, made more precise overtures to Ciano about ceding French territories (except for Corsica), and attacked previous French governments for their poor dealings with Italy; Ciano, knowing Mussolini's thinking, explained that it was all too late. It was a different interview with Loraine who, Ciano noted, spoke with firmness, telling him, 'If you choose the sword, it will be the sword that will decide the future.'[292] Mussolini was looking to the Balkans and Yugoslavia in his proposed policy of a parallel war, but Ciano suggested that after the main war was won he could do what he liked.

ITALY DECLARES WAR

Mussolini eventually decided that 5 June would be the date for Italy's entrance to the battlefield, and wired the date to Alfieri in Berlin, to be given personally to Hitler. Alfieri replied that Hitler was 'in fact enthusiastic' but reserved the right to let Mussolini know the precise date once he had conferred with his generals. Hitler was making sure that Mussolini recognised him as supremo, but Mussolini instructed Ciano to draft the communiqué for the declaration of war, which constitutionally had to be announced by the king.

As it became obvious that Italy was about to declare war, Ciano decided he would return to being a pilot. Ciano observed that this delighted Mussolini, but it may have pleased the Duce more because he was aware that his son-in-law held differing political opinions. What Ciano did not know was that many Germans regarded him with even more suspicion than Mussolini, even believing him a traitor. News of the invasion had been leaked, and Canaris, head of the Abwehr, had been given the task of investigating. Canaris, as is now known, was anti-Nazi, and the investigation identified the source as leaks from Ribbentrop's entourage to Ciano.[293] This suited Canaris, because Ribbentrop was hated and Ciano was already suspected; it was an attempt to kill two birds with one stone.

The Italian people were aware that war would happen. Although football continued, the music and dance halls had been closed, Milan's cathedral windows had been replaced with canvas and foreign music was discouraged; the future was becoming all too clear. Mussolini and others were excited. Some had reservations, but Ciano had to shift his position, and becoming a pilot again helped that transition.

In June the world watched Mussolini attacking France moments before the French capitulated, but the Italians had military problems in even this small venture. Hitler claimed that they had been too cowardly at first, but were now in a hurry for spoils. This had been predicted by Hitler as early as January 1940 when he stated that 'Italy will enter the war only in the event of great German success, and preferably only against France'. He saw no great advantage for Germany in Italy's participation, in view of the fact that 'Germany would probably be burdened with the obligation to make more deliveries to Italy'.[294] It was a prescient insight by the German dictator, and Mussolini told Badoglio 'I only need a few thousand dead so I can sit at the peace conference as a man who has fought'. This was the month when Mussolini stopped prevaricating and set Italy on its disastrous course with its long-lasting ramifications.

During June the rest of Europe was in turmoil, too. The Soviets occupied all three Baltic states, but this was all but overlooked in Western Europe because of events there. As June opened, the evacuation of Dunkirk was coming to an end, and became in Churchill's words 'the miracle of deliverance', and as the Luftwaffe obliterated the town of Dunkirk 'the smoke from the smouldering buildings and overcast skies provided enough cover to get the troops out'.[295] The signing of the French armistice was made as humiliating as possible; Hitler had chosen the woods at Compiègne, using the same carriage in the same place as at the end of the Great War. This was sweet revenge for Hitler, but bitter for the French. Shirer, the American journalist, was there and wrote: 'I drove out there and found German army engineers demolishing the wall of the museum where the old wagon-lit of Marshal Foch, in which the 1918 armistice had been signed … had been preserved'.[296] It was a disastrous month for defeated France, with Britain in rapid retreat to its own home shores.

In Italy on 1 June Ciano had visited the king, who concluded his interview with Ciano by stating 'those who talk of a short and easy war are fools'.[297] There is little doubt that the Italian king was more astute than Mussolini, and it was because of Mussolini's decisions that the king later lost his crown. On this significant day Ciano was back on the golf course talking to Bottai 'who had not lost his head' and 'suggested we form a new party: Party of the Interventionists in Bad Faith'.[298]

Five days later, on 6 June, Ciano found the Duce angry with the king over the question of the supreme command; Mussolini had assumed the king would 'yield it' to him, but the king had 'assumed the command'. Mussolini told Ciano that 'when the war is over, I shall tell Hitler to do away with all these absurd anachronisms in the form of monarchies'.[299] This was a curious insight, insofar as Mussolini had always assumed he was the supreme fascist yet there was already a suggestion that he needed Hitler's support to abolish the Italian monarchy. Despite his ambitions Mussolini stooped to the Nazis by restoring the Italian Ambassador Rosso to Moscow, and a Soviet ambassador was accepted in Rome, which Ciano knew would please Ribbentrop.[300]

The Germans asked that the Italian declaration of war be postponed for a few days. Ciano gathered that Hitler had decided to attack French airfields and did not want French planes heading towards the Italian front. Mussolini was pleased yet annoyed with this change, preferring 11 June because this date was 'a good omen for him'. The Germans then changed their minds and wanted Italy in the fray as soon as possible. Mussolini claimed more time, thereby demonstrating some independence by choosing the date himself. He chose 10 June, and spoke from his balcony on the Palazzo Venezia to a hastily assembled crowd. He expounded that 'we go to the field against the plutocratic and reactionary democracies of the West, who have repeatedly blocked the march and even threatened the existence of the Italian people', telling his listeners that 'our conscience is clear, and a people of 45 million souls cannot be free if it does not have access to the ocean'.[301]

Ciano talked to the military commander Balbo, who had been against the war, and found he was preparing to go to Libya, noting that 'he is a soldier, and he will fight with energy and determination' even though he 'hates the Germans'. But on 29 June Balbo was shot down by his own side while landing at Tobruk. In Britain Colville in his personal diary wondered whether Balbo had been killed intentionally, and George Orwell thought it likely.[302] Later, on a trip to Berlin in July 1940, when Ciano was surround by ladies he dropped a hint that perhaps 'Balbo's death was not an error', and followed it with a wink.[303] This was probably just Ciano showing off to the enamoured ladies.

In his own preparation for war Ciano had chosen to be a 'soldier-minister' rather than a 'minister-soldier', by taking command of a bomber squadron in Pisa. He noted that the French were fighting with 'traditional bravery' now they were on their own soil; and despite contrary comments made about French soldiery this carried some validity. Ciano bade farewell to the British ambassador, who pointed out that 'the British are not in the habit of being beaten'. The French Ambassador Françoise-Poncet stated that he would like to arrange a separate peace, but he had no idea of his government's intentions. Given the state of military affairs in France this was not surprising, because the French government had no idea of which way to turn. Ciano described Françoise-Poncet as emotional, which 'neither of us was able to conceal. Poncet is a man like us: he is a Latin'.[304] Françoise-Poncet told Ciano it was a 'dagger blow at a man who had already fallen', and this observation was accurate. Loraine was 'more laconic and inscrutable' but at the door 'we exchanged a long and cordial handshake'.

As the reports poured in about gallant French resistance Ciano noted that the Duce was following the events with 'anxiety', but Mussolini was pleased that the French were resisting because it would 'weaken' the Germans; he did not want them to be too strong at the end of the war. On 10 June Italy formally declared war, though for months most observers had been anticipating it, with the more cynical understanding that Mussolini was waiting for it to be safe enough for him to do so.

On 11 June Ciano joined his squadron in Pisa, where he recorded searching for French ships which had shelled Genoa, but without success. After Mussolini's declaration of war, the British 11th Hussars crossed the Libyan border, heading for Fort Maddalena and Fort Capuzzo, and took 70 prisoners. Unbelievably 'the Italians were most upset. Nobody had bothered to tell them that their government had declared war'.[305] On 12 June the RAF bombed Turin and Genoa; the Italian population were horrified not just by the attack itself but also by the total lack of anti-aircraft defence systems.

A week later, after a flying mission, Ciano was told that Marshal Pétain had taken Reynaud's place. Peace was in sight (Ciano thought) and following a phone call from Anfuso he was ordered back to Rome as the French were seeking an armistice. There he discovered that the Duce 'was an extremist', wanting the whole of France occupied. He was also unhappy that Hitler had won the war in Western Europe without any serious military support from Italy, realising he would only be consulted by Hitler (as he believed), knowing he would not be on the major stage. Ciano found the Duce 'bitter' about the Italian people and the armed forces.

In his diplomatic papers Ciano noted that Ribbentrop was now seeking peace, and while Ribbentrop agreed on Italian ambitions in North Africa when Ciano mentioned Algiers and Morocco he was evasive, claiming he had no instructions on these two countries. The reason was simple: Hitler was aware that Franco had ambitions there, and he was working to have Spain as an ally, not least because of Gibraltar. Hitler wanted the Belgian Congo, to complete the German Empire, and he desired to retain the *status quo* in the Danube basin and the Balkans.[306]

Mussolini was angry that Hitler was prepared for the French to keep their fleet, which he rightly conjectured would remain a powerful asset to Hitler and a danger to the Italians in 'his' Mediterranean Sea. When Ciano saw and heard Hitler in Munich, he thought he spoke with 'reserve and perspicacity', adding that 'I cannot be accused of excessive tenderness towards him, but today I truly admire him'. Even the interpreter Paul Schmidt had noticed Ciano's change of attitude, writing that 'a completely changed Ciano sat facing him … the lightning victory over the French and British armies had obviously had its effect, and he seemed to have lost his high opinion about the Western powers. Now he had gone to the opposite extreme, at any rate for the time being.'[307] Ciano had apparently fallen for the *vox populi* feelings that success in war brings popularity. Mussolini, Ciano observed, was embarrassed because of the lack of involvement by the Italian military; the Duce, he wrote 'sees that unattainable dream of his life, glory on the field of battle, fading once again'.[308]

Inexplicably, Mussolini now proposed to attack the French in the Alps, which Badoglio vehemently opposed. Ciano used his influence in support of Badoglio, and as a result the attack was limited to a small sector near the Swiss frontier. Mussolini realised he had to move with caution for fear of causing problems with Berlin. The Italian troops had advanced but stopped before reaching the first French fortification, and in Libya an Italian general had allowed himself to be taken prisoner. None of this augured well for the Italian military effort. Starace, returning from the front, told Ciano that the attack on the Alps had demonstrated the total lack of preparation of the Italian army, an absolute lack of offensive capability, and the complete incompetence of the top officers; this view would become commonplace in the years ahead.[309] The Italian army had few jeeps or cars, and their tanks were small, so became bogged down in mud and sand all too easily.[310]

On 23 June, after the German French armistice had been signed, the French plenipotentiaries arrived in German planes. The Italians gave them the Roman salute, but the French simply nodded and, as Ciano noted, 'they are dignified', showing no pride and no humiliation. The meeting lasted less than half an hour. The French were irritated at having to attend the Italian conference since Italy had played no part in their downfall, but they were under German instructions.

By the end of the month Hitler had not responded to Mussolini's offer of planes to help attack Britain, and Ciano wondered whether Hitler really wanted Italian help. As Hitler went to Paris, Mussolini visited his own tiny sector of the war zone – a demeaning comparison with the German effort. The summer was almost a tragicomedy from the Italian perspective as Mussolini came on and off stage like a dramatic strutting clown. Ciano believed that Mussolini was taking

Italy to war so he could go down in history as the warrior-leader, but he had left it too late to make any difference to the German victory, and Hitler did not allow him to attend the French armistice, so all Mussolini had was a small and reluctant French diplomatic party obliged to attend a brief meeting, like crumbs from the master's table. Ciano had noted that the future did not look promising, and he sensed that the Germans did not need their assistance; but conversely the Italians needed German help throughout the war.

Churchill claimed that one man had started Italy down the course of war, and most historians have tended to agree. It is a debate which has tended to be one-sided but there are other viewpoints which should not be dismissed. It has been cogently argued that Mussolini always had an intuitive fear of the growing Nazi power and was looking to Italy's survival. There are 'grounds for doubting the totality and singularity of Mussolini's powers'; Italy's monarchy was constitutional, but not as in Britain, and by June the Church was becoming reconciled to the fascist point of view.[311] This debate will probably never end, but in my opinion Mussolini allowed himself to be caught up in the Nazi conflict and whether through his concern for the safety for his country, or by seeking personal warrior status, he blundered.

At the beginning of July Ciano arranged to visit Germany because he needed to build bridges, realising he was not trusted. A perception that some Germans even regarded him as a traitor may have crossed his mind. Later Mussolini would express concern that captured French documents would disclose too much about Ciano's dealings with the French and British in previous years. Mussolini had returned from his 'frontline visit' in the Alps and was pleased with what he had seen. Ciano was aware that there had been no breakthrough as Mussolini declared on the Alpine Maginot Line; they had occupied some towns and villages, allowing the French to encircle them, and it was therefore fortunate the Armistice was declared when it was. Mussolini was furious when he heard that British ships and planes were finding refuge in Greece, and he informed the Greeks that it could mean war. Ciano gave the distinct appearance that at this stage every country was taking stock as to where they stood, and who was with or against them. A few days later the Greeks officially assured Ciano of their neutrality, obviously concerned about Mussolini's reaction and in the hope of keeping safe in an uncertain world.

Ciano, who appeared to have a sneaking regard for the Royal Navy, heard about an interchange of fire between the French and British fleets at Oran.[312] It was no more than a skirmish but was in fact, as Ciano later noted, a 'very momentous event'. This was because the French fleet was a potential disaster for Britain if used by the Germans, and 'it was regarded as an intolerable risk by the British government'.[313] The British had been concerned because they knew that Article

8 of the Franco-German Armistice had indicated that French vessels should return to their home ports. As, however, Hitler's promises could never be trusted, of course, it took little imagination to understand how easy it would be for the Germans to take control. So the British felt they had no choice but to neutralise or sink the French fleet, which they eventually did on 3 July at Mers-el-Kébir in Algeria, having failed to make an arrangement with the French.

In mid-afternoon on 9 July the Italians clashed with the British fleet; their cruisers exchanged fire at long distance, and the British battleship HMS *Warspite* moved ahead to join the cruisers when the Italian battleship *Giulio Cesare* and its sister ship suddenly appeared. The *Warspite* fired at the *Giulio Cesare* and scored a hit at the stunning range of over 13 miles. Under a smokescreen the much-treasured Italian warships withdrew. There were further attacks by Italian aircraft which accidentally hit their own ships. In the end, little damage was done by either fleet, but Admiral Cunningham was probably correct when he speculated that the British had unnerved the Italian navy. There followed the Battle of Cape Spada in the Mediterranean, and on 19 July there was another significant clash. An Allied squadron was patrolling the Aegean Sea when it came upon two Italian cruisers, and in the running battle which followed, the *Bartolomeo Colleoni* was irreparably damaged, eventually to be sunk by three torpedoes.

These sea battles had gone badly for Italy; Admiral Cavagnari was distraught, and Mussolini was depressed by the sinking of the *Colleoni*. On 4 July, Bastianini, fresh back from London, had talked to Ciano. He believed that everybody in England, 'aristocracy, middle class and the common people' were embittered, tenacious and proud, and morale was high; he may have exaggerated, but the British determination to fight on was real enough. Bastianini explained that Britain with its empire was 'building an imposing military machine', and the situation with the British would be different from that of the French.[314]

BERLIN

Alfieri informed Ciano of an invitation to Germany, and before Ciano set off for Berlin on 6 July he took Mussolini's guidance on the issue of Italy's being invited to fight alongside Germany in the proposed conquest of Britain, because he did not want to be 'defrauded of any booty'.[315] Ciano arrived in Berlin for what would be his first of two visits that month. He was met by Ribbentrop appearing more belligerent, echoing his master's mood. He visited the Maginot Line, Metz and Verdun, then went on to the Channel coast, to Dunkirk, then to Lille. The Germans were giving the cynical Ciano a *tour de force* of their military power.

Ribbentrop hosted a dinner for Ciano at the Hotel Adlon.* Later he attended

---

*   Still a luxury 5-star hotel in Berlin.

a reception by Alfieri at his villa at Wannsee. An exiled white Russian émigrée, Marie Vassiltchikov,* was presented to him, together with other pretty girls, undoubtedly because of his predilection for beautiful women. Marie described the scene, noticing Ciano's habitual playboy lifestyle of intimately 'dancing cheek to cheek' with a beautiful woman.[216] While in Berlin he also met Hitler in the Chancery for two hours. Hitler told him how the Italian armistice had helped facilitate the agreement with France. He was in fact deluding Ciano, because it had been the Germans who had obliged the reluctant French to sign a separate armistice with Italy. Hitler actually disclosed little to Ciano, telling him that plans against Britain had yet to be confirmed. Ciano explained that the Duce was keen to participate and had promised 10 divisions to assist and 30 squadrons of planes. Hitler did not accept the offer, but he was pleased to hear of Mussolini's plans in North Africa, and offered to send German planes to bomb the Suez Canal.

Ciano raised the issue that the French 'would try and work their way into their camp'.[317] In time Vichy France, especially under Pierre Laval and even more so under Admiral Darlan, would pursue this policy, but Hitler never trusted the French. Ciano then raised the issue of Yugoslavia; Hitler replied that it was a problem to be resolved, but only after the British were finished.[318] Ciano described this meeting as 'cordial', and over lunch with Keitel he gathered that the anticipated landing on the British coast was not considered an easy exercise, especially as the Royal Air Force was still effective, with an estimated 1,500 planes. And, like Hitler, Keitel wanted Gibraltar.

Ciano returned to Rome on 11 July, reporting to Mussolini, who was happy about his report and becoming excited at the prospect of adding Egypt to the empire. It was at this moment that news of the naval conflicts with the British, mentioned above, were arriving, and Mussolini was pleased that the Italian planes 'had annihilated 50 per cent of the British naval potential in the Mediterranean'. In fact, as Ciano would note later, it was 'not 50 per cent but naught'. This was later confirmed by the Germans and the Italian navy, leaving Ciano to admit once again that the 'Italian air force tends to exaggerate'.[319] 'Once the war began, Italian production remained derisory; in 1942 the USA could turn out from its factories in a week more planes than Italian industry could manufacture in a year', yet senior air force officers were able to impress Mussolini that they had the necessary numbers.[320]

By 19 July Ciano was back in Berlin, holding a conference with Ribbentrop, only to discover that Hitler's latest hint to the British for a suitable peace, which Ciano had thought was 'unusually humane in tone for Hitler', had met with a cold reaction.[321] In a conversation with Hitler, Ciano was told that the British had

---

* She used the German name of Wassilchikoff.

rejected all peace moves and Hitler was preparing for war. The Romanian and Hungarian issues were discussed, and Hitler concluded his session with Ciano by expressing his regard for Italy's war effort – manifestly a diplomatic nicety. As it was, Hitler was not especially interested in Ciano's or Mussolini's views, but Ciano allegedly told Bottai that 'Hitler was a genius' – indicating, if that were true, that Ciano was doing a *volte face*.[322]

Ciano visited Göring's magnificent country retreat, Carinhall, and found his host somewhat 'rude and haughty towards me, as he flaunted his Italian award of the Annunziata from his neck' – the very award that Ciano had organised for him so reluctantly in the face of monarchical opposition. Ciano was interested in Göring's mansion, entering in his diary 'it is an ever-increasing show of luxury, and it is truly incomprehensible how, in a country which is socialistic or almost so, people can tolerate the extraordinary pomp displayed by this western satrap'.

Back in Rome Ciano reported his news to Mussolini, who remained convinced that the British would sue for peace, with Ciano noting that this 'would be sad for Mussolini, because now more than ever he wants war'.[323] Ciano took some family time in Florence to visit his son Marzio, who had been ill for a few days. It was more than ever apparent, with Ciano's professional life, his golf club, and his liaisons, that he and Edda were each living their lives in their own way as major events unfolded.

On 27 July Ciano attended a meeting between Mussolini and the head of the Romanian government, Gigurtu. Ciano noted in his diary that he found the Romanians 'simply disgusting. They open their mouths to make honeyed comments'.[324] However, despite Ciano's cynical remarks it was clear that the Romanians wanted to live at peace with their neighbours, and Mussolini stated that they were popular in Italy but had trusted too much in the League of Nations and the French and British promises, adding that the Romanians' geographical position made such support impossible.

Mussolini was correct in his criticism: Britain and France, despite their assurances, had not been able to help Poland – and had known that at the time of making those promises. These international guarantees had all been part of the pre-war diplomatic dancing and when impossible to fulfil were morally questionable. Mussolini also warned Gigurtu to 'eliminate Jews from the life of the state and to restrict their activities'.[325] When Mussolini used the term 'eliminate' it was not meant to be taken in the same way as the German 'liquidate', but he was to all appearances edging alongside Germany, and the next day Mussolini instructed Ciano to offer more pro-Soviet comments.

Italy barely fought in the land war and had suffered against the Royal Navy, and for the Italians the military future did not appear promising. 'Mussolini's methods of administration as a military commander did nothing to overcome national inadequacies', as Ciano had noted.[326] As war started thousands of Italians were unemployed, even in the larger industrial cities, and food supplies were scarce; Italy was unprepared for war. Ciano had long known this, but the German victory in France had turned his head as if swept by the tide. He had tried to repair his reputation in Germany, and knew it was now necessary, for his own safety, to walk alongside his master, the Duce.

Hassell, who had been recalled as ambassador to Italy by Hitler in 1936, was now working with the Italians on seeking better economic relationships. He regarded 'his work with the Italians as a tragi-comic situation', and he noted that 'Berliners grin when they hear the word Italians'.[327] He was finding it difficult to fathom Italian intentions, writing that they were concerned with their attacks on Egypt and the preparations for their involvement in the invasion of England while feeling anxious about the apparent lack of enthusiasm on Hitler's part, especially with his desire for peace with Britain. They were anxious about the USA and its possible intentions to enter the war, and about the apparent German–Soviet relationship. Hassell was astute in his observations in August, which was the time Ciano, for safety reasons, appeared to be adjusting his views.

Ciano's August diary indicated the haphazard approach of the Italians: reluctant generals, ignorance of the British front, being kept in the dark by the Germans, and Mussolini's mood swings. In addition to these issues, Mussolini's foreign policies were constantly changing, and his attacks on Italian attitudes gave the impression of uncertainty if not a lack of reality. Hassell had been reasonably correct in his reflections on the Italian situation. During August Mussolini turned his thinking more from Croatian ventures to an attack on Yugoslavia and a growing tendency to look towards Greece. On 3 August Ciano demanded that the Greek minister should withdraw their consul in Trieste, and just over a week later Mussolini was discussing the 'political and military plans for action against Greece'.[328] On 6 August Mussolini even suggested that Ciano should visit Moscow to smooth the way for his proposed ventures.

Mussolini was frustrated by the lack of progress in North Africa; the Duke of Aosta had started his offensive in British Somaliland, and it had appeared to start well, but by the end of the month the absence of headway was annoying Mussolini. On 8 August Ciano heard from Alfieri that the delay in attacking Britain had been caused by bad weather, but according to General Marras it was because of secret negotiations, leading to Ciano's angry outburst that 'we know nothing. The fact is that the Germans keep us in the dark about everything, just as they did when we were neutral, even though we are now fighting beside them'.[329] Operation Sea Lion was not looking comfortable for the Germans; it was not just poor weather, but the British RAF was showing stubborn resistance and the Germans were nervous about the British fleet. However, the Germans probably had good reasons for keeping Mussolini's Italy in the dark, and would soon regret they were their allies. Even so, the next day the Luftwaffe asked for some Italian planes to be sent to join the attack on Britain. Curiously, Ciano was not in favour, for political and technical reasons.

According to his diary on 14 August Ciano went to Livorno to visit his children. There was no mention of Edda, just the children, as he and Edda persisted in leading their own lives. Ciano's diary reveals a growing sense of frustration, not helped when Alfieri reported a conversation with Ribbentrop. Ciano stated it was almost like receiving instructions, informing the Italians that the German regime did not want Mussolini and Ciano making 'too close a rapprochement with Russia', when initially they had been encouraged – which at the time they had found objectionable. It does not take much historical knowledge to assess what would have been fermenting in Berlin, with the prospect of Barbarossa. Ribbentrop phoned to ask the Italians not to attack Yugoslavia, and stated that any action against Greece would 'be unwelcome by Berlin'. The major effort, Ribbentrop pointed out, must be concentrated on crushing Great Britain; this was the 'question of life and death'.

Mussolini ordered Rodolfo Graziani to 'march into Egypt' as soon as the Germans invaded Britain, but Graziani sent a report from his generals indicating some reluctance. By 18 August there was a series 'of significant hints' from Berlin that Britain was about to fall. Mussolini thought there would be peace in September, and therefore his troops needed to 'move fast' in Egypt. Ciano and Mussolini were listening to the hints arriving from Berlin about the Balkans, and a letter was written to Jacomoni in which Ciano pointed out that while Germany was fighting England, and following the rapid victory in Somaliland, there had to be a slowing down in the pace for the projected moves against Yugoslavia and Greece, until further orders.[330]

Mussolini was interested in 'occupying Egypt', claiming that Keitel thought 'taking Cairo is more important than the taking of London'. Ciano observed that Keitel had never expressed this unlikely thought to him. Mussolini heard from Hitler that he had not been able to take Britain because of bad weather, and he would need at least two weeks of good weather 'to neutralise British naval superiority'. Ciano rightly speculated this amounted to a 'definite postponement'.

Before he met Ribbentrop, Hitler had asked to meet Ciano at Berchtesgaden, where he explained the problems over the projected invasion of Britain. As soon as the meeting concluded Ciano cabled the contents of Hitler's conversation to Mussolini under various headings. First while Hitler was sending Mussolini congratulations on the Italian success in Somaliland, he was also, applying his usual pressure, asking about Egypt. Hitler then explained that they needed larger landing craft for the cross-Channel invasion, plus artillery on the French coast – and then there was the need to destroy the British fighter aircraft; there was the need for good weather, and it was essential to destroy the Royal Navy. The next point was to resolve the issues between Hungary and Romania, and thereby not weaken the Axis. Ciano felt that both Hitler and Ribbentrop were appearing more hostile towards the Soviet Union. His final note was that Hitler appeared optimistic, but he (Ciano) felt that the war might last through the winter.[331]

VIENNA

Ciano travelled from Salzburg to Vienna to participate in the Romanian–Hungarian dispute, which was finally settled on 30 August according to the German wishes. Ribbentrop explained to Ciano he wanted to give Romania and Hungary 'some friendly advice' but 'accompanied by threats'.[332] The Hungarians were the aggressor and threatening to take matters into their own hands; Ciano found Czaky reasonable and Teleki somewhat hostile. But finally the Romanian–Hungarian issue was resolved, with the Hungarians content. The Romanian Mihail Manoilescue fainted at the discussion table.

In Vienna Ciano had found the atmosphere dreary; 'the people on the streets are badly dressed and listless' and 'they are eating less and badly … and Austrian morale is not good either'.[333] This observation that 'Vienna was truly grey' was reflective of most of Europe during this year. To finish this so-called triumph, Ciano 'went hunting with Ribbentrop', but for ordinary people the future appeared bleak.

Ciano's September diary began on the first day of the month with a concern about Mussolini's mentality; Mussolini was pleased that the war 'would last beyond the month, and maybe beyond, and maybe beyond the winter, because this will give Italy time to make greater sacrifices and this enables him better to assert our rights'.[334] Ciano asked himself whether, if the war did extend so far, that it might not be favourable for Italy, and observed that 'this is a question that is worth asking, and one which many Germans who have their heads screwed on the right way are now asking'. In the long term Ciano was correct, Italy's entry into war accentuating his view that Mussolini was seeking glory on the world stage, reflecting Hitler.

Mussolini was concerned about Romania, where the Ribbentrop plans had simply not worked, and Ciano noted that Romania's King Carol II had paid for his 'silly buffoonery, his betrayals, and his crimes'. The dictatorial king had made many errors and was infamous for his hedonistic lifestyle, but with the crisis in

Western Europe this attracted less attention. Later in September Ciano also heard that the Hungarians were printing propaganda leaflets claiming 'the Trianon is dead. Vienna, too, will die'.[335] The idea that a brief meeting dictated by Ribbentrop would heal these issues is beyond belief.

On 7 September Mussolini informed his council that a German landing in Britain was certain, and he wanted the Italian navy to seek out and destroy the British. Graziani had already asked that the Egyptian venture be delayed for a month, and within the safety of his office Mussolini spent his time grumbling about this request, being suspicious of his military commanders, and speculating about what could happen next. This image, which Ciano painted in his diary, again exposed an inept leader concerned with his own image. The Duce threatened his leading commanders with their immediate sacking if they did not move into Egypt instantly, and 'Graziani obeyed at once', not wishing to clash with Mussolini for fear of losing his rank. Ciano made the cynical comment that 'never has a military operation been undertaken so much against the will of the commanders'.[336] Mussolini had assumed that the responsibility was his, and anticipated the glory.

On 13 September Ciano heard that Ribbentrop wished to come to Rome just when the Italian attack on Egypt had started. Ciano heard that the British troops were withdrawing, and that Mussolini was already regarding it as a 'great victory', though within days he was concerned at the lack of speed of the advance. Mussolini was pleased that at Mersa Matruh the Italians could use the airstrip to attack Alexandria with bombers.* There was still no news of the projected invasion of Britain, and Ciano hoped to hear more from Ribbentrop's visit. Ciano and Mussolini were still in the dark, Ciano complaining they knew nothing about what was happening with Britain, and had no information about what Graziani was doing in Egypt. However, the Italians were surprised at the speed of the British withdrawal, many wondering where and when they would stop and fight. Ciano observed that 'Mussolini is radiant with joy. He has taken the entire responsibility of the offensive on his shoulders, and he is proud that he was right,' (for the time being, at least).[337]

On 15 September Ciano returned to Livorno to preside at the annual memorial ceremony for his father. Ciano appeared to be closer to his dead father than to the living Edda. Ribbentrop arrived on 19 September, to be greeted by what Ciano called the 'applause squad', with a briefcase full of details about a military alliance with Japan. The argument was that the Americans would be more concerned about Japan than Europe. Ciano quietly differed, thinking that Washington 'will increasingly favour the British'. He was right insofar as

---

* Italian troops crossed the Egyptian border and occupied Sidi Barrani, which the British bombed two weeks later.

America would need allies and if Britain survived then its fleet and empire would be important to the Americans. As for the invasion of Britain, Ribbentrop claimed that the poor weather was still hindering the event, but that it would happen very soon. Ribbentrop further asserted that British defence was 'non-existent', and a single German division would bring about a complete collapse. Later Ciano heard from a friend called d'Aieta, who reported 'that Ribbentrop's optimistic forecasts are not shared by his associates, who think this may be a long war'.[338]

Ribbentrop held his formal conference with Mussolini, and Ciano was present. The German foreign minister explained how Britain would not cope with the bombing, and that although the ruling elite were full of bluff, the ordinary people had had enough.[339] He expounded his theory that Russia would be irritated by the Tripartite and the Vienna agreements, and would 'throw themselves into the arms of the democracies'.[340] He agreed that Yugoslavia and Greece were within the Italian orbit of interest, and spent some time on the topic of Franco appearing to join the Axis. As ever, Ribbentrop was belligerent, often exaggerated and told lies, still treating Europe like a chess game, which pleased Mussolini.

Later Ribbentrop posed the question to Mussolini of the Axis breaking diplomatic relations with America, which Ciano thought would be an error, because such a declaration would provide Roosevelt with the excuse that America was being attacked. Ciano wrote that 'anyway, the decision is not imminent, and I hope that I shall be able to put in my oar'.[341] This demonstrated Ribbentrop's simplistic views, always based on his belief that Germany would succeed, and aimed at pleasing Hitler.

BERLIN AGAIN

To sign the treaty with Japan, Ciano had to travel to Berlin, but his train was stopped at Munich on Hitler's orders, because they were entering the British bombing danger zone. He continued by air, and although he made no comment in his diary he must have wondered about the German claims of success, if they were so worried about attacks by the British between Munich and Berlin. The pact was signed on 27 September and Ciano noted that it was like the occasion of signing the Pact of Steel but the atmosphere 'was cooler'. The Tripartite Agreement was based on the policy of mutual defence, but also the right for Germany and Italy to impose a new order in Europe and for Japan to do the same in Asia. There seems to be little doubt that Hitler had always had the invasion of Russia in the back of his mind, and with the British refusing to capitulate, he anticipated that the Japanese invasion of the Russians' territories in the Far East would distract them.

Ciano observed that the traditional congratulatory crowd outside was 'composed mainly of school children' with a sense of 'regularity but without conviction'. He wrote that a winter war would be 'hard to bear' especially as in Berlin food was scarce, and that the 'window displays promise much more than is actually inside'. The people were also 'depressed' by the constant bombing raids and having to hide in cellars, and he observed that although the 'bomb damage is slight; nervousness is very great'. He wrote that in the bomb-shelter life 'there is promiscuity between men and women', which was of course hypocritical.[342] He noted that the 'spirit of Germany' was not the same as in previous months. Churchill and British bomber command would have been gratified by reading this at the time of its writing. Ciano gathered that Hitler wanted to meet Mussolini at the Brenner, but he heard no more 'talk of the invasion of England', observing that 'Ribbentrop is more nervous'.

With the benefit of hindsight, it is now clear that all German machinations 'in the summer and fall of 1940 could only be understood if they [were] seen in the context of the new plan', the invasion of Russia.[343] There had been a start on improving road and rail links to the east, and during October the Luftwaffe started aerial reconnaissance over the USSR. Hitler had even toyed with the idea of encouraging Spain and France against Britain.

Ciano's October diary started with reflections on the domestic issues in Spain. The Spanish Foreign Minister Serrano Suñer had arrived in Rome to be met by Ciano and the Spanish General Queipo de Llano, but the two Spaniards did not greet one another.* As Ciano observed, 'all this has symbolical meaning; it represents the situation in Spanish public life today'.[344] Both men were subservient to Franco, but in Spain there was internal dissension on how far, or if at all, the Spanish should be involved in the world war.

Ciano speculated that there were problems in London, because he heard Chamberlain had resigned from the government. Ciano admitted his information was 'scarce and uncertain', and he obviously had not gathered that Chamberlain was seriously ill. On 4 October Mussolini had a brief meeting with Hitler at the Brenner. Ciano heard that Mussolini was happy with the meeting as Hitler had 'put at least some of his cards on the table'. Ciano kept a diplomatic note of the meeting, in which Hitler explained how the weather had stopped the Sea Lion operation, how the British could not endure the German bombing and that they were foolishly relying on American or even Russian help, but he had 180 armoured divisions ready.[345] Mussolini chipped in to say that the air attack 'has had a profound effect on Britain', but quite how he had gleaned that information

---

* General Queipo de Llano was not to Franco's political tastes. Queipo de Llano once said that 'the only thing that Franco ever sacrificed for Spain was his moustache'. See Preston Paul, *Franco* (London: Fontana Press, 1995) p.142.

was questionable; he probably said it to imply that he 'was in the know'.

Mussolini and Ciano had no idea of Hitler's intentions against Russia, and Hitler was content merely to be cynical about that country. The possibility of supplying Spain in return for intervention was raised, but Ciano was amazed at the next item, which he described as 'fantastic as it may seem'; Hitler was reflecting on French help, with the caveat that France should never be allowed again to have a prominent role in Europe.

Mussolini spoke about Spain's demands on French Morocco, Corsica, Nice, Tunis and Djibouti, to which Hitler appeared to agree. Mussolini showed his plans for Egypt to Hitler, who asked where he could help. Mussolini promptly responded that help was unnecessary except for 'armoured cars, a number of heavy tanks, and some formations of Stukas' which must have made Hitler blink.[346] Ciano's main overall impressions from the meeting amounted to the fact that the invasion of the British Isles was now on hold, and it was no longer talked about. Secondly, that there was a possibility that the French could be attracted into the 'anti-British coalition,' because it was 'now realised that the Anglo-Saxons are still a hard nut to crack'.[347] Thirdly, that greater importance should be attached to the Mediterranean area; and finally that Hitler was anti-Bolshevist, reflecting Hitler's plans for Barbarossa.

GREECE

A few days later Mussolini's mood changed again; when notified of Germany's incursion into Romania, he asked that Italian troops be used, but Ciano reported that Ribbentrop received the suggestion coldly, and the operation went ahead without the Italians; the Germans had ostensibly decided to move into Romania to protect their oil supplies. Mussolini claimed 'Hitler always faces me with a *fait accompli*. This time I am going to pay him back in his own coin.'[348] Mussolini was thinking of an attack on Greece, which Ciano observed 'will be useful and easy'. The date for the attack on Greece was projected to be 26 October. This attitude by Ciano that it would be 'easy' quickly prompted the rumour that the attack on Greece was Ciano's idea; this seems unlikely, though he was clearly supportive in a way he had not been in the matter of aligning Italy alongside Germany in a major war. The historian Douglas Porch believed that it was because of Ciano's enthusiastic support that it became known as 'Ciano's war'.[349]

The general staff, including Badoglio, were still pessimistic about these plans, Ciano noticing they did not want a prolonged war (as indeed Hassell had predicted in his own diary). Mussolini was furious and in 'bad humour' with the news of Badoglio's pessimism, saying he would 'go personally to Greece to witness the incredible shame of Italians who are afraid of Greeks'. Ciano was more supportive of Mussolini on this issue, pointing out that Greece was 'isolated', and that Turkey 'will not move', nor would Yugoslavia, and Bulgaria would be 'on our side'.

On 20 October Ciano heard from the German ambassador that Hitler intended to meet Franco and Pétain to discuss his plans, which the Italians had heard something about at the Brenner meeting. Mussolini wrote to Hitler on 'the general situation' and alluded to 'our impending action in Greece' but did not specify the form of intended action or dates, because he feared 'that once again an order might come to halt us'. This fear of German reaction underlined the relationship between the two countries. Italy under Mussolini wanted to be regarded as a great military power – but too late: Italy was already subservient to Germany, a situation Mussolini had to accept, however bitter it made him.

When Mussolini heard that a limited air attack on Greece was planned, he demanded a full and vigorous onslaught and Ciano agreed, writing 'if we leave the Greeks too much time to reflect and to breathe, the English will come, and perhaps the Turks, and the situation will become long drawn out and difficult'.[350] There is a distinct impression that Ciano was becoming more belligerent about invading Greece than indicated by his previous diary entries. He probably believed that Greece would be an easy victim for Italian expansionist hopes.

On 24 October Ribbentrop phoned from 'a little railway station in France' regarding Hitler's meetings with Franco, then Pétain. According to Ribbentrop, Hitler had claimed he was 'satisfied with the results achieved'. It is now known that in fact the meetings had been a disaster: Franco had demanded material and offered no help, and Pétain had not been as easy for Hitler to deal with as he had assumed. Many historians have regarded the meeting as Franco skilfully warding off Hitler when in fact it was simply two tyrants seeking to utilise one another, and Franco and Hitler never obtained what they wanted. Hitler and Franco certainly gathered personal insights into one another, and Churchill, in an amusing broadcast on these meetings, said, 'Each one hopes that if he feeds the crocodile enough, the crocodile will eat him last. All of them hope that the storm will pass before their time comes to be devoured.'[351] Ribbentrop also spoke of the necessity of another visit by Hitler projected in some northern Italian city; it must have been obvious that Hitler's sudden frenetic meetings portended some hidden agenda.

Ribbentrop designated Florence as the meeting place on 28 October. On the day beforehand, Ciano told German, Japanese, Spanish and Hungarian diplomats about the Italian ultimatum to the Greeks. The diplomats 'were rather surprised'.

Back in August Mussolini had suggested attacking Yugoslavia, but Ciano had suggested Greece as the easier option. The Germans had warned against such action, but Mussolini had stopped faltering on a decision once he had heard that German troops were in Romania, with a sense of 'childish petulance'.[352] 'Ciano's agents in Greece had told him he could buy off the Greek military commanders, and he believed them' – an almost incredible opinion, especially since his military attaché in Athens had warned him the Greeks 'were no pushover'.[353] The proposed invasion was no secret, and the American ambassador was able to enlighten Washington on 21 October. Ciano was confident about it, and told Bastianini that it would be a 'military walkover ... everything is arranged'.[354]

On 28 October the attack began, from Albania, the same day as the brief meeting with Hitler in Florence. Hitler had heard the news at Bologna railway station. He was angry with Mussolini for not informing him – which, given the German lack of communications, was hypocritical – but he offered his best wishes. He questioned why they had started the attack in late October, and he was right to do so, especially when it was realised the Italian troops had not been equipped with winter uniforms, and the weather would make the assumed 'easy task' dangerously impossible.

Ciano observed that 'the advance continues' and, as no one appeared to be making a move to help the Greeks, 'it is now a question of speed, and we must act quickly'. However, Ciano noted the weather problems, that the general staff had hoped for an Italian–Greek diplomatic resolution, and that they were failing in their military preparations, thereby indicating a possible impending disaster. Within days of this localised Balkan war Ciano was finding excuses in the weather and, like Mussolini, blaming the military commanders. It has been justifiably claimed that the attack on Greece, Mussolini's first major war decision, was the blunder which started to destroy or at least diminish the Italian people's support for him.[355] The descent was to become terminal in July 1942 when Rommel failed in his North African advance, but it was from Greece onwards that Mussolini's fascism was in decline.

The month of October made sense of Hassell's jibe that Hitler and Mussolini were like caged tigers throwing themselves at the bars; Hitler was dashing around Europe planning and plotting, and Mussolini, almost on a whim, and in reaction to Hitler's dominance, had started a war with Greece. It was sheer ambition on the part of Mussolini as he tried to show the world, the Italian people and Hitler that he could win his own wars – which he never did: 'Mussolini's motives seemed as petty as his ambitions were grandiose'.[356]

Mussolini was almost a tragicomedy in himself but more tragic than comedy because he appeared to have no sense of military command, and with his limited resources and hopeless planning created more suffering. He wanted to be on the same assumed elevated podium as Hitler and be regarded as a military hero, which he never would be. A curious feature of Ciano's diary was that for a man who regretted the warlike policies of his Duce, for a man always suspicious of the Germans, he had in the matter of the Greek war suddenly become bellicose, believing the war against Greece would be easy.

Ciano started his month of November by going to war as a pilot, and he carried out a 'spectacular bombardment of Salonika'. He was somewhat concerned when he was attacked by Greek planes, writing 'I must confess that it was the first time that I've had them on my tail. It is an ugly experience'.[357] He was fortunate that he was not attacked by a swarm of Spitfires and Hurricanes experienced in pursuing bombers, but he was more fortunate than others, because on landing he was instructed that he was obliged the next day to go to Taranto 'to confer with the Duce', and then back to Rome. From the Italian capital he went to the Sudetenland, ironically on All Saints Day, where he met Ribbentrop at Schönhof, near Carlsbad.*

This meeting with Ribbentrop was unpleasant; at least Ciano was out of the danger zone, but Ribbentrop explained he was waiting for a telephone call from Hitler for instructions.[358] The first discussion concerned the secret protocol for Spain's entry into the war, which to German frustration never happened. Ribbentrop and Ciano discussed keeping Russia neutral and talked of Molotov's impending visit to Berlin, in a week's time. Ribbentrop explained that 'Russia's dynamism' should be anti-British and directed south towards Afghanistan and Persia; Italy should focus on the Mediterranean; and Germany would concentrate on equatorial Africa. Ciano noted that Ribbentrop made no reference to the Balkans – and he should have been more curious about Ribbentrop, as he was obfuscating Operation Barbarossa. Ribbentrop further suggested that the Montreux Convention should be dismissed, making the Black Sea Russian as would be access through the Dardanelles. He spoke with total authority.

According to Ciano, Ribbentrop kept repeating the World War I German claim that 'the war was already won'; he then reported how a German army major had quietly said to him 'this phrase was given to us in 1914, in 1915, in 1916, and 1917. I believed it. In 1918 I wished I were dead'. Ciano was impressed by Ribbentrop's calm sincerity and sadness, but he wrote 'let's hope that too many Germans don't think like this in any way'. Even though he had experienced the fighter plane attack a few days earlier, Ciano still had to learn about the fear and brutality of war.

He gathered on his return that Mussolini was unhappy about the start of the Greek war. Ciano felt a little more confident, writing that 'I don't think that we have come to the point where we must bandage our heads although many are beginning to think so'.[359] This was a war that Ciano had strongly supported, and he still believed it would be easy to win. Some, including Hassell, thought Ciano

---

* now Karlovy Vary

was the instigator; he had certainly encouraged Mussolini in this nationalistic enterprise. The news from the front contained conflicting information, and Mussolini was angry with Badoglio, who was still demanding another 'four months'. Mussolini always wanted instant success. It was about this time that Ciano heard of Chamberlain's death, about whom he expressed a degree of affection, but Mussolini simply stated to Ciano that Chamberlain 'had missed the bus', and told Ciano to enter it in his diary, which he duly did.

On 13 November the news came through of a British assault on the fleet at Taranto, in an innovative attack by Swordfish aircraft armed with torpedoes, launched from the carrier *Illustrious*, taking the Italians by surprise.* Three days later an Italian cruiser and two destroyers were damaged in an attack off Sardinia.

Ciano nevertheless remained hopeful at this point, and told Bottai that they would all be in Athens by Christmas Day.[360] However, by 15 November he was told that the 'Greeks have resumed their attack all along the front, and with considerable forces'. Ciano noted that 'we lack guns, while the Greek artillery is modern and well-handled'.[361] This accentuated the Italians' appalling lack both of preparation and of reliable information about the enemy. The next day he noted 'we are putting up a strong resistance in Albania', from where the invasion had started; this small hope appeared almost ridiculous given that although they were fighting Greece they were still inside Albania, virtually pushed back to their starting line. When he heard that a 'Comrade de Vecchi was thinking seriously of offering his resignation', Ciano noted that this man was 'one of the most active, indeed the most active inciter of Mussolini in the war against Greece'. Whether Ciano was beginning to shift the blame away from himself is a possibility, but at this stage he was probably wondering where it would end. On 15 November Goebbels entered in his diary 'now the Italians are in the soup and are having to plan, organise and prepare everything anew. Ciano was responsible for the whole affair and against the views of the majority. Another windbag, a companion for Ribbentrop.'[362] Some Italians still believed they could win, but when on 17 November Ciano left for Salzburg, he recognised that 'an eventual withdrawal is not to be excluded'. Ciano remained hopeful but was becoming realistic.

In Salzburg he met Ribbentrop, who was gloomy about the Greek situation, and they lunched with Serrano Suñer, whom Ciano found somewhat outspoken in his criticisms of the German failure to reach an agreement with the French. On 18 November Hitler received Ciano and Serrano Suñer, both of whom he distrusted, at Berchtesgaden; Ciano was not present, however, when Hitler and Serrano Suñer met. Hitler was angry with the Italian failure against Greece and

---

* This attack highlighted the importance of aircraft in naval affairs, and it has often been claimed that when Admiral Isoroku Yamamoto planned Pearl Harbor he had studied the Taranto attack.

concerned that the British might gain bases from where they could bomb the oil wells at Ploesti. (He was correct; the RAF were eager for bases in Greece for that very reason.)[363] He instructed Ciano, as only Hitler could, that Mussolini should bring Yugoslavia into their orbit. He informed his nervous guest that it was necessary to close the Mediterranean and to seek accord with Turkey, thereby encouraging Romania and Hungary. Ciano wrote to the Duce, stating that Hitler 'sees the problem within the vaster framework of the European conflict', which aspect should have been more on the minds of Ciano and Mussolini.[364] Ciano described how Hitler delivered a lecture surveying the map, making him appear more like a 'senior estate manager'. Hitler informed Ciano that the Germans were in Romania to deter the Russians, prompting Ciano to observe that since Molotov's visit there had been less mention of the Soviets. Hitler informed Ciano that when Italy had secured Mersa Matruh he would be willing to send Stuka squadrons to attack British shipping. Hitler wanted Hungary to accept German transit trains ferrying troops across it to Romania, and again demanded that Yugoslavian relations with Italy be improved, which Ciano tried to counter, asserting that they were already sound. Hitler ended his conversation by informing Ciano that when in Italy he had already been aware of the Italians starting the Greek war, scoring, as it were, a point.[365]

On 20 November in Vienna Ciano joined in the document-signing ceremony for Hungary to join the Axis, in the anticipation that Slovakia and Romania would soon follow, prompting the cynical comment 'I do not attach much importance to these states joining: they are vassals of Germany'.[366] It apparently had yet to cross Ciano's mind that many Germans thought the same about Italy.

When Hitler wrote to Mussolini on these matters Ciano was surprised to find that his master did not appear concerned; he had anticipated a 'violent reaction'. Ciano believed that the Duce would refuse 'all military help in the matter before he has taken revenge on the Greeks'.[367] How such a revenge could be exacted without German help was becoming questionable.

Pavolini reported that Badoglio was blaming the Greek fiasco on the Duce.[*] This had been, according to Ciano, a 'confidential' conversation of which 'Pavolini dutifully' informed the Duce. Mussolini called Badoglio a series of names, including 'traitor', which Ciano thought were 'strong epithets for him to use about his own chief-of-staff in war-time.' Ciano, in a cable from Germany, had informed Mussolini of a conversation between Badoglio and Keitel in which Badoglio had explained he had opposed the Greek invasion. None of this helped. By 26 November, following criticisms in the *Regime Fascista*, Badoglio handed in his resignation. By the end of the month the internal dissent in Italy was more

---

[*]   Pavolini, a friend of Ciano, later ensured Ciano was executed.

evident, with further Greek pressure threatening to penetrate the Italian defence lines.

The month ended with a cynical note by Ciano, observing that General Cavallero was 'called in', and that this general was one of those optimists who had full faith 'in our ability to take the offensive once more'.[368] Mussolini did not offer Cavallero any post at this time, and as Ciano noted, 'Badoglio continues to shoot pheasants' in his retirement. The Italian failure on the battlefield in Greece and later in North Africa has often led to the belief that that the Italian soldier 'lacked the stomach for fighting', which is absolute nonsense. They lost these battles because they were badly equipped, poorly led and had weak commanders, with Mussolini making unrealistic demands without appropriate preparation. Italy was facing a potential disaster, and Ciano felt even more gloomy because he had once considered it to be an easy task to occupy Greece, a view he had undoubtedly transmitted to Mussolini, who was emotionally unstable, still seeking military success to compete with Hitler. By the end of the month on the Greek–Albanian front the Greeks made more advances after heavy fighting. 'The humiliating set-backs suffered by Italy's armed forces on the Greek Front in November, accompanied by the Taranto raid, was soon followed by the collapse in North Africa, and shook the fascist system in Italy.'[369]

At this point Ciano's popularity was in freefall. The Italians believed that their sons had died in a needless 'war instigated by him to expand his grand duchy, and many called for him to be fired', and the rumour spread that he would soon be appointed an ambassador to somewhere in South America.[370] Later Ciano would argue that it was Mussolini, not him, who always made the decisions, and although many critics, both then and now, blame Ciano he was in fact correct in this argument. Undoubtedly, however, he encouraged the Duce. Whether Mussolini would sack Ciano as an effort to shift the focus of blame from himself is not known for certain, but it has been suggested that an intervention by Edda saved Ciano.[371]

Ciano and Edda's relationship had been continuing along the same hedonistic lines, generating gossip that Edda was leaving him for her long-time lover Pucci; in November Rachele Mussolini allegedly received an anonymous letter informing her that Ciano was having an affair with a Delia Di Bagno, one of Edda's friends, and that Delia's husband was having a similar encounter with Edda.[372] Political life in Italy was as murky as the personal behaviour of their leaders. The immorality of their mores extended beyond their personal lifestyles; on 10 November Mussolini had commanded his troops to 'raze all Greek cities with a population of more than 10,000', which, although it may have been seen as 'a gesture of increasing impotence' was still appallingly immoral.[373]

During the final month of 1940 Mussolini and Ciano watched as their military efforts failed abysmally, not just in their proposed occupation of Greece but in North Africa as well. The Italians were still short of equipment and had only a few reserves. Mussolini blamed everyone but himself, and his impulsive demands for immediate victory were evidently absurd. On 6 December Marshal Badoglio resigned as the commander-in-chief of the Italian armed forces, and later General Ugo Cavallero was appointed in his place; two days later the Italian Navy Admiral Cavagnari was replaced by Admiral Campioni.

The world was amazed by the Greeks managing to defeat the Italian military. Many Italians wondered why they had attacked Greece in the first place, because they had no irredentist claims on that country; in Albania thousands of men were dying, and the Greeks had pushed the Italians so far back that even Port Edda was occupied. If during this month of December Mussolini was frustrated by his failure in Greece, the situation in North Africa was even worse. All too typically Ciano started his duties in December not in relation to military or international matters, but in response to an order from the Duce that he approach the Vatican demanding the abolition of three religious festivals, which fell too close together, he felt, at the beginning of the New Year. With such serious problems in Albania and Egypt, it must have seemed bizarre that Mussolini was concerned with religious festivals.

In between these ecclesiastical liturgical issues Ciano was aware of the military failures, with General Soddu suggesting a truce be arranged through Hitler. Ciano was unhappy, stating that 'I would rather put a bullet through my head than telephone Ribbentrop'. He phoned Jacomoni in Albania and, on hearing that 'Tirana was more calm than Rome', concluded that they were receiving mixed messages – not, of course, that he should have assumed, as he did, that Jacomoni was correct.[374] This emphasises one of the ongoing problems with the Italian military weakness, namely the lack of a unified command and differing opinions from senior officers along with little reliable information. Badoglio was considering withdrawing his resignation, but Mussolini told him it was too late, that he was 'too tired' and that 'the king himself encouraged him to accept it'.* On 6 December Cavallero was appointed chief of the general staff. He went straight to Albania and returned with the news that the situation was 'critical but on the way to a solution'.

If Albania were bad news the British attack at Sidi Barrani came 'like a thunderbolt'. Initially the news did not appear too serious but, as Ciano admitted, the subsequent telegrams from Graziani 'confirm we have had a licking'. It was a

---

* Badoglio was appointed prime minister after Mussolini's downfall, and survived the war; he managed to avoid criminal trials for his savagery in North Africa.

disaster for the Italian military, but Ciano observed that 'Mussolini, whom I saw twice, was very calm', and 'he commented on the event with impersonal objectivity'. Ciano was more worried about the reaction of the public, which 'had already been shaken and too much divided to receive this news and heavy blow calmly'.[375]

The Italians had arrived in Egypt and simply dug in while the British pretended that they were better armed than they were.[376] Despite their paucity of arms and materials Churchill decided to send tanks and men to that area. On 9 December the opening of the British offensive started by breaking through the Italian lines at Sidi Barrani. The British surrounded the entrenched camp of Nibeiwa, killing amongst others General Maletti, still in his pyjamas such was the speed and surprise of the attack. Over four days collapse all but ensued, and the critical area was in British hands. Four Italians divisions were wiped out and 38,000 prisoners were taken, including four generals; British casualties were 624 dead. The remnants of Italian troops retreated west. In two months, the British success was immense: 'they had advanced 500 miles and captured 130,000 prisoners, 380 tanks and 1,290 guns, all at the cost of only 500 killed and 1,373 wounded'.[377]

As the news percolated through, Goebbels was busy attacking Ciano and Mussolini, writing in his diary on 7 December 'Mussolini would do better to sack Ciano too. He deserves it most', three days later adding 'he is sacking one commanding officer after another. He should fire Ciano, and the Führer should do likewise with Ribbentrop', and the next day 'Ciano is trying to push it on to Badoglio … and claiming he was not consulted … an appalling orgy of dilettantism'.[378] When Goebbels heard about North Africa he wrote 'London claims to have recaptured Sollum. Italian public opinion blames Ciano, quite correctly', writing two days later that 'feelings in Italy are turning against Mussolini and the Fascist Party, Ciano is the object of general hatred. He deserves it'. Goebbels' information, for once, was reliable.[379]

Ciano too listened to Hitler's speech, which gave the impression that 'Italy was playing a secondary role'. Mussolini had once considered himself as *primus inter pares* with Hitler, but Ciano had a more realistic perspective of the relationship. As Hassell had noted, the Italians were regarded by the Germans with contempt, viewing Italy as the lame duck needing constant first aid. Ciano finally reached the conclusion that 'something is the matter with our army if five divisions allow themselves to be pulverised in two days'.[380] As usual the blame was cast on the generals, and Graziani was criticised by Ciano for being too fearful for his own life, and having too many guards surrounding his own residence, even in Italy. Cesare De Vecchi resigned, Admiral Cavagnari was replaced by Admiral Riccardi, and Badoglio had resigned. Ciano accused the generals of suffering from more jealousies than women (yet again demonstrating his prejudice).[381]

When Graziani telegrammed that he was thinking of withdrawing to Tripoli, Ciano found Mussolini 'very much shaken', and spoke to him about raising the morale of the people. Mussolini had good reason to be shaken by the news – not least because, as he observed, 'five generals are prisoners, and one is dead. This is the ratio of Italians who have military qualities and those who have none'.[382] Mussolini decided they would have to build a professional army. Such a decision being taken only at that point illustrates his immature approach to a national dilemma by going to war so badly prepared.

On 14 December Ciano dined at the German Embassy, where he gained the impression that the German attitude 'towards us is grim; in German eyes we are not yet guilty, but we are under suspicion'. Ciano was ordered to write to Alfieri, asking him to seek an interview with the Führer requesting resources, especially, he added, given that the Germans controlled the resources across Europe. He suggested a tactic to Alfieri, suggesting that 'when talking to the Führer you can call his attention to the fact that since it is Italy which is bearing the weight of the conflict with Great Britain at the present time and presumably for the duration of the winter, our consumption had shown a rise … which justifies our requests'.[383] Hitler had been confronted by Spain's extensive shopping list, and now the Italians were claiming they were fighting the British when in fact they were causing more damage to the Axis than was Spain by staying isolated. Spain might have been irritating to Hitler, but Italy was proving to be a burdensome partner.

There were major factions in Italy who were against the war and fascism, but Ciano merely latched onto the jealousy amongst the generals. On Christmas Eve Mussolini remained in a grim mood, accusing the Italians of being 'a mediocre race' and 'good for nothing'. Ciano noted that the Duce is 'sombre' and 'more tired than usual', which worried him because the 'Duce's energy at this time is our greatest resource'. It is possible to detect here either a change from Ciano's more cynical views of Mussolini expressed earlier in the year, or a concern that his diary might be read by his master. Having watched the German military victories Ciano appeared more inclined to be pro-German, and in her later reminiscences his wife Edda wrote that when he had disagreed with her father he should have resigned, but with German supremacy seeming unchallengeable the 'events made it seem that my father might be right'.[384] It was an appalling start to Mussolini's projected concept of the 'parallel war', and after a few weeks Mussolini was having to ask Hitler for assistance. For Ciano the month of December 1940 was a record of Italian military disaster and political ineptitude, and this would be an ongoing picture for the Italians for most of the war until they capitulated. The fault would be that of Mussolini and his cohorts, with their political sense of nationalistic expansionism and wanting a place on the world stage; this would lead to disaster for Mussolini, Ciano and many others.

SUMMATION OF 1940

1940 had witnessed German victory in Western Europe and Italy's declaration of war at the very last moment. For Italy it was one disaster after another in Greece and North Africa and in naval conflict, and there were deep German suspicions about their partner. Mussolini and Ciano were rapidly losing what popularity they had had in Italy, and Ciano was distrusted by the Germans.

Hitler and his cohorts were becoming more concerned by Mussolini's failures; Hitler was equally unhappy about Franco's lack of support, and he had proposed Operation Felix for the German takeover of Gibraltar, because he knew it could block the Mediterranean for the British. Even France was causing him concern, because the seeming pro-German Laval[385] – the man who had claimed he 'foresaw chances of a beautiful French–German collaboration in British Africa' – had fallen from power. It was easy for Hitler's men to restore Laval and to ignore Spain, but Italy was becoming a nightmare. By 13 December Hitler had issued Directive Marita, which would despatch 24 divisions to the Balkans; if his plans for Russia were to succeed, then he needed the Balkans and south-eastern regions of Europe under his control

The next directive of any substance to leave Hitler's desk was the one on 17 December outlining his plans against Russia – unknown to Mussolini and Ciano and, as it turned out, the greatest military blunder by the Nazi regime. Somewhat ironically, the very day before that, Ciano had written a letter to Alfieri in Berlin about their Ambassador Rosso in Moscow. Italy was keen to improve relations with Russia, which was driven by trade necessities, and to restore the Russian–Italian relationship to 'a sense of normality'.[386] Italy was, as usual, being kept in the dark, and the Italian situation was falling apart – but with Hitler's plans so was the whole of Europe.

On the Albanian front the conditions remained disastrous as the temperature plummeted to -20°C. In Italy there were serious shortages of food, especially in the bombed cities. Significantly, just before Christmas Ciano had found time to go to a local village, Cortellazzo, named after his father, and noted that 'soldiers in the know were already grumbling that Mussolini spent every afternoon with Claretta Petacci and was frequently impossible to contact'.[387] Ciano had spent many sentences in his diary on being somewhat critical of the Duce's shifting moods, even accusing him of being unbalanced, but now others were becoming aware of 'a leader whose ageing physique was collapsing under the weight of office and the evidence of failure'.[388] It has been suggested that sometime during this last month of 1940 Ciano put out peace feelers in Lisbon, but as Eden was now the British foreign secretary the feelers were 'snuffed out'.[389] Ciano had realised that the war was going badly for Italy, and this was leading him to clash with Mussolini in an ongoing downward spiral. In a matter of just a few months from the declaration of war Italy was in chaos, Mussolini was proving himself incapable, and Ciano was not strong enough to apply any brakes.

7

1941 – TOTAL WAR

Barbarossa; the brutality of total war
(Polish Archives, author-unknown)

FACING HITLER

Between 1939 and 1941 Ciano fluctuated from belief in certain defeat to hope of
an Axis victory. After June 1941 he again became sceptical about winning against
the Allies, a reaction reinforced by his distrust of the Germans. The year had
started with his concerns over his mother's health, and with Cavallero announcing
a strategy of attacking Greece along the coast, then on 4 January there was a
meeting of the council during which Mussolini was sombre about Greece but
optimistic about North Africa. Ciano recognised that Greece remained a serious
problem, and the news from Africa was not hopeful, which raised the question
as to whether Mussolini was playing politics with his ministers or was removed
from reality. Ciano heard that Grandi was worried because Farinacci had written
to him to be open; it was understood that Grandi had been 'reserved about the last

two months', implying he was unhappy about Mussolini.[390] This could be regarded as the first serious signs of dissent within the Mussolini government; Grandi had always been pro-British, never comfortable with Mussolini's inclination towards Germany. The war dilemma worsened the next day with no Italian radio connection from Bardia (in east Libya), and Mussolini still waiting for Cavallero to strike his promised attack against Greece.

On 6 January Ciano met the king, who remained sceptical and raised the question as to whether the British were intending to invade Italy. The king told him that he had decided the Germans would win because they had 'unified Europe' (a strange way of articulating military occupation).[391] The news of the fall of Bardia to the British shook Italian public opinion after so much political optimism, but even with this news Mussolini remained unperturbed, with Ciano writing that the Duce 'these days seems really superhuman', and describing him going through the military lists of senior officers, pondering who should be replaced.

When Mussolini warned Pavolini, Bottai, Renato Ricci and Ciano that the time had arrived for the fascist leaders to join the fighting, there was a sense of desperation. Ciano decided he would resume his air force command in Tirana, but many of the fascist leaders, now much older, were fearful of themselves facing such a prospect. Mussolini persisted in this plan, however, and demanded that the members of the government, the Grand Council and the Chamber and indeed all fascist officials take up arms. There was evident disquiet. Bottai wondered if it were an embryonic *coup d'état*, and whether other political forces were to be introduced, which surprised Ciano, but he thought Bottai was wrong, and it was not a time for such domestic issues.[392] Grandi, aged 45 and the ex-ambassador to Great Britain, was ordered to 'put his Alpine boots on' – not that he ever did so. It is feasible that Mussolini was putting his fascist supporters in 'their place', and had decided that he did not need their advice. He was confident, telling Ciano that Greece would be finished in a few months; as it turned out he was correct, but only because the Wehrmacht arrived.

On 10 January the German ambassador came to arrange Mussolini's trip to Berchtesgaden, which made the Duce happy, and all the more so since he had heard the news that in a naval clash in Sicilian waters the British were losing. The news was, however, again exaggerated, which meant he was unable to announce a victory while in Germany; and there was no good news, either, from Cavallero in Albania. Frustrated, Mussolini went to Foggia to meet the military leaders from Albania. In his absence, Ciano heard from Alfieri in Berlin that the anti-Ciano rumours 'had made the rounds', with Ciano noting that 'the Germans harbour an old resentment about my non-belligerency and cannot conceal this resentment even when they try to save appearances'.[393] Ciano complained that they thought he wanted the war with Greece, when he claimed 'I wanted no war at all'. Whether this was true at the time or a later addition to his text remains questionable.

In mid-January Mussolini and Ciano departed by train to Salzburg for their Führer conference. They met Hitler at a small railway station, and Ciano described the meeting as 'cordial.' Mussolini later disclosed to Ciano that he had found the Führer anti-Russian, and for his part Mussolini explained to Hitler his issues with the king and the emerging problems with Badoglio. General Guzzoni was there, and Ciano amusingly described his 'tightly stretched paunch and his little dyed wig', realising that his appearance had made a poor impression on the Germans. The main task was Hitler instructing Mussolini to bring Franco into the conflict.* Hitler had found Franco difficult, but with a diplomatic touch he suggested that the main source of the problem was Serrano Suñer and the influence of the Church, upon which Franco had depended for support. Hitler explained there were tensions between Pétain, Weygand and de Gaulle, claiming that all they had in common was hatred of the Axis powers.[394] (They were more than tensions, however, and de Gaulle would later be denounced by Vichy as a traitor.) The same type of conversation was orchestrated between Ciano and Ribbentrop in their discussion, the latter having carried out his habitual survey of relationships between the Axis powers and others, featuring Franco's leaning more towards Britain, Gibraltar being essential for unlocking the Mediterranean, and King Boris of Bulgaria tending to favour the British, but critically the thorny problem of Soviet Russia. Ribbentrop admitted that the Italians had been asked to draw closer to Russia, but not quite as cosy as they had become.[395] He then changed the subject to the embarrassing question as to what was happening in Libya.

It has been suggested that during this meeting Hitler gave Mussolini a secret file on Ciano prepared by Himmler, but if indeed that file existed, Ciano, unaware of it, wrote that the 'Italians know I am the only one in Italy who has the courage to stand up to Mussolini'.[396] There were no post-war discoveries of such a file, but nevertheless there was plenty of evidence to indicate that Ciano was distrusted. He should have realised that he was unpopular in Italy by being associated with the Greek disaster, a general discontent in government rule, and his apparent closeness with Mussolini. In February, with the bad news from North Africa, Goebbels wrote that 'reports from Italy mention the profoundest defeatism. These days, the Führer is their only hope, Ciano is absolutely finished, and the Duce's popularity is approaching zero level'.[397] Later he wrote 'the Duce is making a host

---

*   On 7 December Canaris had purportedly informed Franco of the decision to take Gibraltar from Spanish territory in Operation Felix, but it is now known that Canaris had in fact advised Franco *against* the risk of the action.

of psychological errors, in his private life as well. To the common people, Ciano is the devil. And he must be incredibly corrupt. The Italians will continue to give us plenty to worry about.'[398]

When they returned Ciano followed the request to try and bring the Spanish into the war, writing to Serrano Suñer suggesting there should be a 'propitious meeting' between Franco and Mussolini, perhaps on the Ligurian Riviera near Genoa.[399] He then made sure that Ribbentrop was aware of his efforts.

By 22 January there was the bad news that Tobruk had fallen. The news from Greece was no better, Cavallero still promising action with Ciano writing 'I am waiting without excessive illusions but with faith'. Before he left for his military duties Ciano gave a letter to Mussolini from a Professor Faccini in Livorno, complaining that his teenage son had been mobilised and sent to Albania the same day 'without knowing what a firearm is'.[400] This singular letter indicated yet further that the Italian military was reckless and lacking professionalism.

In late January Ciano prepared to travel to Bari, having said farewell to Mussolini the day before. Ciano felt that Mussolini was not as friendly as he could have been, and 'made certain observations which he should have kept to himself'. It may have been that Ciano had spoken to him too brusquely a few days before, or that the Himmler file existed and Mussolini had read it. Whatever the facts of the matter, Mussolini stopped keeping Ciano informed, and according to one Italian historian Ciano now believed that Mussolini hated him.[401] Anfuso recalled that when he asked Mussolini whether he would like Ciano present, he was simply told, 'Count Ciano will remain in Bari.'[402] There was a distinct impression that Mussolini was unhappy with his son-in-law.

It was not helped when Mussolini was made aware of reports about Ciano and his flying comrades. It was reported they had been celebrating a bombing raid on the Albanian border and were revelling, with rumours of setting off 'fireworks'. Mussolini demanded an investigation; Ciano had to appear before a general, and was furious. He was so angry that he wrote and complained directly to Mussolini, which 'no one else would have dared'.[403]

While Ciano was dropping bombs in the Balkans Mussolini was meeting Franco, as Ciano had arranged, and in his diplomatic papers Ciano explained that Mussolini's efforts had failed. Franco embarrassed Mussolini by discussing the Italian defeats, which Mussolini attempted to explain by claiming that the British 'attack succeeded because in the front we had Libyans, who are excellent troops, but not when faced by mechanised forces'.[404] In their conversation Mussolini suggested that 1941 would be the end of that conflict.[405] Franco explained that all his guns were surrounding Gibraltar and he would rather the Spanish accomplished this, though he had let the Germans investigate, which they did without any collaboration.* Franco demanded grain, manure and 32,000 mules or tractors, and Mussolini assured him that the Germans were true to their promises, as they had been with his coal. It should have been obvious to Hitler and Mussolini that Franco had no intention of going to war.

MORE DISASTER

Rommel had taken El Agheila, which looked promising, but the war was not going well, and on 28 March the Italian Navy suffered its greatest defeat in its history at the Battle of Matapan, where it lost three heavy cruisers. This was not the only sea disaster, because the British sank the Italian hospital ship *Po* just off Albania, with Edda on board. Ciano had noted that Edda was on a hospital ship in the capacity of a nurse, and although there are many photographs of her in this role Ciano had merely alluded in passing to her new life. She had not at this time completed her two-year Red Cross course, but having used her influence to be taken on as a nurse was now swimming for her life. In her memoirs she claimed that 'Mussolini and Ciano had been making an inspection trip in this area' which was not true, but she may have been told this by her distraught father.[406] When she was rescued, Mussolini was notified and telephoned Rachele immediately, and Ciano arrived the next day. In addition to all this Mussolini ordered a spring offensive but, as soon as the Greeks counterattacked, it ground to a halt.

BACK WITH HITLER

At the end of March Ciano returned as foreign minister, prompting Goebbels to make the acerbic comment that 'he bounced back from the depths'.[407] Ciano's first task was a meeting in Vienna on 25 March with Hitler, who wanted to ensure that Yugoslavia either stayed neutral or joined the Tripartite Alliance. Yugoslavia signed the pact the same day, but two days later there was a *coup d'état* and Yugoslavia's new government promptly backed out of it, then in response to an armed incursion was forced to surrender the following month, on 17 April. When Ciano told Hitler of Mussolini's movements in Albania the Führer noticeably 'did not reply'.[408] When England was discussed, Ciano noted that Hitler only mentioned his U-boat threat. He was becoming more sceptical about Vichy France, was sure that Turkey would arrive in the Axis camp for safety reasons, and felt that the Soviet Union was becoming more hostile, hence the necessary build-up of German troops along the borders. Ciano met Hitler again on 20 April

---

*   The Germans had planned Operation Felix but 'Canaris and others pointed out that travelling from the north to Gibraltar would be hazardous because the communication links by train were dubious, the roads were not always ready for traffic, and the journey involved steep mountainous passes'. Sangster, Andrew, *Probing the Enigma of Franco* (Newcastle: Cambridge Scholars, 2018) p.151.

in lower Austria, when Hitler complained that had Spain cooperated the British situation in the Mediterranean would have been vastly different. Hitler told Ciano that he would like another meeting with Mussolini. The next day Ciano met Ribbentrop as they discussed the new plans for the Balkan region, especially Slovenia, causing Ciano to tell Mussolini 'I reaffirmed our deliberate decision to claim the whole of Dalmatia for Italy', with Ribbentrop making the suggestion of giving Hungary an outlet to the sea.[409]

THE BALKANS

In the meantime British troops had arrived in Greece, but too late and too few; many people have regarded this move, instigated by Churchill, as a serious mistake. Mussolini ordered another advance in Albania on 10 April, and the Greeks had to withdraw in order to avoid German encirclement. The Germans were rapidly advancing, the British were having to evacuate, and Mussolini was attempting to be regarded as the victor. He refused to sign the proposed armistice while any Greeks remained on Albanian soil; this irritated the Germans, and they sent units forward to stem the so-called Italian advance. Mussolini protested but signed the agreement on 23 April. He was desperate to go to Greece to accept the surrender personally, but it took place before he could arrive. He announced that the Greeks had already been in retreat from the Italians, but few believed this assertion. The Italian historian Mario Cervi wrote 'in the Greek campaign the Italian troops were, without doubt whatever, the worst-led troops in the world. They deserved better of their country.'[410] The tempo of the Balkan conflict was rising, and in early April the free state of Croatia was declared by Ante Pavelić. He had taken refuge in Italy and was the head of the fascist ultranationalists known as the Ustaše, infamous for persecuting minorities, with the support of the Nazi regime. As these developments occurred, Ciano continued to apply pressure to gain Italy's right to occupy the whole Adriatic coast, while Ribbentrop was insisting on a German outlet to the sea through Croatia. The opening months of 1941 had been successful for the Axis powers, but it was more than ever evident that Italy appeared to be a handicapped partner, and for most of April Mussolini tried to establish some sense of victory and spoils, against a dominant Germany.

Ciano met the king, and discovered that he wanted the restoration of the royal Petroviches in Montenegro, and later in April was 'insisting' on it. The king was perceptive about the Nazis but was attempting to extend royal power; Mussolini and Ciano accepted this if it were a means to gaining some spoils of war.

As Ciano prepared to meet Pavelić, Mussolini ordered him to keep Croatia within Italy's orbit of influence. Ciano found 'Lubliana' freezing*, but he noted that although Pavelić said he needed time he did not rule out a union under one royal head. Ciano observed that 'our humane treatment as compared to the inhuman treatment by the Germans should gain us the sympathy of the Croats'.[411] Ciano probably believed this, but by the end of the war in the Balkans it is now known that Italian behaviour in their areas of occupation matched the atrocities of many German units.

As the German invasion succeeded Mussolini became excited and took Ciano's advice by sending Anfuso to Greece; he promptly returned, however, stating that he had found no Greek or German delegations, and informed Mussolini that it was a matter of finding a government which had some legality. Mussolini instructed Ciano to ask the Germans about Italian government for the territories they claimed. One thread of welcome news was when Casertano, the minister to Zagreb (the major city in north-central Croatia) visited Mussolini regarding the royal crown, and Ciano wrote to Pavelić telling him that Mussolini was 'pleased with his majesty's acceptance of the crown of Croatia for a prince of Savoy'.[412]

Ciano, back in office, was indicating his concerns about military failures, and also about where Mussolini was leading the country. Many more Italians opposed the war, 'criticism of the regime' was becoming more widespread and more outspoke; this suggests that it was from about this point that Ciano 'began to plot seriously against his leader'.[413] The month of May 1941 was perplexing in Italy, with developing tensions with the Germans, the use of the distrusted royalty to extend influence, internal wrangling over appointments, news of events from overseas which was often muddled, and signs of internal dissent – and when Ethiopia was occupied by the Allies, Mussolini was bitter at losing the pearl of the empire.[414] Ciano wrote that there was 'a general feeling in the air that Italian domination in Croatia is to be temporary'. He revealed a degree of humanity when he heard that Badoglio, whom he disliked, had lost another son, in a car crash in Libya; he 'felt sorry for the man'.

German issues were causing irritation, not least when Mussolini heard that Rommel had reproached Italian commanders in North Africa, and there were further tensions with the Germans in Albania. Alfieri in Berlin was sounding alarms, and advised that Mussolini and Hitler should meet to 'settle the main issues'. Following this warning Ciano organised a meeting between Pavelić and Mussolini at Monfalcone, close to the border as Pavelić could not afford to be too far from home.† When they arrived Pavelić was surrounded by the Ustaše guards, giving Ciano the impression of a 'wild west character'. The ceremony of 'crowns'

---

*   now Ljubljana
†   Monfalcone is located on the Gulf of Trieste.

was set for 18 May, with Ciano wondering whether he could arrange a monument for his father at Buccari.*

The game of thrones was being played out, and was now part of empire-building by Mussolini, who as we know normally had no time for royalty unless they furthered his ambitions. The new throne was to be given to the Duke of Spoleto, whom Ciano tracked down in a hotel room in Milan with 'some young girl'. Spoleto had no idea of what to do, and Ciano explained to him that he was a 'lieutenant-general with a crown in the service of the fascist empire', adding that 'we must keep the reins tightly in our grasp'.[415]

The king of Italy was delighted and took himself off to Tirana, where, according to Ciano, the people were 'enthusiastic'. The king was still demanding royalty for Montenegro, next door, and wanting the old 1914 borders re-established. When he pressed this matter, Ciano reflected that such an action would cause unrest in Albania. Later Ciano heard that a discontented Albanian student called Mihailov had fired a shot at the king – reflecting the lack of enthusiasm in Albania for Italian efforts – but had missed.

The Montenegrins made it clear they were not in favour of the crown being offered to Prince Michael, but preferred his mother, the queen, to which the king of Italy immediately objected. He then suggested Prince Roman, a son of the Petrovich family, but he was not interested, and it was a matter of turning back to Prince Michael. The machinations were medieval, and all to do with the political manoeuvring to gain control and influence. In July Prince Michael would turn down the offer, on the grounds that he believed the Axis would be defeated.[416]

SIGNS OF INTERNAL DISSENT

It is difficult to accurately understand Ciano's views in this quagmire. He heard a speech given by Hitler and wrote 'that I like the oratory of this man more and more; it is strong, persuasive and an informative speech'.[417] He did not comment on the nature of the contents, but later writing that 'recent vicissitudes, and above all tension with German troops in Greece, have opened his [Mussolini's] eyes to many things'.[418] There was more dissension in Italy, which was also surfacing amongst some of the fascist leaders in a clandestine fashion. Ciano appeared to be talking more with fellow fascists whom hitherto he had only mentioned in passing. Later in the month he noted that Bottai was more anti-German, becoming pessimistic about 'our internal situation'. At the end of the month, Ciano wrote that Bottai was even more sceptical about the 'progress of public affairs in Italy', and he spoke to Ciano about the cold atmosphere emanating from Mussolini towards the fascist

---

*   Buccari is Italian for Bakar, a town in western Croatia.

leadership. The fact that Bottai could speak openly to Ciano about such matters indicated that he had detected a sympathetic ear.

Administrative changes were being made, and may have been initiated by Mussolini's domestic life. Rachele had a favourite nephew, Augusto Moschi, who according to Ciano held the keys to his powerful aunt's heart, but Augusto told Ciano that his place had been supplanted by a man called Pater, an entrepreneur and builder, disturbing the 'peace' and Villa Torlonia.* Ciano, in a rare mention of his wife, wrote that 'Edda, who is intelligent and outspoken', referred to the 'strange games' that Pater was playing with her mother, and explained it as 'the consequences of menopause'.[419] The influences of the Mussolini home were tense and gossiped about; Rachele and Pater on one side, and Mussolini's lover Petacci and her family on the other. This domestic embarrassment added to the unease within the fascist leadership, as it was known that these elements influenced him.

As these Italian domestic problems increased, the news became more disturbing. Haile Selassie was returned to his throne in May by the well-known Orde Wingate and his Gideon Force. There was news that Hess, Hitler's deputy, had died in a plane crash, then it transpired he had landed in Britain. Mussolini made the crazy suggestion that he had been on his way to stir up a revolt in Ireland. Then Ribbentrop hastily arrived, looking embarrassed, as he tried to explain what had happened in the high command. It was, as Ciano noted, a matter of 'patching up things', and to this day the circumstances of Hess's flight remain somewhat confusing.[420] Ribbentrop for once was in an embarrassing position, with Bismarck telling Anfuso that Ribbentrop 'is such an imbecile that he is a freak of nature'.[421]

Ambassador Phillips informed Ciano that he could not guarantee that America would stay neutral, and Mussolini told Ciano that in his opinion the war would probably last until 1948. The only good news appeared to be that the Germans would clear Crete of the British, who eventuated on 1 June, but this spark of hope was countered by problems in Iraq, where Ciano was critical that the Italian air force had apparently not left the ground.† The war brought confusing news, and Ciano was aware that the Italian people remained doubtful. On a visit to his mother in Livorno he discovered that his newspaper was not selling, reflecting the lack of enthusiasm for him. Alfieri paid a visit from Berlin, stating that the war 'is won. All we have to do is find a way to stop it'.[422] Mussolini thought the tone of the Italian–German relationship was deteriorating, and Anfuso let Ciano know that the Germans had broken the Italian cypher code, but Ciano was happy because they could now read what he wanted them to hear. When Roosevelt gave

---

*   Mussolini rented Villa Torlonia for one lira a year; after 1945 it fell into decay but is now opened as a museum.
†   Since 1930 Iraq had granted Britain many privileges and the Germans had tried to unsettle this by organising a revolt under Rashid Ali, an ardent Arab nationalist, but it collapsed at the end of May 1941.

an important speech with potential ramifications, all Mussolini could do was pontificate that 'never in history had a nation been led by a paralytic'.[423]

Ciano's conversations with Bottai during this month, and many of his observations, indicate that he was unhappy about the way Italy was being governed. His American biographer, Ray Moseley, refers to a letter sent by Washington, asking whether it was conceivable that an Italian *coup* might happen, and an offer of peace be sent to England. This was based on the work of Giorgio Nelson Page, who claimed that Ciano was the author of this letter.[424] It suggested whether Mussolini and the king might be overthrown and replaced by the Duke of Aosta. An OSS agent called Evans organised a meeting with Ciano at his golf club, using a code name. How far this episode can be trusted is questionable, given that the main source for this knowledge was Page, an American with an Italian mother; he had taken Italian citizenship in 1933, joined the fascists and held positions in the ministry of popular culture, and was later interned by the Allies. In 1958 he founded a right-wing satirical tabloid. He was known to Ciano and may well have been one of his friends, but this plot would certainly have helped his book sell, especially in Italy. The book did indeed sell, and inspired a film by an Alberto Sordi.

During these weeks Ciano frequently mentioned Mussolini's anger towards Germany, caused by his treatment during the Greek armistice, the German interference and interest in Croatia and trade deals, and now probably also based on his awareness that he was regarded as the junior partner. There is no question that Ciano was talking to unhappy fascists such as Bottai, but it is unclear whether he had been manipulating plots with the enemy at this stage of events.

BARBAROSSA

June was a critical month: the free French with British support launched a campaign in Syria; on 14 June America froze German and Italian assets; Croatia joined the Tripartite Pact; and on 22 June Operation Barbarossa started, with Italy and Romania declaring war on the USSR the same day, and Hungary following on 27 June.

For Ciano, the month started with a journey to the Brenner, leading to another conversation with Ribbentrop, though Mussolini could not fathom the necessity. Mussolini had the impression that Hitler had wept over Hess and that the Germans would like a peace settlement. If Hitler had indeed wept over Hess it was probably from rage, and as Hitler was planning the attack on Russia any peace possibilities were extinct; Mussolini appeared to have some whimsical notions. Ciano's conversation with Ribbentrop was the usual *tour de force* of other countries, but he gathered the general impression that Hitler had no definitive plan of action. Ribbentrop told Ciano that rumours about Russia were best avoided, and the problem was in fact the build-up of Soviet forces along the border. The truth was the converse, of course, with many observing the massive trainloads of German troops heading east. Mussolini had instructed Ciano to strengthen his ties with Ribbentrop because 'he knew the mind of Hitler'.

On 4 June Ciano met the new Hungarian minister for foreign affairs, a László Bárdossy, who had come to power since the deaths of Czaky and Teleki.* Ciano decided that Bárdossy was a career man who loved tea parties and the drawing rooms of unknown countesses, and forgot he was responsible for his country's policies.[425] This was a curious observation by Ciano, a playboy himself with similar habits. The festering problem for Italy was the continuing widespread shortage of food and essential supplies. The trade negotiations with Germany were not going well, there were fewer coal supplies, and increasing transport problems with oil. Mussolini was unhappy and told Ciano that he could 'wage an *ersatz* war'. Later, when Ciano raised this with Ribbentrop, he was told there were no problems, and that Clodius, with the Italian Trade Minister Giannini, had everything under control. But the shortages remained a serious problem.[426] The news of French and British activity in Syria arrived, with Mussolini blaming the Germans, and the next day the Hungarian minister for defence, a General Bartha, informed Ciano that a German–Soviet clash was highly likely.

By 21 June Ciano was certain that the Germans were about to start their attempted invasion of Russia. Everyone but Stalin was aware that something was happening, but Stalin's reaction is for another study. Either way, Barbarossa had 'caught the Soviet government both strategically and psychologically ill-prepared', and it was Molotov who broadcast the news on Sunday 22 June to a shocked Russian public.[427] Even though many apart from Stalin had worked out the German intentions, the move came as a shock to the rest of the world. At three in the morning Bismarck came to Ciano's home with the letter from Hitler, and Mussolini ordered that Italy declare war on Russia immediately. The Germans had hinted that the war would only last eight weeks. Ciano had to seek out the Russian ambassador, who was holidaying on the beach with his staff, and 'he received the communication with rather a lackadaisical indifference', with Ciano noting 'that is his nature'.[428] The initial news gave the appearance that the German confidence in an eight-week war was realistic, and Ciano heard that some 1,700 Russian planes had been destroyed.† It was a moment when everyone stood on the edge, and Ambassador Phillips told Ciano how sad he was that Italy was in the conflict,

---

*   Bárdossy was executed in Budapest in 1946.
†   There was some truth in this, though the precise figure can never be certain. The Luftwaffe Field Marshal Kesselring had found the Russian planes lined up like targets in a shooting gallery.

because it was unlikely that America would remain isolated. Mussolini wanted to send divisions to the front, but it was apparent that Hitler was not eager for Italian assistance. Mussolini was unhappy, claiming that the Italians were better soldiers and well equipped, and went to Verona to review a division he proposed to send as a southern flank. Ciano was unconvinced; he believed the soldiers were first class, but he had doubts about their equipment, and others questioned the ability of their officers.[429] Mussolini was excited, however, and some welcomed the attack on Bolshevist Russia, 'the campaign against communism pleased many elements in Italy – the Church for one – and the ideology of fascism could revive'.[430]

On 27 June Ciano went to his father's graveside, no doubt reflecting on his position. Mussolini was angry at Hitler's attitude towards Italian soldiers, blaming it on the Italian military commanders, especially Graziani, and he remained prone to outbursts about the Germans. Ciano reported that even Ribbentrop was in a bad mood because of infighting amongst the Nazi leaders, and when Alfieri had told Goebbels that Ribbentrop was causing him problems Goebbels replied 'together with Ciano, these two statesmen are making all our lives a misery'.[431] Meanwhile, the Eastern Front bulletins were indicating German progress, there was continuing bad news for Mussolini from East Africa, and Ciano was concerned about tensions over the Albanian–Montenegrin borders, though the future now focused on the Soviet–German conflict.

Summer 1941 witnessed the German onslaught into Russia faltering at times but pressing on relentlessly, with the capture of Smolensk and German air raids on Moscow; later, Kiev fell – all with a horrific loss of life. On 9 August the Atlantic Charter was produced,* and in late August the British and Russians started to invade Iran.† It was a short summer for Ciano, undergoing a throat operation for tonsil problems and not returning to his desk until mid-September. During August Edda left to be a nurse on the Russian front, still maintaining her gambling habits, and 'being attractive'. It was observed that she dressed inappropriately when news of her brother Bruno's death arrived; he had been killed in a plane crash at Pisa, which Ciano noted with deep regret.‡

There was gathering unrest in Italy, continuing food shortages. bombing raids, and concerns in political circles about Germany; its soldiers were fighting a war they were not convinced about in distant places, and in fascist circles there was growing concern about the style of leadership. Ciano naturally never mentioned

---

* An agreement between the USA and Britain, setting out their plans for a post-war Europe; it was to lead to the formation of the United Nations and NATO, and some trade agreements.
† A declaration of eight common principles arrived at by Churchill and Roosevelt which would provide the ideological basis for the United Nations.
‡ Mussolini wrote a book called *Parlo con Bruno* (*I talk to Bruno*), as he had once done when his brother Arnaldo had died.

this last aspect in his diaries, but was aware of the grumbling. On the first day of July, according to Bottai, he lunched with Ciano, with Bottai writing that 'I follow the slow, discontinuous approach of the man towards an anti-Mussolini decision'.[432] Two months later in London, the American ambassador and a Myron Taylor (who had been sent by Roosevelt as his personal representative to the Pope) called in to see Eden and left information regarding the general Italian situation; the memo from Taylor read: 'that morale was certainly very low … Count Ciano, in particular, who had once had some popular support, now enjoyed no general regard at all. Mr Taylor added that he knew that, during the period before the war, we had the impression that Count Ciano was genuinely anxious to keep Italy out of the war. It was Mr Taylor's conviction, however, that Count Ciano had been deceiving us throughout this time'.[433] Generally, Ciano had not wanted war with the West, but he was still subservient to Mussolini, and many foreigners, including the Germans and Americans, did not understand Ciano's attitudes – mainly because, in my view, Ciano was uncertain himself, his viewpoint fluctuating with the unfolding events.

At the beginning of July the news from the Eastern Front varied as the Germans pushed deeper into Russia. Mussolini told Ciano that he hoped the 'Germans will shed a lot of feathers', but when the next day Hitler proposed that the 'two chiefs' should meet at his headquarters Mussolini was delighted.[434] At a council of ministers Mussolini gave a long talk on the political and military situation, stating that America would intervene but that this aspect had been taken into account, and that Russia 'will be defeated in short order and Britain would follow'.[435] How far this fell on sceptical ears is difficult to ascertain, but many in the party had long been nursing doubts about Mussolini's leadership and his so-called political insights. Guido Buffarini, a politician and army officer, in conversation with Ciano 'painted a dark picture of our internal situation', and expressed a feeling that anti-fascism was taking root everywhere.[436]

Although the war was being fought on the Eastern Front, in Italy it was the peripheries which were of greatest concern. As Ciano had predicted, with the king's insistence on the restoration of the 1914 Montenegro borders there was now trouble in that country, which although important to its inhabitants was a minor issue on the world scene. The Hungarians had annexed the Mura territory, taking advantage of the situation, but it was the Alto Adige area which raised Mussolini's fears more than anything else. The Italian consul in Innsbruck had transmitted a warning of German agitation in that area, causing Mussolini to forecast a possible 'conflict with Germany', telling Ciano 'to note this in his diary'.[437] Later in the month Mussolini even toyed with the idea of placing guns along the borders of the Veneto. Mussolini told Ciano that he suspected the 'war will be long and exhausting for Germany, and ... it may end in a compromise which will save our independence'.[438] Mussolini must have wondered whether Italy was now another vassal state of Germany, especially in July when Hitler asked if the German OKW (High Command) could take over the Italian air and naval commands.

There was a feeling of discontent in the Germans, which Ciano had detected from the Italian Admiral Fioravanzo, and Anfuso had talked to Frau Mollier, wife of a German press attaché, hearing that the German ruling classes (whoever they were at that point) were concerned about the Russian war, and that despite Göring's boasts Britain was constantly bombing Germany. Naples was also suffering from British bombing, and in early July many of the oil refineries were destroyed. Mussolini thought the bombing would harden up the Italians and 'make them more Nordic' – and he even organised, according to Ciano, dummy air raids on Rome to stiffen the fighting spirit of the people.

During July Mussolini had inspected returning troops, telling Ciano that there 'are no more perfect soldiers in Europe', but the king was annoyed because he considered such inspections his role.[439] According to the historian Susmel, the king was becoming critical of Ciano's attitude towards the Germans, opining that 'Ciano does not succeed in keeping his tongue between his teeth and mouth closed', which would have surprised Ciano, as he and the king often agreed and Ciano enjoyed his cordial welcomes.[440] Italian social gossip was rife, and it may have come to the king's attention that Ciano had repeated the king's views – which, given Ciano's propensity for his remarks in social circles and his golf club, seems possible. It has also been suggested that the king had heard of the rumour of Ciano's purported plot with the Americans, mentioned above.[441]

Mussolini was finding aggravation everywhere he turned. A factory in Florence had promised to produce thirteen anti-aircraft searchlights, but now announced it would only have eight produced by the end of the year. In comparison to the output of Britain, Germany and America, the Italian efforts were bewilderingly pathetic. Mussolini was also upset by the surrender of Italians in Debra Tabor, Ethiopia, in which Ciano noted that two Italians were killed and four wounded out of 4,000 men. These Italian soldiers may have wondered why they were fighting in some distant desert for a war they did not understand or want to be involved in, especially given their paltry equipment and lack of mechanised forces. Mussolini was equally furious with a newspaper article written by Ansaldo which referred to the war in Russia as being under Hitler's direction. The Duce, Ciano recorded 'will cause the people to think that only Hitler is directing the war'. Ciano was bewildered by Mussolini's suggestion that he was equal with Hitler, and he wrote 'are we joking or are we serious?'[442]

On 25 August Mussolini met Hitler without Ciano present, but a brief record of their meeting was kept in Ciano's diplomatic papers. The meeting had two sessions, starting with Hitler praising Mussolini for eradicating the Greek problem before Barbarossa started. Mussolini may have taken the praise at face value, but Hitler was in fact angry at having to rescue the Italians; it had been the Wehrmacht which had accomplished the job since the Italian troops were still ensnared in Albania. Hitler said he wanted Italian troops to take over Crete to release the Germans for the Eastern Front, expressed bitterness towards Spain and suspicions about Sweden, Switzerland, and admitted the Russians were fighting better than his military intelligence had suggested. He put this down to the dedicated Marxists and the stubborn peasants, and he thought the war might last until spring. He praised the Italian troops, but when Mussolini said he could send more Hitler demurred. It seemed a meaningless meeting, apart from a busy Hitler pumping Mussolini's ego to ensure his own southern flank was secure.[443]

GROWTH OF DISCONTENT

During the fraught summer months as the world anticipated concrete results on the Eastern Front, another tragicomedy was being played out in Italy. Mussolini was concerned about his image, his fellow fascists were worried about his leadership, the people were starving and bombed, and there was an ever-developing atmosphere of uncertainty about the future. Ciano had time to contemplate this for the rest of the summer months while he was in hospital and recuperating.

His first diary entry after that was to 'find the chief in good shape, physically and spiritually', so it may be that Hitler's meeting had done some good.[444] Mussolini told Ciano what he had expressed to Hitler, that the Italian people were uneasy because they were not participating in the war. Ciano wrote in his diary that he disagreed, making the more realistic note that the people were more concerned about the 'lack of foods, fats, eggs, *et cetera*'. Ciano had not changed his attitudes; he may have written in his diary that the chief was in good form, but according to Bottai Ciano believed that Mussolini was a spent man.[445]

Mussolini never appreciated personal criticism, and it was no help when Alfieri told him there were rumours circulating about him in Berlin. When Ciano investigated, he found Alfieri annoyingly vague, but Alfieri was correct insofar as nearly everything Italian had become a joke in Germany in the street bars and the barracks, and amongst the leaders. More upsetting was when the diplomat Emilio Cecchi informed Mussolini that Italian labourers in Germany were being treated badly. Mussolini was furious, and asked Ciano to talk to von Mackensen, but although it would always be denied it was undoubtedly true.

On the military side Ciano spoke to Cavallero, who saw the Mediterranean situation 'in dark terms' with the 'continuous loss of merchant ships'.[446] This was because the British warships and aircraft were patrolling the Mediterranean, making supply routes to North Africa hazardous, and it was suggested that Libya might have to be abandoned. Malta was one of the keys to the situation, but the Axis never invaded the island, which would have been a more effective move than their invasion of Crete. Ciano was becoming cynical about Cavallero, hearing that he had found a 'secret entrance to Mussolini's heart', and he 'would cause trouble'.[447] When Ciano spoke to General Gambara he noted that he saw a future full of black clouds and dangers, and thought it a mistake to attack Tobruk; he too was unhappy about Cavallero. The discontent was growing throughout the fascist structure.

At the end of September Phillips, the American ambassador, came to say farewell. He had assured Ciano that the American press was no longer attacking the Italians and that the Atlantic War was being won (correct but somewhat premature), and he spoke in cordial terms. Ciano was aware, the Italian secret services having decoded the American cyphers, that Phillips' reports were not always benevolent.* Following his previous instructions from Mussolini, Ciano wrote an unusually pleasant, if not friendly, letter to Ribbentrop, signing off with 'my renewed friendly greetings'.[448]

September ended with Ciano expressing concern that German units were settling in all the major Italian centres. Mussolini appeared to think he had won a naval victory – which was denied by London – and that the Italian expeditionary corps was doing well in Russia. Ciano may well have appeared cynical, but to use modern parlance there is a distinct impression that Mussolini was living in cloud cuckoo land. It was later estimated that of the 230,000 Italians fighting on the Russian front 41 per cent were already missing.[449]

On 2 October Operation Typhoon, Germany's offensive against Moscow, started, and Bryansk, Vyazma, Mariupol and Odessa were evacuated by the Red Army; on 19 October the siege of Moscow was announced. Kharkov was taken, and to all appearances German victory in the east appeared imminent, but the loss of human life was colossal. The Italians were more concerned about Greece, which had a powerful German administration with a few Italians in places, but the Germans were insisting that Italy was responsible for food supplies to Greece. An infuriated Mussolini told Ciano that the Germans 'had taken shoelaces and blame us for the economic situation'.[450] Mussolini continued to blame the divided command, but later in the month ordered that 7,500 tons of wheat be sent to Greece, Ciano admitting it was not much, and 'we are tightening our belts'.[451]

---

* In the reports Phillips used what was called the Black Code, but it had been stolen by the Italians and deciphered by the Germans.

Ciano heard about the grumbles on the Roman streets – grumbles which were becoming sarcastic. Sicily was in an exceptionally bad state, not helped when Mussolini had suddenly removed the civil service from the island, making it almost ungovernable. Later, when the Allies were arguing over whether to invade Sicily or Sardinia, Eden appeared informed of the Sicilian situation, arguing that it meant there would be little resistance, and indeed many Italian troops would later surrender quickly there, the Allied forces finding cooperation from the locals who were hoping for freedom and food.

Ciano found the news from the Eastern Front encouraging, but the Italian concern over Germen hegemony continued to escalate. At the beginning of October he heard of Hitler's speech to the nation, which Ciano noted had none of the usual 'fulminating threats against the English', but 'we were given no particular attention' and 'we are lumped with the others which will not produce a good impression in Italy'.[452] As these worries intensified, Ciano expressed the concern that after the war Italy, like other countries, would become 'a province of Germany', a policy that they would have to accept or 'be reduced to a colony'.[453] This concept was further agitated by General Marras, who told Mussolini that post-war Germany would be the political and military centre, and other areas would become agricultural; the same concept was later projected about Germany by the American Morgenthau Plan.*

As the economic situation deteriorated the growing fears of German intentions increased, and Mussolini was preoccupied, wishing to send Italian divisions to the Eastern Front as part of his self-conceived image as the warrior chief. His aspiration was further damaged when it was announced that the Romanians had taken Odessa, making him angry because he felt it meant that Italy would be seen as second to Romania. At the beginning of the month Admiral Ferreri had expressed concern over Libya because of the continuous sinking of merchant ships, and as Ciano observed, he was 'openly anti-German'.

The Italian command was divided; the commanders were personally critical of one another, and prone to exaggerating to keep Mussolini happy, especially with Mussolini threatening to court-martial Graziani, but one of the chief aggravations in Ciano's opinion was Cavallero. Ciano had already clashed with this general when the Albanian interim government had offered him a parcel of land in gratitude for his victories and Ciano had agreed, thinking they were giving Cavallero a burial plot.

---

* The Morgenthau Plan was intended to de-industrialise Germany to stop further aggression. It had some influence but was never adopted.

Ugo Cavallero
(Narodowe-Archiwum-Cyfrowe)

When he discovered that the plot in fact amounted to some 2,500 acres, he was furious, protesting to Jacomoni, and he persuaded Mussolini it was all nonsense. The king had an interview with Ciano on 15 October and made it clear that he had no time for Cavallero, especially with his insane boast that he could send 96 divisions to Russia. He said they did not even have that number of rifles, having given so many to the militia, and was concerned that Germany might make a pact with France or even London, leaving Italy out in the cold. Later in Germany, Ribbentrop would press Ciano for information on the king, as his views were probably known. A week later Cavallero informed Ciano that he had resolved the well-known motorisation problem, because his infantry could now march some 18 to 40 kilometres a day, and he had 92 divisions ready. Ciano thought this was a 'shameless lie', ignoring the fact that in modern warfare motorisation was essential. He challenged Cavallero, who retracted his exaggeration the next day, admitting that they could only send six divisions, and that the Germans would have to supply motor transport.

These attitudes and behaviour patterns by leaders during a war defies belief when people were dying on the battlefields and at home from starvation. Ciano himself was still enjoying life, noting in his diary that he spent much time between the countryside and the beach, and was having his portrait painted by Giorgio de Chirico. Ciano is rumoured to have claimed, however, that 'if the war continues like this we will be hanged before the portrait is hung'.[454] Mussolini was also angry about a rumour which he had heard that on his recent trip to Germany someone had overheard the comment 'there goes our Gauleiter* of Italy'.[455] Ciano was charged with demanding that Alfieri elicit the truth of the matter, but it was a common joke amongst many Germans. Alfieri reported on a conference he had held with Ribbentrop, who according to Alfieri was 'singing his usual song of victory is achieved'.[456] In the meantime, Ciano attended a luncheon party at Attolico's to honour their guest, Frau Goebbels, whom Bismarck derided for her sexual habits and those of her husband. Goebbels was indeed a sex addict, but it seems that the personal attack on Frau Goebbels was somewhat malicious

---

*   a Nazi party official in charge of a district in Germany.

and exaggerated. Ciano wrote 'this is how Bismarck talks about the wife of one of the most outstanding men in the Nazi regime'.[457] Quite how Ciano came to this conclusion about Goebbels is mystifying; Goebbels and his wife were both infatuated with Hitler, and Ciano may have held a different view had he had access to Goebbels' diary.

A HITLER MEETING AGAIN

Ciano was in Germany for several days from 25 October; it was supposed to have been Mussolini's visit, but he was suffering from his habitual stomach pains. In his diary Ciano wrote that he had been warned that Hitler was tired which he wrote was untrue because 'I found him in top form, physically and mentally'.[458] Ciano found Ribbentrop friendly, talking in a 'confidential tone' and questioning him about the king, drawing the response from Ciano 'I beg you, my dear Ribbentrop, don't listen to gossips'.[459] Ribbentrop told Ciano that the Reich would bring a thousand-year peace, but after what seemed like some unusual banter between the two of them they agreed a hundred years was more realistic. Ciano thought Germany looked in good heart, but he was probably comparing it to Italy, where hunger was serious – and where, because of his and Edda's lifestyle, they were becoming ever more widely unpopular.[460] He saw labouring POWs and found their conditions distressing, especially the threat of their being shot for any relationships with German women. He met Hitler and wrote his reports for Mussolini, pointing out that the military operations, according to Hitler had achieved more results than expected.[461] This was typical Hitler, who exuded confidence to the bitter end, and it questions the claim that Ciano showed Bottai a report in which Hitler was alleged to have told Ciano that had he known all the facts he would not have attacked Russia.[462] Either Ciano or Bottai were misleading or the evidence was untrue; it defies belief that Hitler would have admitted this to anyone, especially the distrusted Ciano.

Hitler told Ciano that when the Russians were finished he would continue the air offensive against Britain. This led to Ciano adding in his missive to Mussolini the amusing concept of the 'decline of slogans'.[463] First, Ciano explained, the slogan was the invasion of Britain, then it became the penetrating air attacks, then the submarine warfare. The current slogan, as Ciano perceived the situation, was 'European solidarity,' a cultural and moral policy arising from the idea that with Russia defeated Europe could reorganise itself under German hegemony. Significantly, Ciano finished this section by noting the rising areas of resistance in Prague, France and Serbia.

Hitler continued his monologue, claiming that the loss of men and material by the Russians meant that the Soviets could not continue. There was an admission that it was difficult to estimate the potential size of Russian forces (which was later to astound the Germans), and although the removal of industry to the Urals and Siberia was noted, it took time to realise that this was a clever manoeuvre to protect their industrial output. Hitler had decided that Leningrad would be starved into submission (which in fact it would not be), and this conversation was so impressive as to cause Ciano to write 'that if one of the sides in this winter campaign must suffer the fate of the Napoleonic armies, it is certainly not Germany which must fear the threat'.[464] It was also believed that both America and Britain considered that Russia was finished. It is true that some leading military men such the British General Alan Brooke wondered about this possibility, but he like many others hoped for a better result. Ciano also decided that the democracies, by sending supplies to frozen Archangel, were depriving themselves of necessary weapons, indicating his ignorance of the American and even the British industrial output.

Ciano, when he had the opportunity, raised the three issues which Mussolini had suggested. The first was the brutal German attitude towards Italian labour, which Hitler skilfully evaded, explaining that a few incidents 'should not be dramatized'.[465] The second was the question of food in Italy, and again Hitler spoke of the league of grumblers, which they also had in Germany. The third issue was Mussolini's hope (having expressed his wish for some spoils of war) that Italian soldiers could be involved in the campaign, and Hitler suggested the Caucasus was the best area because the Italians would be more adaptable to that climate. Ciano added two incisive observations. The first was Hitler's claim that the war was over, so why was he planning to destroy the railway links with Archangel and Murmansk? The second was that they were still waiting for the 'knockout blow'.[466]

Back in Rome Ciano noted on the last day of the month 'nothing new,' but then mentioned the sinking of the American ship, the *Reuben James*.* Although it was the loss of a single American naval vessel, it had angered the American public as that country drew closer to intervention, and as Russia continued to fight back the overall effects on Mussolini's Italy would be life-changing in the following years.

AGGRAVATIONS

November started with a letter from Hitler to Mussolini full of details about the military situation, with Mussolini being disappointed there was no mention of the Italian divisions. Ciano deduced that Hitler was concerned that the English might just consider invading Italy, and his letter proved that 'fundamentally the Germans don't trust us'.[467] Ciano was correct, because Hitler knew that the

---

* The SS *Reuben James*, an old four-funnel destroyer escorting a convoy, was torpedoed near Iceland by U-552, commanded by Kapitänleutnant Erich Topp.

southern European flank was weak, and Churchill was well known for his concept of the 'soft underbelly' of Europe. It was probably as a result of this reasoning that the Germans announced five days later that Field Marshal Kesselring would be arriving in south Italy to take over the joint command; it was not a request, but a statement of fact. The Italians were obliged to accept, and General Cavallero dropped hints that he should be elevated to the position of Field Marshal to balance this move. This was later agreed, not least to stop the successful Rommel outranking him. Kesselring was one of the outstanding Wehrmacht commanders, but in November 1941 his arrival was not welcomed by Mussolini because it underlined the overall control of the Germans.

Mussolini was concerned that in Croatia Pavelić had claimed that the Croatians were descended from the Goths; this, according to Mussolini, was an effort to garner German sensitivity to their plight. Greece remained a concern, with warnings that riots were likely to ensue, especially when children died from starvation. There was dissension in Kosovo and Ciano spoke to von Mackensen about the issue, knowing that the ambassador could do little in this matter. The leaders in Italy relied on rumour and were powerless to influence major events.

Where they could be active, they failed. On 9 November Ciano heard of the total loss of a convoy to North Africa, with two cruisers and several destroyers. This was a naval disaster which did little to help German–Italian relationships. Italian aerial photographs spotted a British battleship in dry dock, so the Italian navy asserted that it had been sunk. This failed to deceive Ciano, who made the wry comment that it was like 'declaring that a man is slightly dead because he has gone to live near a cemetery'.[468] There was talk in the Italian navy that they should pretend that they had had some success in the Atlantic, that they had sunk two steamships, Ciano noting that the only sinking he had heard about was that of an Italian submarine.* Ciano was astonished that Cavallero did not know the name of the admiral responsible, who transpired to be an Admiral Brivonesi, and this disclosure was followed by Ciano's biting statement that the 'whole navy knows Admiral Riccardi owes his position to Signora Petacci [Mussolini's mistress] which is not a rumour to improve the Navy's prestige'.[469] Excuses, silly propaganda efforts, rumour, and hints of Mussolini's mistress's involvement all failed to cover up the failure of the navy and the dominance of the British at sea. As this infighting was in progress Ciano heard that Riccardi had attacked Claretta Petacci's brother as a crook, claiming 'Dr Petacci is doing the Duce more harm than fifteen battles'.[470] The scandal involving Mussolini's mistress and her family would resound around Italy until the death of Mussolini.

The Germans were pushing forward on the Eastern Front: Kursk and Kerch

---

*   Probably the submarine *Malaspina*.

fell, and the German 4th Panzer Group were 12 miles from Moscow, but Ciano was more concerned that Italy could not pay its own diplomatic agents because it had no foreign exchange left.[471] Anfuso had been appointed as minister to Budapest, making Ciano sad because Anfuso had been a close friend, a confidant and head of his office.

Ciano had mourned the loss of his sister the previous month, and in November he went to Genoa to see a monument opened for his father. Edda was somewhere distant and Ciano barely mentioned his children, but his family of origin remained dominant to him throughout his life. He was having another portrait done by the artist Bartoli whom he thought more highly of than the previous artist, but according to some sources it was never finished.[472]

When he returned to Rome, Mussolini informed him that he had 'told' Rommel to attack Tobruk, but there were the usual scandals, with Mussolini demanding an inquiry into Graziani, and the king wanting the Duke of Spoleto out of Rome because of his outrageous behaviour with women in nightclubs. More to the point, the news was filtering through of a British attack in Libya; this was known by the British as the Crusader Offensive in the western desert.* Mussolini and Cavallero appeared relaxed over Libya, but Ciano noted that the German General von Rintelen was more concerned, not least because another essential convoy had been attacked and forced to return to the relative safety of port.

BERLIN AGAIN

Ciano was occupied with another visit to Berlin attending an Anti-Comintern conference, undoubtedly staged by the Germans to underline the importance of crushing the Soviet Union, thereby demonstrating their new hegemony under the guise of the 'solidarity of Europe'. Ciano wrote a report on the meeting, adding some more indiscreet comments in his diary relating to Serrano Suñer being aggressive but pro-Axis, and the Hungarian Bárdossy throwing the occasional modest dart at the Germans, and noting that the Danish minister wore an old-fashioned frock-coat; in his diplomatic papers Ciano referred to this as being of 'measured correctness'.[473] He even found Ribbentrop cordial, and for the first time he heard praise about the Italian military, probably based, he thought, on the Battle of Marmarica. Quite why Ciano should suggest this battle is ambiguous, because it was a retreat, admitting that although any success belonged to Rommel, Italian troops were showing 'valour' (which was probably because they were fighting under professional German command).

---

*   Operation Crusader was intended to bypass the Axis defences on the Egypt–Libya border and defeat their armoured divisions, relieving the siege of Tobruk. On 27 November, a New Zealand force achieved this.

Ribbentrop spoke about the Vichy government wanting to be part of the new Europe, adding the sarcastic comment that they wanted to change the cards on the table and had 'forgotten they were a conquered country'.[474] Hitler gave another monologue on the military situation, concluding with the anticipated breakthrough in the Caucasus, which he claimed would open the way to the Middle East and the British Empire. He had told Ciano that after the Caucasus victory he anticipated the Italian Alpine divisions to be on hand.

Göring grumbled about the Italian embassy but became more affable, telling Ciano he would rather feed the Finns than the Greeks because the Finns were fighting, and there was no need for guns to lead the Russian prisoners – just a soup kitchen with its smell at the front of the column – cynically deriding them as 'famished animals'. He suggested that the Americans should send food to Greece because Roosevelt 'had taken on the role of the father of humanity'.[475]

THE MONTH OF PEARL HARBOR

Ciano had not been in Berlin for 14 months and when he arrived he found the place sluggish, with few party uniforms, unresponsive crowds and a sense of war weariness. Until now the conflict had been a European war spreading its tentacles around the North African coastline, but with the Japanese attack on Pearl Harbor on 7 December 1941 the war expanded into a colossal global conflict with far-reaching consequences in both time and space.

In Italy, Ciano had been conscious of the problem of conveying supplies to North Africa, and he was becoming frustrated by Cavallero, who had told him that it 'is difficult but logical', causing Ciano to state 'God only knows what he means'. The Papal Nuncio had been criticised for the Vatican paper *Osservatore Romano* portraying Italian POWs enjoying concerts and playing football. Ciano had to tackle this following Mussolini's instructions, as he believed it would encourage others to surrender. Mussolini was also angry about losses in East Africa where at Gondor in later November there had been 67 lives lost, and some 10,000 taken prisoner. Ciano observed that 'one doesn't have to think very long to see what these numbers mean'.[476] As war raged and people died, Mussolini again became obsessed about the Christmas festival, referring to it as 'a birth of a Jew' who had given the world 'debilitating and devitalising theories' and was specially contrived to trick Italy 'through the disintegrating power of the Popes'.[477] Mussolini even ordered the newspapers not to mention Christmas, though Ciano noted that the churches were packed. None of this was helped when on Christmas Day the Pope's message made five points, four of them aimed at dictators.

The Japanese raised the Tripartite Agreement with a formal meeting in Japanese style, noting that the 'conflict between Japan and the United States and simultaneously with Great Britain must now be considered possible'.[478] The Japanese ambassador referred to the relevant Tripartite clause and demanded that Italy should immediately declare war on the USA. Mussolini, although happy, replied that he would wait to hear the response from Berlin which, after some hesitation caused by Hitler's preoccupation with Russia, was agreed. Curiously, Ciano's biographer Moseley pointed out that Ciano made no effort to warn Washington.[479] The place and date of the Pearl Harbor attack was not disclosed, but it would have been unusual for Ciano to reveal this information at this stage. Ciano noted in his diary that any idea of peace was receding, and it would be a long war, adding 'who will have the most stamina? This is the way the question should be put'.[480] He would have been more accurate if by 'stamina' he had meant sheer resources, in which both Russia and America had been grossly underestimated.

When the Japanese attacked Pearl Harbor, the 'day of infamy', Ribbentrop was on the phone to Ciano 'jumping with joy', and Mussolini was happy because, Ciano claimed, he had waited for a long time to clarify the position between America and Italy. Churchill – half-American himself –was also overjoyed because he recognised the incipient American power, and the British–American Arcadia Conference was arranged for 22 December, the British intent on focusing American eyes on Germany as the prime enemy.

Ciano set off to Turin for an early December meeting with the French Admiral Darlan. He found Darlan 'small, energetic, calls a spade a spade, boastful and hates the British'.[481] It was Darlan who had agitated for attacks on Gibraltar and the African colonies, and who was later responsible for the disastrous loss of Syria to the British. Darlan often claimed that his hatred of the British stemmed from the time his great-grandfather had fought at the Battle of Trafalgar. Darlan was much more acceptable to the Germans, especially with his bellicose nature towards the British. It has been suggested that Hitler wanted Laval in Paris as a 'threat' to Vichy.[482] Laval was by nature a pacifist, whereas Darlan, the naval man, tried 'to reach the peak of Franco-German collaboration' at a military level.[483] It was said by the Germans 'that when we ask Laval for a chicken, we get an egg; when we ask Darlan for an egg, we get a chicken.'[484] Darlan had told Ciano that since he had become the head of government he had discovered 'the corruption of parliamentary and ministerial circles' which appeared to be his way of appealing to fascism.[485] Darlan raised the question of the Tunisian ports, expressing concern that if they were opened to the Axis there might be a full-scale attack by the British, but Ciano told him that he was not authorised to discuss that issue. Darlan explained he wanted to break 'the ice between the two countries', apparently primarily wanting France to be important in what he perceived to be the new

Europe. After the meeting Ciano made the shrewd comment that 'naturally not all the Frenchmen yet understand the soundness of his [Darlan's] policy'.[486]

On his return Ciano discovered that Mussolini was not in the least interested in hearing about his talks with Darlan but more interested in the 'American war'. The American *chargé d'affaires*, a George Wadsworth, turned up at Ciano's desk when Italy and Germany had declared war on America on 11 December, Ciano treating him somewhat coldly. Wadsworth later reported that Ciano 'received me most brusquely, so unlike his usual, promiscuously friendly manner'.[487] Ciano kept this showmanship up until he was told there was a message from Phillips saying farewell, prompting Ciano to write that 'Phillips is an honest man, and he loves Italy. I know for him it is a day of mourning'.[488] Later Wadsworth would comment that 'Ciano's strongest claim is that Mussolini wishes him as his successor, but the public would never have confidence in him'.[489] This latter point may have been true, but how far Ciano was aware of his increasing unpopularity is ambiguous, and a declaration of war on America was not welcomed by most Italians.

Minor countries hurried to take sides, Cuba and Ecuador declaring war on the Axis, with Ciano being rather conceited with the Cuban minister, claiming 'he was very emotional, and was disappointed that I did not share his emotion'.[490] This arrogance by Ciano was one of his less palatable traits, as the American Wadsworth had discovered. On 15–16 December Ciano was in Venice, meeting Pavelić. Ciano found him confident in his position, and the 'Croatian boat', as Ciano described it, was still floating – but it would depend on Italy. Pavelić informed Ciano that the Croatians were dealing with many problems, not least the Jews, whose numbers had dropped from 35,000 to 12,000, and the Croatians were suspicious, as always, of Hungary.[491]

On his return Mussolini was somewhat sceptical about Croatia, but happy that the Germans were, because of their growing struggle on the Russian front, intending to leave that country to the Italians; Moscow remained undefeated. By the end of the month the Germans had changed their mind, which pleased Ciano because he detected possible trouble in Bosnia, Serbia and Montenegro.[492] As he left his meeting with Pavelić, Ciano noticed that Venice looked 'sad, empty and tired. Never have I seen it so squalid. Empty hotels and deserted streets', and this may have caused him to reflect on the way he had noticed the war had affected Berlin.[493]

Back in Rome, Ciano heard more bad news emanating from Libya, Rommel warning that he would fall back to Tunisia because, Ciano added, he did not want to become a British prisoner. There was trouble in Albania; and Mussolini was pleased that the Germans were not having it all their own way in Russia. There was a sense of loss of balance, and it was not helped when Cavallero talked about

Cyrenaica, claiming that 'all was logical'. This was followed by the astounding news that Hitler had sacked his leading Field Marshal Brauchitsch and taken over the military command himself.*

When Mussolini addressed the Council of Ministers on 27 December he predicted a long war, but Ciano more astutely believed that Mussolini had underestimated the potential impact of America. The news from the Russian front was far from good; only supplies could save Libya; and on New Year's Eve Ciano had a formal conversation with Field Marshal Kesselring, who would soon play a prominent role in Italy's war history. However, Ciano was always suspicious of Kesselring and German motives, and later, as relationships between Rommel and the Italians deteriorated, wrote that 'Cavallero found himself between Rommel and Kesselring like Christ between the two thieves'.[494] The Italians were suspicious of Kesselring, and Ciano wrote that in Kesselring 'Mussolini has swallowed a toad' (suggesting he had swallowed poison or something that would consume him in turn).[495] The year 1941 was concluding with Italy now under German dominance; the Russian front raising doubts; and the Axis now facing America – a formidable industrial power – without recognising the new problem it was facing.

SUMMATION

In the wider context 1941 is frequently regarded as the year of achievement for the Axis powers, but mainly for the Germans who, supporting their weaker military ally, Italy, pressed on with their combined forces eastwards, towards the Libyan–Egyptian border. It was the German military that swept through Yugoslavia and Greece, ousted the British from Crete, placed Pavelić in power in Zagreb, and suddenly attacked Russia. After the Italian failure in Greece, Goebbels referred to the Italians as the worst possible allies; many others thought the same, and although Mussolini pretended that he and Hitler were partners, it was clear that the German dictator was the overall master. Finally the significance of Pearl Harbor, which had brought America into the war, was largely unrecognised by the Axis.

---

* Brauchitsch had suffered a heart attack and was blamed for the failure of Operation Typhoon against Moscow. He entered a period of enforced retirement, and post-war was arrested but died from pneumonia in 1948 before his trial.

8

1942 – DISSENT

Italian troops in Russia
(Italian Archives, World War II, 1942)

BAD NEWS AND INTERNAL DISSENT

New Year's Day started with the customary infighting as Cavallero asked Ciano to explain to the Germans that it had been Mussolini's idea to attack Tunisia, with Ciano recalling that it had been Cavallero who had 'put this idea into Mussolini's head'. Ciano began 1942 with an implied criticism of Mussolini as being prone to persuasion by misleading influences. Ciano gathered that Hitler had written a letter to Mussolini about the Russian front 'offering excuses and not explanations'.[496] Mussolini was in a dark mood for the New Year, and was angry with the Germans for taking the Romanian oil which he had believed had been destined for Italy, and his feelings had not been helped by a captured German General Schmidt explaining that he had been taken prisoner because of the weakness of Italian soldiers.

In January Ciano gave a speech at Bologna and was pleased to hear that Mussolini had appreciated his efforts – but heard, too, that Mussolini had been unimpressed by his half-hearted Roman salute. Aldo Vidussoni, the party secretary, saw Ciano the same day and claimed he wanted to kill all the Slovenes, because on the north-west border there was some guerrilla opposition to the fascist rule. This may have rung warning bells for Ciano; the police warned him about visiting Zagreb because of potential violence. It was clear to Ciano that Vidussoni was potentially dangerous, and his appointment, as noted earlier, had not been received well by the fascist elite: 'De Felice argued that the appointment was a last attempt by Mussolini to organise the Party in his way, but the selection of Vidussoni is better seen as a gesture of desperation and despair.'[497]

This was the start of the dark period for Mussolini, who was nearly 60 years of age and now really struggling to cope with events. Bottai had written in his diary that Mussolini 'is not just tired, disheartened, sad, but he is no longer winning out over his age'.[498] When Ciano arrived in Zagreb there were anti-Italian protests, but Ciano was more concerned that the Duke of Spoleto was less concerned about Croatia and just needed money. Ciano proposed suggesting to Mussolini that the so-called royal personage should be paid 100,000 lire a month.[499] Whether that suggestion was made to keep the duke quiet, under wraps and in their pay, is not clear, but in fact he was simply a playboy needing cash.

On 14 January Ciano travelled to Hungary to re-stimulate Italian influence in the Danube region; this would be difficult, as would be his second purpose, seeking food supplies. In Hungary he met the Regent Horthy whom the Germans had asked to introduce full mobilisation, but he was reluctant to concur because, not having the benefit of working POWs, there was a shortage of labourers. Horthy was still worried about Romanian intentions and maintaining troops on the borders in case of an emergency.[500] Ciano then met Bárdossy, who was worried about trouble in the Balkans, feared German influence, was desperate to maintain Hungarian independence, and irritated that the Germans seemed to be giving preferential treatment to the Romanians. In his diary Ciano noted that the Hungarians were exasperated, and 'you cannot remain long with any Magyar before he speaks ill of Germany'.[501]

On his return to Rome, Ciano discovered that while the Italians' supplies were not reaching Libya the British forces were well stocked. Cavallero remained optimistic, explaining to Ciano that the Russian counter-thrust was nearly over, that the British could be resisted in Libya, and that the Italian army was being organised 'at a favourable pace', prompting Ciano to write 'we shall see to what extent Cavallero is right'.[502] With the benefit of hindsight Ciano was correct to be sceptical about Cavallero, and Ciano's diaries indicate growing inferences that he was unhappy with developments, noting that Grandi had told him 'I don't know how I was able to disguise myself as a fascist for twenty years'.[503]

As the South American countries one by one decided it was safer to be with the Allies, Ciano for the first time mentioned the problem faced by Italian immigrants: to escape the poverty of Italy over the years many Italians had gone abroad for a better life, some moving to Britain, but many more to North and South America, and even though they might have become naturalised residents of their host nations, many of their neighbours treated them as the enemy because of their origin, betrayed by their Italian names. Many Italians, Germans and Japanese were interned for a time in Britain and America; worried by the so-called Fifth Column threat, both Britain and the USA were guilty of overreaction. Such is the nature of war that an Italian or German name would inspire idiotic vitriolic attacks, and in Italy many had families in America and Britain.

News from the Russian front was, according to Alfieri, not good, and this disturbed Mussolini, who felt relaxed over Libya and believed that sea communications were improving, even though – Ciano cynically noted – the 'jewel of the Italian merchant fleet, the *Victoria*', had just been sunk. Hunger was increasing to critical levels in Greece, and even if Italy had supplies, the Italians had no fleet to transport the food. The attitudes towards Germany were mixed; at times Mussolini was pleased that they might have their wings clipped, but news of an Allied victory would be more crippling. This was not helped when an intercepted message from German military headquarters referred to the Italians as 'macaroni'. This was aggravated at the end of the month when Göring arrived in Rome, ostensibly on military matters, but Ciano saw little of him. He heard that in Göring's opinion Russia would soon be defeated and that the British would lay down their arms in 1943; Ciano sardonically added 'I took it all with a grain of salt'.

The war against Russia appeared problematic; a sense of delicate balance persisted in Libya; the Germans remained confident; but Italy gave the impression of standing on the sidelines with Mussolini anxious to be called upon but beset by accumulating political dissent and personal domestic issues within his household. Ciano had met Arturo Osio, the founder of the Lavoro Bank who had been 'kicked out' over a quarrel with Claretta Petacci's brother, Marcello.[504] There was a scandal with a Venetian countess over property, stemming from the same Marcello Petacci, most of this fiasco resulting from what had been termed 'Mussolini's alternative family'.[505] Claretta's youngest sister, too, was causing gossip, and it was rumoured that although married to Rachele and having a long-term mistress in Claretta, Mussolini was behaving, like many middle-aged males, as a sentimental sugar daddy, with a young typist, Elena Curti, in tow. To any observer with knowledge of the political Italian landscape set against the rapidly developing global war, Italy must have appeared as a subplot – but for the Italian people themselves the events and their consequences were disastrous.

Mussolini was mesmerised by the Japanese success when they took Singapore, bombed the Australian city of Darwin and at the end of the month invaded Java. Ciano suffered a luncheon party with Göring at Cavallero's invitation, when he noted that Göring was 'as usual his bloated and overbearing self'. He was equally cynical about Cavallero, writing he 'would even go so far as to bow to the public lavatories if he thought this would be helpful to him'.[506] Ciano was irritated with the Italian military, who always 'crept' to the Germans, writing that he 'had to swallow more bile than food'. He had to endure Göring's company two days later at the Excelsior Hotel, bidding him farewell before his train journey. Ciano, like others, noted Göring's obsession with jewellery and the rings on his fingers. Göring was widely known for this and for his love of art, which he pilfered from across occupied Europe. Ciano noted that Göring had two loves, 'beautiful objects and making war', both of which were expensive hobbies.[507] He accepted that Göring was liked by many people 'because he has a dash of humanity', and when Göring wished he could be quite amenable, as his post-war captors discovered. By 'humanity' Ciano must have meant 'the human touch', because Göring had full knowledge of the Holocaust.

Ciano was disturbed that the Prince of Piedmont might command an army on the Russian front, and it is easy to understand Ciano's concern that a young Italian prince, albeit heir to the throne, could handle such a position.* A few days later Mussolini, addressing the council, attacked his own generals but praised Rommel. Italy's military leadership appeared weak but was not helped by Mussolini's outbreaks; there were continuous rounds of infighting, and even within the party structure the new appointment of Party Secretary Vidussoni was causing waves. Later in the month Ciano noted that Vidussoni had attended a dinner at the German Embassy dressed in a 'blue-striped shirt and red tie and handkerchief … and he is not very much at ease'.[508] Later Ciano heard that when Raffaele Guariglia (the Italian ambassador to France) had tried to introduce himself Vidussoni turned his back on him, thinking him to be the Papal Nuncio. The fact that this young man took so much space in Ciano's diary indicated the instability of Mussolini's appointments and the importance of the trivia preoccupying Roman society in a time of international crisis.

The cynics grew, with Grandi criticising the social policy of the regime and a growing sense of anger amongst those who dared express themselves, but Ciano, himself critical, remained cautious. When the news of Attolico's death was

---

*   In May 1946 he became King Umberto II for 34 days, then the monarchy was abolished.

announced, he who had been the ambassador to Germany and then the Holy See, Bottai hinted that he would like his post at the Vatican, causing Mussolini to jest that Bottai would end up as 'a sacristan'.[509]

Admiral de Courten told Ciano he was experiencing problems with British planes and that there was a serious lack of oil for the Italian fleet, leaving their naval vessels trapped in ports. A few days later Ciano heard that the *Lucania* had been torpedoed when moving towards East Africa for evacuation purposes. Ciano knew of an arrangement with the British to allow this action, but in war any suspicious vessel was likely to be sunk by submarines unaware of minor diplomatic arrangements; later the British said they would release a captured Italian vessel as compensation.*

FRUSTRATIONS

Mussolini was angry because he wanted to send two divisions to the Eastern Front, but embarrassed because he would need to ask the Germans for anti-tank guns, cars and anti-aircraft batteries. Cavallero, Ciano noted, was 'playing his usual games', and claimed they were producing enough, but when challenged had to step back from his wild assertions, which left Mussolini feeling angrier and Ciano even more sceptical about Cavallero. The situation in Italy was desperate, with growing criticisms. Food supplies were dangerously low, and Ciano was instructed to write an embarrassing begging letter to the Hungarians. In it he explained that payment for wheat could be covered by 'the huge amounts of lire in Hungary' (even though the lire was by now an almost useless currency), and knowing this, Ciano suggested they could 'pay in gold'.[510] Mussolini told Ciano that the people would be 'patient and understanding', indicating yet again how removed he was from everyday reality.[511]

As more news of the Japanese occupation of Singapore arrived, the fascinated Mussolini spoke about them with admiration, and was pleased when he gathered that there were tensions between the Germans and Japanese. He told Ciano that the Germans would not dare to wake the Japanese Emperor in the early morning, as they did him. Alfieri had informed Ciano that Ribbentrop was excited by the news of Singapore and believed that the British would seek an armistice – again failing to understand the enemy.[512]

At the local level, the new Albanian Prime Minister Kruja came to Rome, preceded by rumours that he was a dangerous nationalist, but Ciano thought more highly of the man on meeting him. In Hungary the news came through that Horthy had appointed his son vice-regent, which was not well received in Berlin,

---

*   The submarine was HMS *Una*, commanded by a Lieutenant Martin who at the time of the incident had pneumonia.

and Ciano wondered whether Horthy Junior was up to the job. This information was followed by yet more disturbing news, that within the Reich Protectorate in Prague Italian labourers were being badly treated there as well. Mussolini instructed Alfieri to protest to Ribbentrop, but with 'moderation'.[513] This note of caution by Mussolini indicated that he had recognised his lesser position within the Axis. The Papal Nuncio was less cautious, demanding Ciano investigate whether Padua University was offering Ribbentrop and Goebbels honorary degrees – but it was one of those many rumours which circulated in Rome with no substance; life in Rome was dominated by gossip.[514]

The serious problem for the Italians was the shortage of iron and steel, with coal stocks so low that Ciano believed the railroads would consume the available supply by April. Later, Clodius assured the Italians that the shortage was temporary because of the demands on the Russian front. Mussolini reacted by pontificating on Italian society, telling Ciano that war helped appraise 'the true internal composition of the people'. Mussolini ordered the mobilisation of men aged between 18 and 55, Ciano suggesting it would be 'women next'.[515] What with the shortage of food, the increase of conscription to men in their middle age, the lack of resources, and a war over which most people agonised, it was unsurprising that the regime leaders were becoming a focus of criticism.

During March the Japanese invaded New Guinea, and the British were bombing Germany – which was fighting a war of annihilation against Russia. However, Ciano's life was not as hectic, and for nine days during March he made the diary entry 'nothing new', and apart from a possible student plot his month was the usual round of infighting, rumour and gossip, and a sense of helplessness as the Italian population grew closer to famine.

The internal dissent in Italy rumbled on, Ciano hearing that when Gambara had been relieved of his command in Libya the police had searched his offices. When Ciano investigated he discovered that Cavallero had been the instigator – but he, when challenged, explained that some of Gambara's aides had been under suspicion. Mussolini had read the report on Graziani and was wondering whether to have him court-martialled or retired. The disarray amongst the military commanders and their conflict with the regime was too contentious for a country at war. Mussolini was frustrated, and told Ciano that war was not for the Italian people, who 'do not have the maturity or the consistency for such a tremendous and decisive test. This is for the Germans and the Japanese, not for us'.[516] It never seemed to cross Mussolini's mind that the Italian populace had already realised the war was a disaster, and one which many of them had never wanted.

The Japanese conflict had Mussolini's attention more than anything else, with Ciano concluding that 'I still prefer the white to the yellow race' (reflecting his racial bigotry), and cynically adding that 'Japan is far away, and Germany is close, very close'.[517] The neutral Swedes reminded Ciano of the better side of humanity when they approached him with the possibility that Britain might open the blockade to allow relief food ships through to Greece, though Ciano was unsure whether the Germans or indeed Mussolini would agree.

The Germans were not as self-assured about the Russian war, and Pavolini, back from Germany having spoken to Goebbels, painted a dark picture, saying that the Germans were 'no longer speaking of destroying Bolshevism but just reaching the Caucasus'. A week later, reports were received that the Germans were considering defeat but intended to stay strong in Europe. These reports were not necessarily accurate, but tended instead to reflect some popular opinion, a few disgruntled military men and an anxious population watching the casualty figures rising daily. Ciano astutely observed that it had become a 'war of attrition'.

Ciano, hearing a Churchill speech, decided that he was an orator and could 'move the people' where Mussolini was failing. The dissent was still growing and Mussolini remained overly critical of his own compatriots. He had admitted that the 'people are not in favour of the war' and the incentives were lacking, and he proposed 'to flaunt' the propaganda line of 'the banner of defeat as a threat'.[518] There was resentment, and Ciano was confronted by a nervous young man, Armando Stefani, who reported a plot led by a journalist called Felice Chilanti; he wanted to oust the regime, kill Ciano and impose a socialist policy. This disclosure made it abundantly clear to Ciano that the plot reflected the start of an anti-fascist movement, illumined by the knowledge that it was based on a personal threat against him. The plot involved some 70 young people, and although Ciano had them all arrested he later decided that they were stupid young men, and most were released with a 'kick in the backside'.[519] Two of them, who were soldiers, were punished, and Chilanti was banished to the island of Ustica, a few miles north of Sicily.[520]

Had this happened in Nazi Germany the consequences for the young people would of course have been very different. It was not surprising that within a week of this incident Mussolini addressed the party directorate and in his speech was critical of young people but favourable to the older fascists. It raised the question in Ciano's mind as to whether there was a widening crisis within the Fascist Party, which by this stage should have been evident.

In the middle of March the Minister of Agriculture Carlo Pareschi had informed Ciano that the food situation was desperate. There had been a 25 per cent cut in the bread rations, fertilisers were reduced by a third, manual labour was lacking, and essential agricultural tools were wearing out.[521] By the end of the month there were food riots led by angry women in Venice and Matera.

Most European countries had rationing, but the system was not working in Italy. Infighting, trivia, rumours, political dissent and food shortages typified Italy at this time.

During April Ciano was far from busy, having seven days with nothing to add to his diary; he started his month by recording jokes he had heard about Germany, and noted that Mussolini was furious with the behaviour of a few Italian visitors in Hungary. Pareschi was more optimistic about food supplies, but the crisis was creating reactions, especially in Naples and Genoa. The Hungarians had responded to Ciano's plea for food, offering some 13,000 tons of wheat, which Mussolini derided as a pittance. But in Italy's condition any offer of food should have been accepted, and the Hungarian offer was probably made because it was a 'personal achievement of Ciano' that Hungary, suspicious of Germany, felt close to Italy.[522] The lack of food was causing trouble on the streets, and General Hazon of the Carabinieri* informed Ciano that 'the country had lost faith in the Party'.[523]

It is often necessary when reading Ciano's personal diaries to read between innocent-looking comments to evaluate Ciano's views. He attended a mass and found a large 'devout crowd', and noted that Italy was 'a fundamentally devout Catholic country', thereby exposing his views, which underlined his formal Christian belief instilled by his father – in contrast to Mussolini's vitriolic attacks on Christianity and the Vatican.

By the second week of April Mussolini was furious at the sight of so many men still on the Roman streets when 'they should be in uniform'. Ciano was critical of Mussolini, but it was evident that the Italian conscription system was not working any better than rationing. Bismarck was back in Rome, confidentially claiming that Germany would have to make peace, having spoken on this matter to Canaris, the head of the Abwehr. It is now widely known that Canaris was against the Nazi regime, as was his deputy Hans Oster, and there is a hint that Ciano was possibly aware of this, as he wrote 'personally, I believe that the strength of German resistance is far greater'.[524] Men like Canaris would never have revealed this to a man like the talkative Ciano, but Bismarck loved to gossip about the Nazi leaders and obviously trusted Ciano.† But there was an ever-growing scepticism about Germans throughout Italy; even Mussolini made it apparent by attending a meeting of the Society of the Friends of Japan.

Ciano was visited by Donna Edvige, Mussolini's elder sister, who wanted to express her views on the Mussolini family life and obtain Ciano's opinions, but he realised this was a 'delicate matter'. The critical issue was the ongoing problem of

---

*   the national police (military, as against the Polizei, civilian)
†   One of Bismarck's more amusing jokes was about the German consul general in Milan, who when seeking a home was sent an address which, when he turned up, transpired to be the city prison.

the Petacci 'clan' and the way they were using their influence over Mussolini to make money, thereby creating one scandal after another. Ciano was polite but lost as to how to react, writing 'who has the courage to speak to him [Mussolini] about a personal matter?'[525] Later the same month the Prefect of Venice raised the issue of a Petacci scandal in his city, suggesting that Guido Buffarini was supressing reports in their favour.[526] On 24 April Riccardi had complained again about Petacci's brother 'and his gang', but Ciano decided it was a 'buzz saw I don't want to put my finger in'. As noted above, Mussolini's mistress problems would not go away in his lifetime. Ciano sometimes found the courage to raise issues with Mussolini, was increasingly critical about him in his diaries, and often regarded himself as Mussolini's natural successor, but he was always cautious on family matters and avoided these problems for personal security.

Ciano heard that the Americans had bombed Tokyo, believing this was their first offensive action in the war, as their 'preparation was far too behind'.* Ciano had the sense to realise that the Americans would soon make their weight felt, especially in air power.[527] At the local level Kesselring returned from Berlin with the policy of occupying Malta. This worried Ciano, because although the bombing had been heavy the coastal defences were still intact. Malta was never invaded (in April 1942 the Malta was awarded the George Cross for bravery) and Kesselring was never ordered to invade; the Axis failure to occupy Malta would prove to be an important factor in the Mediterranean campaign. Rommel would become one of Kesselring's scapegoats, Kesselring complaining in his post-war interrogation that Rommel kept changing his mind about Malta.[528] It was a matter of timing: in the Rommel Papers it is clear that Rommel believed 'Malta should have been taken instead of Crete'.[529] The truth is that to Hitler it was just an island. He misread its importance.

MEETING HITLER AGAIN

Von Mackensen informed Ciano that Hitler desired a meeting with Mussolini; he wanted to reschedule the occasion, only to be informed there could be no delay. Ciano and Mussolini set off with Cavallero for Salzburg on 28 April, four days after the German demand. They were met by Hitler and Ribbentrop, who were convivial, causing the sceptical Ciano to wonder what was happening. They were comfortably housed in Klessheim Castle, nearby, and Hitler spoke with Mussolini while Ciano spoke with Ribbentrop, though in both meetings the hosts produced identical monologues. Referring to the Napoleonic war with Russia,

---

*   This was the famous James Doolittle raid, indicating that the Japanese homeland was vulnerable, and providing a boost to American morale. It caused negligible damage, but in Japan it raised the question of the ability of its military leaders to defend their homeland.

Ribbentrop told Ciano that 'the ice of Russia has been conquered by the genius of Hitler'.[530] Russia dominated the talks, with Ribbentrop informing Ciano that Moscow and Leningrad would be left in abeyance as German troops turned south to the Caucasus to cut off Russian oil, which would bring the Soviets to their knees, and England would follow.[531] Ciano, according to his diary, worried Alfieri by challenging him as to how they would succeed. Ribbentrop considered the USA as a 'colossal bluff' and suggested that Britain and America were divided. (The Allies were often split over strategy and tactics, but they remained firmly together to defeat the Axis.) Ribbentrop believed the British Conservative Party was more likely to seek peace than the Labourites, who wanted war to the death, and he was concerned at Laval's return, believing that France 'might try and snap at the heels of Germany'.[532] This was Ciano's twentieth meeting with Ribbentrop, and he always found him a 'faithful echo of Hitler'. He perceived that his German colleague was not as intoxicated with the idea of victory as in earlier years, but remained 'convinced that he will reach port', and for once was treating Italy and Japan as equals.[533]

From his conversation with Hitler, Mussolini informed Ciano that the German war machine was 'still formidable and powerful but had suffered some wear and tear.'[534] Ciano noted that Hitler did all the talking and Mussolini had to listen, to which he was unaccustomed. On the second day of the visit Ciano noted that Hitler spoke for nearly two hours without a pause; Mussolini kept looking at his wristwatch; Cavallero pretended 'he was in ecstasy'; Jodl, after an epic struggle, fell asleep on his sofa; and Keitel, uncomfortably close to Hitler, was reeling but managed to stay awake. In Germany, from what Ciano saw, there were no physically fit men on the streets, and the Eastern Front losses, according to Ribbentrop, were some 270,000, but General Marras raised it to the more likely figure of 700,000.[535] There was talk of the 'brutality of the English' whose bombing had razed Rostock and Lübeck to the ground; Edda had visited them on her meanderings.

In early May Ciano was told that Edda had informed Hitler of an Italian labourer who had been seriously wounded by a German overseer, and the Führer had ordered an investigation. Edda had visited Germany during April, and even Goebbels found her serious, intelligent and earnest, which was a change in the view taken by most Germans about her.[536] Her pro-German observations on the Nazi leaders were contrary to those of her husband and most others. She described Goebbels as the greatest minister of propaganda with extraordinary powers of persuasion and seduction, whereas most regarded him as an obsessed Hitler fanatic, cruel, a liar, and a sex addict. Edda wrote in her memoirs that Himmler did not seem cruel, even though she was writing long after the war ended, with

Himmler confirmed as key to the Holocaust. The king had heard about Edda's complaint to Hitler concerning the Italian labourer, prompting Mussolini to phone her and ask her not to talk about what she had seen in Germany, as he feared the king might use the information to draw out anti-German policies, of which he at times had been equally guilty.[537]

A newspaper man and ex-fascist leader called D'Aroma approached Ciano, expressing concern about public reaction to Mussolini and the regime, but Ciano rejected his concerns, claiming that Mussolini remained popular with the crowds meeting him on their journey back from Germany. Such crowds, as Ciano knew, were summoned, and it defies belief that Ciano was unaware of the growing unpopularity; he had only just finished dealing with a project which had mooted his own assassination.

Ciano heard of the British landings in Madagascar and thought they had been caused by Laval, who had purportedly claimed that he preferred a Japanese victory to a British one. Mussolini followed this with the even more ludicrous view that Laval had deliberately manipulated this situation. Mussolini and Ciano were somewhat naïve in their speculations. Ciano's attention to world-changing events was suddenly diverted as he heard that Vidussoni intended to close golf courses. When Ciano challenged him, he was told by Vidussoni that it was an 'upper-class game', which infuriated Ciano, who claimed that the Italian middle classes were the ones who endured, and the working classes were as 'changeable as the sands'.[538] Ciano found some joy the next day, 9 May, when he accompanied his daughter Dindina to her first mass, describing her as 'pretty as a dream' – but still not mentioning Edda.

The usual internal problems intrigued Ciano more than his diplomatic duties. He heard from the new Police Chief Carmine Senise that he had a strong case against Buffarini, who had been profiting out of Jews trying to escape persecution. He also read the reports on the 'bad boys', the young men who had planned their proposed *coup d'état* badly – that is, in a manner, Ciano wrote, of which 'I greatly disapprove, that is, with my proposed assassination'.[539] Five days later he was concerned at some outrageous drunken party which involved a lady apparently left there by the American Embassy. The issues he dealt were becoming trivial.

SOME HOPEFUL NEWS

At a more pertinent level, Ciano heard from Cavallero of Rommel's preparations to attack in Libya and to take Malta, with the news that the Germans were sending paratroopers under the Luftwaffe General Student, but that a Colonel Casero did not share Cavallero's enthusiasm. Ciano was equally pleased to note that the Under-Secretary of the Air Force Rino Fougier was among those venting their rancour against Cavallero, whom he described as a 'dangerous clown'.[540] It was evident that Ciano was hoping for Cavallero to be sacked, but noted that 'things are not yet ripe for his dismissal'. General Gariboldi was about to leave for Russia, because, as Ciano noted in his diary, Cavallero wanted to get rid of Messe: 'Cavallero is a faithful follower of the theory which calls for the decapitation of poppies that grow too tall'.

Mussolini had been in Sardinia for a week and was pleased because the Sardinians were not grumbling about food. The Duce then went down with a bout of influenza, but not before he had expressed his disagreement with the navy, which had been prepared to allow British hospital ships to Malta. These 'white ships', as they were termed, were supposed to be inviolable – but, as noted, the British had sunk the Italian *Po* with Edda on board, and Mussolini had told Ciano that the Italians had used these types of vessels to transport gasoline to Benghazi. In war, trust and truth are cast aside – and now Rommel was preparing to advance, with the BBC announcing his plans.

On 26 May he started his attack on Gazala, and Mussolini excitedly claimed that Rommel would reach the Delta 'unless he is stopped not by the British but our own generals', a biting comment which Ciano enjoyed recording.[541] Fougier thought Rommel was attacking too soon. Carboni was against taking Malta, and Mussolini's contempt for his military leaders was known – but whereas Churchill, Hitler and Stalin replaced their generals as a result of constant evaluations of their performance, Mussolini tended merely to make cynical comments about his generals. Some news from the Russian front came from the journalist Lamberti Sorrentino, who said the future looked bleak, and Ciano noted that 'the brutality of the Germans, which has now reached the proportions of an endless crime' (which was not far from the truth).

Ciano's month ended with his speech to the Senate, which he said was well received and pleased Mussolini. Ciano decided to take time off in Livorno for fishing. It was the day that the first thousand-bomber raid by the RAF took place over Germany, and while Ciano was busy fishing the Japanese were attacking Sydney Harbour.

In June the naval Battle of Midway occurred; the Lidice massacre took place as a response to the killing of Heydrich; and the Germans launched Operation Blue, their summer offensive on the Eastern Front – but it was the fall of Tobruk which attracted Ciano's attention in his diary. Most of his entries, however, reflected the internal infighting amongst the Italian high command and scandals rather than the major events. This is not just a thoughtful thought on Ciano; it mirrors the situation in Italy at that time.

That same month Riccardi was again complaining about the shady business deals with Dr Macella Petacci, Clara's brother; three weeks later Riccardi was reporting that the Petacci gang was involved in the illegal traffic of gold and that Buffarini was implicated. Near the end of the month Ciano, having been tipped off, found in the diplomatic pouches some 18 kilos of gold, and handed the matter over to the police. He was convinced, probably correctly, that the Petacci family and Buffarini were involved, and judiciously noted in his diary that 'I make no further comment'.[542] Ciano, who kept a safe distance for self-preservation reasons, heard that the investigation was becoming serious and that Buffarini was defending himself, and was told a week later that Mussolini had been informed and was furious. But Mussolini did nothing.

During this month Petacci's sister was married in Rome in a typically high society wedding, remarked on for its extravagance. In 1942 Mussolini's mistress Clara was at 30 a brunette with green eyes, with an ample figure compared to the 'dowdy Rachele', and was known as a mediocre painter and writer.[543] Mussolini's love for his mistress was well known and scorned, but as with Ciano most knew the danger of approaching Mussolini on this subject. According to her memoirs, Edda was supposed to have addressed the issue with her father, but that failed as well.[544] Mussolini was frequently criticised behind his back, and according to one historian, Ciano, by making his views known to Serrano Suñer, was among those who objected to Mussolini's personal life, hypocritical as that may sound.[545] The reaction against the regime and Mussolini was growing yet more, and over lunch with Bottai Ciano heard that in his opinion the Duce appeared 'spiritually and intellectually very low'.[546]

DIVIDED COMMAND

Ciano was attentive to the poor relationships between the Italian military commanders. To the outside observer these machinations of the Italian military command seem to emphasise the impotence of the war machine – a war machine that Mussolini had often claimed was the finest in the world. When in early June Cavallero informed Ciano that the situation in Libya 'was considerable', this vague meaningless statement prompted him to refer to the 'mysterious language of this mountebank general'.[547] When Cavallero later informed Ciano that the situation in Libya was 'logical' – a term he had frequently used in the Greek débâcle – Ciano was again cynical. On the day he entered this biting comment he met General Messe who, as mentioned earlier, was being replaced in Russia by Gariboldi, and noted that he too was furious with Cavallero about the change of command. Serena, when he returned from Croatia that month, was arguing that Cavallero needed 'to be kicked out', and General Carboni, involved in the Malta plans, told Ciano that no one dared complain about the imminent disaster for fear of reprisals by Cavallero. When Rommel was promoted at the end of the month Mussolini decided that Cavallero and Bastico should receive the same promotion, causing Ciano to pluck up the courage to tell Mussolini that if General Bastico were promoted it would make people laugh, but that Cavallero's promotion 'would make them indignant'. Mussolini ignored him.[548]

To counter the grumbling about food, Mussolini suggested that the newspapers could help by stating that during the Great War the crisis had been worse; but Ciano knew that as that war had taken place only 20 years earlier most people, with their own memories of it, would not be taken in by such obvious propaganda. The public reaction to the regime was unquestionably deteriorating, and at a public ceremony for the unknown soldier at Livorno Ciano noted that the subdued public gave no applause.[549]

SOME SUCCESS

As these problems of scandals, military infighting, food supplies and money were being tussled over, the world war raged on. Dino Alfieri had been stopped from visiting Cologne because of the bomb damage, and on 1 June Ciano had noted that 'Tobruk is an impossible objective', but the news was becoming more hopeful. Bir Hakeim, an oasis a short distance to the south-west of Tobruk, was taken, but this delayed the attack on Tobruk itself; some military historians believe that the delay was caused by the Allies' strong defence, and notably the Axis's failure to take Malta. As the news improved from the Axis's point of view, Ciano noted that the Italian destroyer *Usidimare* had been sunk by one of its own submarines. However, on 21 June the news arrived of the fall of Tobruk, and the taking of some 25,000 prisoners of war.

Mussolini immediately wanted to visit North Africa, with Ciano writing that after all 'he is the man behind the decisive victory'. In this statement he echoed Mussolini's own thinking, based merely upon his demand that Tobruk should be attacked, but Mussolini was sent a restraining cable warning him of the dangers of a personal appearance. Meanwhile the prospect of Italy occupying Malta was causing concern; Mussolini sent Hitler a message that he needed 40,000 tons of oil before the attack could take place. Given the situation on the Eastern Front, this was an almost impossible demand. Ciano heard from messages sent by an American military attaché that the English were beaten, and that Rommel could reach the Suez Canal Zone.*

Even while the fall of Tobruk was being celebrated, Mussolini was unhappy that the battle was identified with Rommel, emphasised by Hitler's elevation of

---

* Colonel Bonner Frank Fellers, an American military attaché, was sending reports to General George Marshall in Washington, unaware that their code had been broken by the Italians.

this popular general to field marshal. Unquestionably it was the victory of the much-admired Rommel. Meanwhile, Mussolini's attitude, if faithfully reflected by Ciano, exhibited his self-inflated ego. Mussolini eventually went to North Africa on 29 June. Ciano was pleased that all was going well in Libya, noting that the 'English are going through a serious crisis', and at the end of the month he returned to Livorno to remember his dead father and enjoy some more fishing.

July for Ciano was more of a holiday month spent relaxing in Livorno, helped by Mussolini's absence in North Africa. Mussolini had phoned to instruct him to contact Hitler with a view to appointing Rommel as the military commander in Egypt but with an Italian administrator; Hitler agreed regarding Rommel, but deferred on the Italian suggestion. He later announced his acceptance. The fall of Tobruk was regarded as a victory such that it encouraged Cavallero and Mussolini to expect that they would be within the Suez Canal Zone within weeks – but Ciano rightly asked whether this was putting 'the cart before the horse'.[550] He wondered why the lull before El Alamein, pondering why the attack had stopped, and was aware that the British were receiving the necessary military resources. He was informed, too, that the Axis forces were having problems with water supplies, and that the RAF dominated the skies, hitting any moving targets, water bowsers in particular. In his usual cynical anti-Cavallero campaign, Ciano wrote that Cavallero was having booty flown home, writing in his diary that when it comes 'to grabbing Cavallero can even cheat the Germans'.

On 4 July Cavallero was made a marshal of Italy. The effect of this promotion, wrote Ciano, was negligible, except for unanimous disfavour in military circles. He also heard that the Germans were struggling in Russia, observing that the 'German army was no longer what it was'. The Germans had taken Sevastopol, and near the end of the month would capture Rostov, but it involved bitter fighting and they were not having the success they had anticipated.

DEPRESSING NEWS

Ciano returned to Rome on 20 July, expecting Mussolini back that evening. Ciano gathered that the situation in Egypt was not as rosy as he had believed, and that the general staff were even considering a retreat. However, he found Mussolini in a good mood, believing that they would soon be in Egypt; he had been confident enough of this to leave his personal baggage in Libya. Mussolini told Ciano that he had met some New Zealand POWs who looked at him in such a way that he made sure that he had his pistol handy. Ciano always referred to the British as the English, but the troops were in fact Commonwealth men such as New Zealanders, Australians, South Africans and Indians as well as many others, besides the Welsh, Scots and Irish, who would never describe themselves as English.

Mussolini disclosed to Ciano his deeper feelings. He already knew that many of the Germans held the Italian military staff in low esteem, but had also formed the impression that the local Italians preferred the English to the Germans. He was also furious with his own staff, who had invited him to view a battle – but, as had happened in Albania, it had turned out to be not the best of occasions to watch. Ciano noted that Mussolini was more anti-German than usual and had written a letter to Hitler saying that Rommel and the Germans had been unnecessarily critical of the Italian Sabratha Division.

There is no question that the Germans thought the Italians made poor soldiers, but with the benefit of hindsight we can see that it was a comment on the poorly trained officer class rather than the bravery of individual Italian soldiers, whom Rommel often praised. Nevertheless, of all the armies in this conflict the German soldier, whose training was based on the Prussian tradition, was nearly always the better soldier – and was ably led by professional officers. When at a meeting Hitler asked Rommel if he knew of any Italian commanders able to work with the Germans, the reply was cynically short: 'there is no such person.'[551] Kesselring was better at concealing any contempt he might have felt for the Italian military; later, when defending Italy from the Allied advance, he expressed his belief that the southern temperament was not belligerent, and that the Italians did not make 'natural soldiers,' observing that in the changing of the guard they appeared to have no enthusiasm for their profession.[552] His subordinate, the more perceptive General von Senger, was probably closer to the truth when he wrote that 'the Italian is by nature more critical and therefore politically more mature than the Germans'; he could clearly see that they had realised they were in a hopeless situation.[553]

On the global scene, during August American troops had landed at Guadalcanal; the Dieppe Raid had turned out to be a total disaster; and at the end of the month the Battle of Halfa started as Rommel tried to break through the British defence lines guarding Egypt. It was clear, however, that in North Africa the British had no intention of retreating.

In Italy, meanwhile, the constant lack of food and resources dominated the scene. Even the optimistic Pareschi was, according to Ciano, concerned about the shortages; any chance of importing grain was unlikely, there was no coal, and even wood was rationed.[554] At the beginning of August news came through that some agricultural workers were refusing to hand over their grain, and the situation was potentially volatile. Medical officers indicated that oedema, a form of inflammation caused by malnutrition, was becoming widespread. Ciano, however, still appeared oblivious to the fact that these issues were causing growing hostility towards the regime, and that despite his misperception of how he was personally admired he was in fact strongly associated with Mussolini. He noted that Bottai was more anti-Mussolini than usual, but the fact that Bottai was prepared to listen to critics of the regime was not widely known, because many assumed that he was Mussolini's chief advisor.

The Chief of the General Staff Vittorio Ambrosio told Ciano that the British were struggling with their supplies to North Africa and, although it was widely rumoured that Rommel intended to attack at the end of August, Ambrosio did not think the battle would start until October. He informed Ciano that the Russians were holding out and that the battle for the Caucasus would be another winter campaign. Ciano was also interested when he heard there were problems in Mussolini's home territory of Romagna, where the Mussolini and the Petacci families were 'poking their noses in' and creating further alienation amongst the populace. He attended a ceremony with the Mussolini family as they laid Bruno's remains to rest in the family vault, with Mussolini 'unusually showing a degree of emotion'.

On 11 August the British carried out Operation Pedestal, sending a major convoy to Malta to bring relief to the besieged island. The convoy was attacked by German and Italian forces, and Ciano listened to the results with interest, calling it the 'great English convoy' and noting that the Italian 'big ships' had to stay in port because of lack of fuel. As this battle raged at sea Mussolini held a council on administration matters, but he gave an optimistic account of the war which made Grandi pessimistic and increased his 'hatred' of Cavallero. About midway through the month, the 'Roman midsummer holiday', Ciano noted that 'the people do not wish to change their habits, if they can get away with it, and everyone wants to have a good time. The War? They want to forget it'.[555] This was an unbelievably hypocritical view by Ciano, as he had spent much of July in Livorno and kept returning there for holiday breaks.

He was not as busy as in the pre-war years. The diplomatic service was no longer his principal activity, but instead the military. Bottai recorded in his diary that Ciano's 'evenings were long and empty', and he 'had no popular following in Italy'.[556] Ciano admitted that the 'real enemy of the diplomatic set is boredom', but the way he phrased it indicates that he saw himself above this problem.[557] He attended the funeral of Horthy's son Stephen, who had died in an accident in Hungary; at the funeral he met Ribbentrop, who had changed from claiming the 'the war is won' to 'we cannot lose this war'. It was probably these occasions which helped Ciano believe he was still active and even popular.

One of the questions often raised by historians was whether Ciano was plotting and planning for better times, even if it meant clashing with Mussolini. Unusually for him, at the beginning of the month he had written in his diary about Edda, who was attacking him 'violently' about his anti-German attitude. How far this was a clash with her more pro-German views or whether she was trying to alert Ciano of potential dangers is ambiguous. She warned him that the Germans were aware of his views, so it should have crossed his mind that someone else was behind her outburst.[558] There were rumours that behind the scenes he was putting out feelers to look for a peace settlement, and that this was purportedly happening in Spain.[559] It made sense of his diary entry of 29 August, that Grandi had been about to go to Spain but his hosts had cancelled his visit at the last moment, which Grandi accepted 'without any problems'. It is probably correct that Ciano never wanted a major war, was critical about what was happening, disliked the Germans, and would prefer peace. How far the 'peace feelers' were serious is difficult to estimate.

Rommel launched his attack towards Alam el Halfa, a short distance south of El Alamein, and although the prospect of imminent victory may have altered a few perspectives, Ciano's habitual approach was one of caution, as he was constantly worried about Mussolini and his 'change of minds'.

September started with the encouraging news that the British were withdrawing towards the sea and offering little resistance, but this was rapidly followed by more depressing information: Rommel had been forced to stop because of fuel shortages. Military historians have often emphasised that the North African war was more of a coastal war than one covering the vast desert hinterlands, and that the materiel, which the Axis now lacked, was a major factor. Rino Fougier underlined this issue by informing Ciano that Germany and Italy were producing between just a fifth and sixth respectively of the numbers of planes and pilots that the Allies could produce.[560] The British superiority at sea and in the air was a critical element in this war. Ciano noted that three Italian tankers had been sunk, which underlined that the 'desert war' was in fact dependent on the conflict at sea, which remained in favour of the British. Cavallero remained optimistic but the German General Rintelen, recently returned from Africa, was less certain, and Ciano noted that Mussolini was in a dark mood, barely mentioning what was taking place in Libya. Ciano admitted that with the mixed reports it was difficult to work out what was happening, but he gathered that Rommel was drawing back on his left flank, and may have cancelled the advance because of limited supplies.

As the month progressed Ciano felt that the ever more depressing news of the battle was leaving a bad impression on the Italian people; by the end of the month it was clear that the attack had failed. Rommel appeared in Rome, meeting Ciano before returning to Germany for six weeks' rest. Rommel was not well, and Mussolini suggested that he would not be returning. Mussolini was, furthermore, angry with Rommel because he had complained that Italian officers had leaked his plans.

In Spain Serrano Suñer had persistently argued that Spain should enter the war on the side of the Axis, but was replaced in September by Jordana, who was far less inclined to do so; he was purportedly an Anglophile so his appointment was a great relief to the Allies.[301] Ciano noted the immediate impact; the Italian submarine *Giuliani*, under repair in San Sebastian, was virtually interned, which would never have happened under Serrano Suñer. News from Germany was not as encouraging as in previous years, and Bismarck was as usual predicting that Germany would lose the war, and felt that Italy would escape the final catastrophe – because, as Ciano was pleased to note, of 'Ciano's own personal efforts with Britain and America', an opinion that would have bemused the Allies.

DISCONTENTMENT

Ciano spent much of his time away from his office, first with a bout of flu and then in his favourite home at Livorno. In the safety of the distance from Rome he spent two days with the angry Bottai who, like Bastianini, saw a 'dark future', and raised the issue that the war was technically illegal in the first place because the Grand Council had not been consulted. This was dangerous chatter, and Ciano merely noted the view without further comment, though the nature of the confidential conversation implied that Ciano was listening to anti-Mussolini elements.

Ciano, unusually for him, attached to his diary a letter from Edda. She was concerned about Mussolini's state of health and about her mother. The main concern was Mussolini's stomach ulcer; she wrote that he had not received appropriate medical advice, only surveys of his body. She finished her letter with 'dear Gallo, let's take it as it comes, chin up! I urge you to get to work about the doctors'.[562] They were still leading their separate lives, but there was an impression from this letter that apart from her concern for her father, she recognised that Ciano was feeling depressed. If he were, he cheered himself up at the end of the month by relating that Cavallero had made a *faux pas* at a meeting of Axis diplomats. Ciano was evidently in the doldrums seeking more retreat time in Livorno, but a juicy piece of scandal relating to Cavallero was like a tonic for him.

During October, despite the hopes of victory in Libya, there was a sense of impending gloom. Ciano was receiving pessimistic reports from Germany, and the problems in the Balkans were increasing. The Greek obligation to supply money to the Germans was rapidly becoming a serious issue, as was the food shortage. The Germans had imposed an indemnity on the Greeks for having to invade them, and the Greeks were supposed to find some 53 billion drachmas every month, an amount which had been seriously misjudged. Mussolini told

Ciano that the 'Germans had made Europe as hot and treacherous as a volcano'.[563] More startling was the news from General Amè, Head of the Intelligence Service, that the Anglo-Saxons (as the Anglo-Americans were frequently labelled) were preparing a major landing in North Africa. This information was correct despite the efforts of the Allies to operate in secret, and prompted Ciano to write the pessimistic entry: 'how long shall we have the strength to resist a determined, strong, and methodical air and naval offensive?'

On 11 October Ciano met Himmler at the station in Rome; he had recently returned from the Russian front and appeared somewhat depressed. According to Ciano, Himmler said nothing of great importance in itself but, significantly, spoke of sacrifices and difficulties. He had arrived to discover what was happening in Italy, and Ciano claimed that he praised the Italian monarchy for its loyalty and the Vatican for its discretion (which seems highly improbable unless Himmler was doing his best to be deceptive). There is no doubt, however, that Himmler was there 'to sniff the political air in view of the increasing reports of the decline in Mussolini's health, and to investigate the intricate balances of forces behind the scenes', hence Himmler's interest in the monarchy and the Vatican.[564]

As Himmler departed a few days later, Göring announced he would be briefly in Rome to pick up his wife, who had been visiting, and he demanded to see Mussolini at 11 a.m. on Monday morning – an arrogant demand which was not going to be easy to meet, because Mussolini had dysentery. Then von Mackensen reported that Göring was suffering from the same complaint, which would 'not allow him to leave his throne, even for ten minutes'.[565] This communication raised a few eyebrows, and Bismarck enjoyed the comment.

If a graph of the regime's popularity had been available, it would at this point have indicated another sharp decline. Farinacci and Bottai expressed their exasperation to Ciano about the internal situation and the inadequacy of the party leaders. Ciano also heard that the party federal secretaries had openly discussed Petacci, which caused Mussolini some anger a few days later. Mussolini meanwhile was more preoccupied by Taylor (the American envoy to the Vatican) whom he thought was feeding intelligence to the Allies, and he wanted him 'handcuffed'. The following month the Vatican became furious about an article Farinacci had written blaming the Vatican and Taylor for the 1943–44 bombing of Rome's industrial outskirts. Farinacci was ordered to retract the article, but told Ciano he was unhappy about that because it had been Mussolini's suggestion in the first place.

The 20th anniversary of the March on Rome was about to be celebrated, and Ley had arrived from Berlin. It was a subdued ceremony, the only event being the inauguration of the new quarters for the exhibition of the 'Revolution'. The celebration had originally been intended to mark the world exhibition, but the 'historical significance of the occasion was unhappily dwarfed by the harsh realities of war and the first perceptible signs of the disintegration of the very structure of the regime'.[566] Mussolini had been due to address party leaders near the end of the month, but suddenly cancelled the arrangement, and Ciano appeared out of touch because he had been left to speculate on Mussolini's reasons. He wondered whether it was because Mussolini was ill, perhaps anticipating changes in the party structure, or was hoping for better news on the Libyan front; Ciano decided it had to be the last reason. He may have been correct, because it was on only the previous day that it had been announced that the British had attacked in Libya – the start of Montgomery's Second Battle of El Alamein.

As this battle started it became clear that the anticipated Axis victory was becoming elusive. Ciano noted that 'the tactical situation is good, the logistical situation dangerous' – and barely had he written this when he heard another vital oil tanker had been sunk. Even Ambrosio, who had always been full of 'rosy predictions', was pessimistic. The misreading of the situation by Mussolini, who thought the military situation was good, underlined the paucity of reliable information arriving in Rome. Mussolini had made this forecast on about 2 November, the day that Rommel had informed Hitler that without fuel and ammunition his army faced annihilation. Hitler had naturally told Rommel to hold fast, which he attempted but failed. Ciano had written that Hitler had 'nailed Rommel to the spot'. Ciano was right about the logistical situation, and Montgomery had methodically built up supplies, giving the British an overwhelming superiority.

For the Italians October was a month of depression and widespread gloom, and Mario Farnesi, a Fascist Party official, told Ciano he felt that the 'earth was giving way' under his feet. Ciano noted that 'I did not conceal from him that on many issues I disagree with the present leadership of the party, for reasons of substance and form'.[567] Ciano was in a vacuum and becoming more critical of the party, and many were aware of his attitudes.

November started, as had the previous month, with more bad news and a sense of despair, with Ciano writing that 'for some time a sense of irrepressible pessimism has overtaken the Italian people', which was not surprising when it was evident that the much-vaunted Libyan front was collapsing.[568] On reading Ciano's diary it was becoming clear that although he still represented Mussolini in meetings in Germany he had become a mere observer of events. Mussolini still fluctuated wildly between optimism and depression, even stating that the Libyan loss was perhaps a good thing, because it would save the merchant fleet.

Ciano was somewhat disturbed when Mussolini asked him whether he was maintaining his diary, on the grounds that it would demonstrate that the Germans had acted militarily and politically without his knowledge. Ciano wondered, 'what does his strange question really hide?' His personal notes, revealing what others had told him and with which he often concurred, were such that it would lead to disaster if Mussolini took too much interest; Ciano may have wondered whether Mussolini was considering some form of future personal defence.

As Ciano pondered this question, further news was received of Allied convoys, with the speculation that their objective might be Malta or to land troops at Rommel's rear as he retreated west at, according to Ciano, 'breakneck speed'. The next day, however, the issue was resolved with an early morning call from Ribbentrop announcing that Allied troops had landed in Algeria and French Morocco. This rekindled Mussolini's desire to seize Corsica. General Amè, Head of Intelligence, told Ciano that there would be some resistance but that the Americans and de Gaullists would overcome this, nevertheless adding the painful note that 'army morale is dramatically low'. Amè seemed to be one of the more informed generals within the Italian structure. The Allied invasion of Morocco and Algeria was known as Operation Torch, and although there were occasional problems it was finally successful.

To Hitler again

Operation Torch caused concern in the Axis partners, with a frantic call from Ribbentrop informing Ciano that he or Mussolini were to travel immediately to Munich for a meeting with Hitler in the presence of Laval, the French prime minister. Mussolini's ill-health meant that Ciano went in his place, meeting Hitler the same day; he understood the issue was France, with Hitler apprehensive that the French would turn against them. He was concerned that General Giraud was the dangerous man, and considered that it was necessary to have France and Corsica occupied at once.* Over the next two days a conference between Hitler, Göring, Ribbentrop, Laval and Ciano took place, and as Laval could not promise the gift of Tunis or Bizerte, he smoked in one room while the decisions were made in another. On 11 November, the 1918 Armistice anniversary, while the conference concluded, German troops occupied Vichy France without opposition. The question was not Laval but where Admiral Darlan stood, as he had once wanted to cooperate militarily with the Germans. Darlan had paid a visit to North Africa to see his sick son, and had taken command. When Hitler invaded the unoccupied zone of France, Darlan was uncertain about his authority, and prevaricated; he tried to establish a neutral zone in line with Vichy policy but, having finally understood Anglo-American determination, changed sides. There

---

*   Giraud had been captured in 1940 but had escaped.

was a post-war rumour that Pétain had encouraged Darlan in secret telegrams, but although Darlan claimed Pétain's support there is no evidence of this in any records known.[569]

By the time Ciano returned to Rome, Mussolini's optimism had resumed. Ciano was pleased to hear that Mussolini was irritated with Cavallero, who had been sent to Libya to find out what was happening only to rush back in fear for his personal safety. Ciano rightly reflected that the French response was ambiguous, and that if Tunisia fell Italy would lose its last important defensive bastion; this was accompanied by the disturbing information that the Italian consul general in Tunis had left because he had decided that the situation was no longer tenable.

On 19 November Ciano met the king with the usual exchange of views, curiously noting that the monarch had advised him 'to cling to any thread which might yet be reknotted even if it was as thin as a spider's web'. This comment followed a conversation concerning relations with Washington and London. It appeared that the king and Ciano both hoped for peace. Mussolini, however, did not share this view, and two days later at a council appeared unduly optimistic, He informed the members that the food situation was better than the forecasts; that the enemy could be stopped in Cyrenaica; that the Axis would gain the upper hand; that the internal situation was excellent apart from a few alarmists; and that Hitler, acting on Mussolini's advice, would send Italy 100 anti-aircraft batteries. None of this was anywhere near the truth, and Ciano wrote that 'in the country, pessimism and concern are growing beyond all measure. One cannot speak with any person of any class or station in life without hearing these things'.[570]

On 27 November the key French naval base of Toulon was occupied by the Germans, but the resident French fleet scuttled itself and Ciano again retreated to Livorno. While there he heard that Rommel had left North Africa somewhat hurriedly and that Göring was back in Rome. He also heard a Churchill speech, and as a result was worried about the future, not being able to see how the Italians could 'frustrate Churchill's programme of a scientific and destructive offensive against our country'.[571] In Livorno he talked to his father's old friend Vergani, who according to him had been told by Ciano that the war was useless and there was no point in continuing.[572] Curiously, Vergani must have been aware that because of Ciano's views he (Ciano) might be in some danger, and advised him to leave the country.[573] Ciano may have regarded his views as private, but it was apparent that many were aware of his criticisms.

On 1 December Ciano did not bother to note that Abyssinia had declared war on the Axis but observed that Mussolini, whom he had not seen for ten days, was looking very thin. Göring and his staff were in Rome, full of confidence about the future, and evidently irritating Ciano by their presence. Bismarck was around the edges, confiding that in his opinion North Africa was lost and the Germans were only preserving Rommel's reputation because he was a public hero. Ciano pondered whether Göring was thinking of appointing himself as *Reichsprotektor* of Italy, and when he heard that Göring was holding meetings he was pleased to learn that Buffarini reported that Cavallero was far too servile.[574]

On 6 December Göring and Mussolini held a personal conversation in which the Duce outlined his ideas.[575] Mussolini had decided the best policy was for Germany to end the war against Russia and establish a reliable defence line, and move the necessary resources to North Africa and Western Europe, pointing out that Croatia was looking precarious. It was about now that the word *Tedeschi* (Germans) was taking on a pejorative meaning, as the Allied threat increased alongside that of a possible German takeover of Italy on the excuse of defence.

A major issue was the possible bombing of Rome, which was raising serious concerns in the Vatican. The British representative at the Vatican, a Sir Godolphin d'Arcy Osborne, had not helped by pointing out that Rome was not the only Catholic city, and if Rome were to avoid bombing raids it was suggested that the military command should be removed from the city Mussolini was not averse to this idea, stating that 'it may not be said that he has remained under the big umbrella of Catholicism to protect himself from English bombs'.[576] Osborne insisted that the Germans had to leave as well, and later Eden demanded that the evacuation should be supervised by Swiss agents. It was something of a relief when Ciano heard from an intercepted cable that the Americans objected to Eden's more 'draconian measures'. One of the critical factors was that Rome was a hub for communications by river, road and rail.

Revealingly, when Ciano commented on Mussolini's speech to the chamber he noted that the reception was warm, 'but [it was] easy to recognise people in the hall who privately disagreed'. This telling note would have been more illuminating if Ciano had disclosed whether he knew this because he knew who they were, or because of their facial expressions. During this month Ciano had another dangerous conversation with Vergani, in which Ciano pointed out that whereas Churchill visited bombed areas Mussolini never did.[577] It was not surprising that Vergani had suggested Ciano leave the country. The sense of impending gloom was not helped by the news that the British were attacking again, and everyone knew, despite Mussolini's and Cavallero's optimism, that they had insufficient fuel and arms to resist.

During this month there were sound reasons to believe that Franzoni, the Italian minister in Lisbon, was making discreet approaches to Eden, and the American Cordell Hull was looking for some form of peace, a move which appeared to have emanated from Ciano.[578] Apparently, this situation remained in place until July 1943. It was clear that the German dissident Hassell had picked up this information as well, stating that a group of moderate fascists were trying to reach an agreement with Britain.[579]

Von Mackensen arrived to arrange another meeting with Hitler, and Mussolini said he would only go if he could eat alone (he did not want the Germans to see his diet of rice and milk, all part of his medical treatment). A few days later the meeting had to be postponed, and it was proposed it should then be in Hitler's war headquarters, where they anticipated receiving Ciano, knowing that Mussolini was unwell. Mussolini gave Ciano strict instructions, which were generally the same he had discussed with Göring: principally to stop the war with Russia and to concentrate on the south and west of Europe. By the autumn of this year many in Italy, including those in the fascist regime, were wondering how to extract Italy from the war, but were equally aware that overthrowing Mussolini could simply lead to a German invasion. It was a devastating choice.[580]

Ciano left for Berlin with Cavallero, picking up Alfieri with a senior embassy official called Lanza. Lanza mentioned Ciano's table talk as 'brilliant and amusing, but he is disconcertingly vacuous and extremely monotonous', and 'the Germans seem to be his favourite target, and he enjoys himself by talking to them in the worse possible way'. Lanza then added that we 'never see Cavallero whom Ciano addresses as that bum with short legs'.[581] Ciano referred to the 'delinquent Ribbentrop and that criminal Hitler', and there is no doubt that the Germans detected Ciano's attitude. The railway carriage may well have been bugged, but even without that, Ciano's state of mind would have been easy to read.

When they arrived in the forest of Görlitz, Ciano described the atmosphere as 'heavy', a humid forest, boring, living in the barracks of command, and waiting rooms filled with people smoking, eating and chatting. Given other sources of information, this appears to have been a realistic picture. It was not an easy time for Ciano, as he was told that part of the Russian front had collapsed because Italian soldiers had fled; Hitler asked Ciano to request that Mussolini should tell his soldiers to hold firm.[582] Lanza claimed later that Ciano had given the impression of 'having lost his nerve. He does not stay still for one moment. He gets up and down. He jokes then goes sullen'.[583]

Hitler explained there was no formal agenda and launched into a diatribe on the dangers of Bolshevism infecting the whole of Europe. Ciano managed to present Mussolini's ideas of ending the war with Russia in order to concentrate on the other fronts, which naturally Hitler rebutted, whereupon Ciano weakly pointed out that the 'Italians only wanted to know his views.' Curiously, this Italian suggestion had already been proposed by the Japanese, whose principal goal was the defeat of Britain and America.[584] One aspect of this meeting was that 'Ciano's credit as foreign minister had evaporated … and 'equally clear the Germans had their reservations about him' and distrusted him.[585]

Back in Rome Ciano heard that Darlan had been assassinated in Algiers, that a Princess di Gangi had 'opened her heart' on the Petacci clan, that there had been reports in Tirana over gossip about himself; he must have felt at home again after Hitler's headquarters. He heard that his childhood nanny, Emilia, had died in Livorno, and as with his father and sister he felt deeply moved as yet another part of his family background evaporated.

DID CIANO SAVE FRENCH JEWS?

Ciano's biographer Moseley makes the point that Ciano may have been personally involved in saving Jews in the Italian-occupied areas. The Italian historian Renzo De Felice had written that 'the Vichy and Nazi documents present Galeazzo Ciano as the *deus ex machina*, the inspirer of the policy of the protection of the Jews in the occupied territories', especially in their portion of Vichy France.[586] There has been considerable discussion as to how far Ciano was involved in saving French Jews from the Holocaust. France had once been considered a natural resource for refugees, often declaring itself 'une terre d'asile' (a land of refuge): there had been a degree of truth in this until anti-Semitism raised its head again in the 1930s. Laval had once protested that in their zone the Italians were trying to protect the Jews from the French police. It is known that nuns in Notre Dame de Sion rescued nearly 500 Jewish children, finding them places in Christian homes, and a Capuchin brother in Marseille talked the Italians into accepting some 30,000 Jews into their zone.[587] Technically the Italian zone had been subject to Vichy legislation and there was tension between the French and Italians over the Jewish population, especially during 1942. The Italian General Lazare di Castiglione forced Vichy to release arrested Jews, and in Annecy (in the Alps) Italian soldiers forced a gendarmerie, at the point of a gun, to release its Jewish prisoners. Ribbentrop confronted Mussolini over the Jewish problem, but over the ensuing months Mussolini made promises he reneged on or 'simply changed his mind on a variety of clever and slippery excuses'.[588]

How far Ciano was personally involved is difficult to establish; it seems more likely that the general Italian attitude and individual Italians found the Nazi persecution of Jews difficult to comprehend. There were claims that Ciano 'hoped to buy sympathies for Italy should they lose the war'.[589] The impression was that it was more a general Italian attitude than a direction from Ciano, but it cannot be ruled out. For all his faults, there sometimes appeared a glimmer of genuine humanity in Ciano.

SUMMATION OF 1942

During 1942 there were significant signs that Germany could no longer be assumed to be the ultimate victor. The news from the Russian front was not good for the Nazi regime, which blamed it on the weather and anticipated that the spring and summer would be better. The Axis advance in North Africa had wavered, the year ending with the German and Italian forces defeated there. In Italy, Mussolini was suffering from widespread criticism, was in pain from his duodenal ulcer, was suffering domestic scandals from his 'alternative family', and was to all appearances living in a world of his own. Ciano was becoming more sceptical, proving to be more of a realist than his master and, as his biographer Moseley wrote, he 'was playing with fire, his opposition to Mussolini but, as always, he remained incapable of acting on his conviction that the Duce must be stopped'.[590]

9

1943 – THE END DAYS

Allied soldiers on Italian soil bringing food
(National Museum of US Navy)

THE DOWNFALL OF CIANO

At the beginning of 1943 the war was turning against Germany. In Italy, hope was rapidly diminishing: in northern Italy there had been serious industrial strikes, caused not by political motives but by sheer hunger, and in the south there was fear of invasion.[591] Ciano noted with dismay the news from the Casablanca Conference which had concluded with Roosevelt's demand for unconditional surrender; in late January British troops entered Tripoli; on 2 February Stalingrad fell to the Russians, and six days later the Red Army took Kursk. In Stalingrad and North Africa the Germans lost hundreds of thousands of men, killed,

193

wounded and taken prisoner. On 6 January Ciano wrote 'I have the impression that the Axis is like a man who is trying to cover himself with a bedspread that is too small'.[592] In the case of Italy his analogy could have been better expressed as seeking cover from a pillowcase. Ciano noted that Mussolini was looking unusually thin and that this worried Edda, and Ciano wondered whether it was caused more by circumstances than illness. Peace with Russia was implausible and the Balkans were ablaze, but Ciano and Mussolini appeared more concerned about giving Göring gifts for his 50th birthday. The good news for Ciano at the end of January was the replacement Cavallero with Ambrosio, which annoyed the Germans, although as Ciano cynically noted the Germans always felt free to sack their generals. After years of plotting Ciano had managed to remove the hated Cavallero, asking his private secretary to send for the Prince of Bismarck to let the Germans know; Ciano was delighted.[593]

He was still hoping for some form of peace, and he tended to associate with the discontented elements. On 15 January Mussolini phoned him to ask if it were true that he had enjoyed lunch with Bottai, Carlo Scorza and Alessandro Tarabini; Ciano noted that it was a mere 'banal conversation'. He knew that Bottai and Farinacci were furious about the events unfolding, and he had talked to Ambrosio and Vercellino, whom he described as patriotic and equally concerned about the future. Ciano from his earliest days had been known for his love of rumours, which probably explained him writing in his diary on 5 February, when summoned to Mussolini's presence, 'I can guess what he is about to tell me' predicting his sacking as foreign minister.[594] Mussolini explained that he was changing his whole cabinet, including Grandi, and offered Ciano the post of governor in Albania, which Ciano promptly refused – but he did take on the role as ambassador to the Holy See, even though Mussolini had once, as mentioned earlier, dismissed it as the role of a sacristan.* Before Ciano left Mussolini asked him if his documents were up to date, which Ciano immediately assumed was a reference to his assiduous diary keeping; Ciano replied they were, and said that they documented all the treacheries perpetrated by the Germans against Mussolini and Italy.

Outside observers such as the German General Westphal noted that the public took Mussolini's action as a 'proof that the dictator was at last resolved to rid himself of his corrupt and incompetent ministers'.[595] The threat from the Allies was growing exponentially, and there was concern that Italy would soon be invaded; changes were needed. The problem was that Mussolini wanted 'Italy to be defended by Italians and shut his eyes to the fact that the appalling state of his forces made such an idea impracticable'.[596]

---

*   a lowly church official, equivalent to a housekeeper

One of the many problems in this saga is sorting out fact and fiction from the differing sources available. Various characters involved in the unfolding drama have left their own memoirs, diaries and notes with their versions of what happened, along with their views of the intentions or impulses which drove events. Sometimes these sources have been treated by historians as gospel – which some sources may have been, others less so. Occasionally the question is not that important: for example Vergani claimed he had met Ciano the next day and heard that Ciano never met Mussolini but had heard the news over a radio broadcast. That point is more or less irrelevant, because either way Ciano was sacked. Later Rachele claimed that Ciano was sent to the Vatican because thereby Mussolini had a possible peace negotiator. However, she never liked Ciano and later in the year Edda recalled that her mother had stated in front of the children that 'Ciano should be judged and punished', an indication of not only the diverse feelings of the day but the confusion caused to historians by the many mixed messages.[597]

What is known is that the Germans were aware of Ciano's views – as were the Allies – and many suspected that a plot was developing to overthrow the Italian regime. In Switzerland Allen W. Dulles, who headed the OSS (Office of Strategic Services, later the CIA) had sent information about such a possible plot via the Black Code which (as mentioned in a footnote earlier) the Germans had deciphered.

It was this that led to Ciano's downfall: the report arrived on Hitler's desk, and he sent a copy to Mussolini, who a few days later sacked his son-in-law. Mussolini had been aware of the dissidents, hence his phone call to Ciano in January questioning him about his luncheon guests. There is considerable evidence that the Germans had long been cognisant of Ciano's views, with the Abwehr denouncing him as a traitor. Goebbels wrote in his diary that all the cabinet rearrangements by Mussolini were to draw attention away from Ciano's downfall, whom he called 'the ringleader in the plot against his own father-in-law'.[598] Mussolini had also sacked Grandi, Bottai and Buffarini, the last one more probably because of his dealings with the Petacci family, whom Edda blamed for her husband's downfall. Von Mackensen, caught by surprise, asked for an interview with Mussolini, stating that he was surprised by the changes, to which Mussolini blithely replied, 'That is just my way. You must gradually get to know it.'[599] Mussolini was aware of the mounting criticisms in his failing war; some historians believe that he sacked Ciano because Ciano was viewed as a defeatist, and Mussolini needed to purge the moderate fascists.[600]

Ciano handed his foreign office to Bastianini (Mussolini had formally assumed the role), whom von Mackensen described in comparison with Ciano as having a 'lucid personality ... who embodies the best type of the old fascist, loyal to the Duce, and who above all does not avoid expressing his opinions openly to him'.[601] Ciano then took himself off to his new embassy, a beautiful palazzo in the Via Flaminia. In her memoirs Edda painted an amusing picture when Ciano took his family to be presented to the Pope and their son Marzio, fascinated by the golden telephone on the Pope's desk, picked it up, causing a tussle for it with the Pope.[602] The whole episode was somewhat embarrassing, and it is easy to believe this anecdote for that reason alone. In any case, Ciano settled into his new post, pleased to be in Rome as an observer, and he continued with his habitual intrigues, though there were times when he wanted to lead an ordinary life (which given his history would have been impossible). He had barely settled into his new function when on 25 February he had a surprise visit from Ribbentrop, who gave him a famous painting for his 40th birthday, on 18 March. Ciano was much taken by this gift, and even felt some warmth towards his old adversary.

THE PLOT

A journalist friend called Yvon De Begnac caught up with Ciano in his new offices not long after he had settled in, and found a changed man, who appeared to be 'worried, nervous and plotting like everyone else'.[603] In Germany, Hassell, when he heard Ciano had gone to the Vatican, wrote 'there he will have every opportunity to contact the enemy'.[604] Ciano may have felt he retained some influence, one observer claiming that at least ten generals or admirals visited him each day, which sounds exaggerated. In contrast, the American representative Myron Taylor claimed that Ciano had no followers, which either questions the previous statement or throws doubts on Taylor's observational powers. It has been claimed that Ciano was holding secret talks with the British and Americans, but another question arises, in that it was unlikely that the Allies, even in the hope of overturning the totalitarian regimes, would not have dealt with party members, though some talking may possibly have taken place between Ciano and Osborne, British representative at the Vatican.

Mussolini still appeared to have no comprehension of his own unpopularity, many people referring to him as 'Baldie or Big Head'. Much of the criticism focused on the fact that Mussolini had 'personalised the war by becoming commander-in-chief in addition to occupying all three ministries'.[605] The military failure was therefore placed on his doorstep, and Grandi with others recognised that it was Mussolini who was the main obstacle to any peace negotiations. In sacking Grandi, Bottai and Ciano, Mussolini had made a gross miscalculation, because it had driven them into active revolt.

How far Ciano was actively plotting or was on the fringes is difficult to ascertain. According to Anfuso on a visit back from Budapest in March, Ciano was 'immersed up to his neck in the fascist plot with Bottai, Carboni, and Castellano'.[606] Many remain convinced that Ciano was at the centre of a growing plot with Bottai and Grandi, with Ciano hoping to play a major role in the post-Mussolini era. The historian Porch wrote that 'Ciano conspired to replace him', which Ciano may have wanted, but he was now more realistic.[607] His intention was to use the king to seek a separate peace with the Allies.[608] The king had long considered the possibility of removing Mussolini, but knew that to do so would be playing with fire, so it was not until late July that he decided to do it. On 21 April when some of the dissidents had met the king and urged him to remove Mussolini, it is noteworthy that Ciano was not present even though Castellano had kept him informed and shown him the plans.[609]

On 12 May Italy lost its last foothold in Africa and the following day Ciano heard that the Germans were sending troops to Sicily and Sardinia – obviously intending to defend the two areas which the Allies might invade – and that Mussolini's military hopes were disintegrating.* The next day Ciano met Mussolini, who was again alerted to Ciano being a critic, having read a report that Ciano 'on various occasions had not hesitated to criticise even the work of the Duce'.[610] Mussolini had also heard from the Germans that Ciano had held talks with the British and Americans (but if that had indeed occurred it was of little importance, given the Allied success and their attitude towards the fascists), though as mentioned earlier Ciano probably had talked to Osborne in the Vatican. Those whom Mussolini had fired from their posts earlier in the year had been meeting one another, but again it is impossible to be certain of what precisely was happening. Ciano was tucked away in his new office, keeping a low profile but nonetheless being observed, while Edda was a nurse in Sicily, where the serious poverty was generating its consequential health problems.

On 10 June the news came through that the tiny island of Pantelleria (between Tunisia and Sicily) had been occupied by the Allies, a tangible warning of Allied intentions. Mussolini's opponents met the king and Ciano, but the king promptly informed Mussolini of Ciano's views, and Mussolini promptly demanded from Ciano to know whether he was betraying him. The king was part of the growing conspiracy, and it can only be conjectured that he informed Mussolini in case Ciano – who was now expendable to him – remained loyal to Mussolini, or became another Duce. At this stage there is a distinct impression that Mussolini still hoped to trust his son-in-law despite the rumours, but Rachele was quick to inform the SS Colonel Dollmann that Ciano was the 'bane of the family' and that his past behaviour meant he could never be trusted.[611] A few days later a

---

* They were correct, because the American and British had indeed been debating which of these islands to attack.

German counter-espionage group drew up a report entitled 'The Ciano Group' which implied that for them Ciano was central.[612] At their home, Edda, who had returned from Sicily, met her long-term lover Pucci, who had become a celebrated pilot but now a friend rather than a lover. In the terms of their peculiar marriage, Ciano appeared to accept this.

In early July news came through of the Allied attack on Sicily. This was Operation Husky, which the outnumbered Germans strongly resisted but lost, and was the precursor to the Allied invasion of the Italian mainland. It was observed that although some Italian soldiers fought well, many had been happy to surrender at the first opportunity. This was not the silly popular myth of Italian cowardice, but sensible men voting with their feet. The Allied attack on Italian soil sent panic waves through the regime and concentrated the minds of those who wished for a change in leadership. Almost immediately Ciano met General Gambara and agreed it was better to have the armed forces under the control of the king; in most opinions – and prominent in Ciano's writings – it was clear that despite his projected belligerence Mussolini was an incompetent military leader. But there was no guarantee that the king would be an improvement. Ciano even told his erstwhile enemy Farinacci where he stood, which was a risky confidence. The general feeling was that the enemy despised Mussolini and if power were returned to the supreme command it might suit the Allies and help the fascists. It had not crossed those Italians' minds that the Allies were opposed to both the Italian and the German varieties of fascism, and not interested in any differences. The king intimated that he was not that keen on a government with politicians, evidently preferring a monarchical dictatorship.

Edda recalled that on 15 July Ciano had received a phone call to go to Rome to see Mussolini, noting that Ciano had said there were tensions in Rome.[613] Ciano resisted the summons, claiming that he was bedridden with an ear infection, which Anfuso referred to as a 'diplomatic illness'. Four days later American bombers hit San Lorenzo, on the outskirts of Rome, increasing the sense of political instability. Italian nerves were probably not helped by a joint broadcast from Churchill and Roosevelt on 16 July, communicated by Algiers Radio. In Churchill's inimitable style he stated that: 'Mussolini plunged you into a war which he thought Hitler had already won … your sons, your ships, your air forces sent to distant battlefields … the sole hope for Italy's survival lies in honourable capitulation to the overwhelming power of the military forces of the United Nations … the time has come for you to decide whether Italians shall die for Mussolini and Hitler – or live for Italy and for civilisation'.[614] The timing of this broadcast was significant.

The critical moment arrived when Mussolini announced that there would be a Grand Council meeting at 5 p.m. on 24 July. This caused a flurry in the dovecotes, and Ciano met Grandi, Bottai and others to discuss their approach. Apparently, this meeting was an open secret, yet although Cavallero sent a message to Mussolini via Farinacci to warn Mussolini, he simply brushed the warning aside, saying he was aware of the opposition.[615] Such was Mussolini's self-confidence that he failed to see the ramifications, and was deceived when he saw the king, who assured him that he would always be his friend. Although Scorza had revealed Grandi's proposal demanding that Mussolini relinquish his powers to the king, Mussolini persisted in believing he would cope. Rachele had warned Mussolini that her son-in-law was a traitor, but as he knew she detested Ciano he ignored her.

A few days earlier, the king had agreed with the opposition and Badoglio had accepted the position of prime minister. Despite the warnings and advice, Mussolini decided he could weather the storm. It was apparent that he knew about the dissidents' plans, but there were other plots being hatched and he knew nothing about the military plan of the king and Ambrosio – which turned out to be the decisive danger.

Edda always claimed that Ciano had had no intentions of dislodging her father, and how much Ciano knew of the precise details of the plot can never be absolutely certain, but overall he appears to have been central to events; many claim that he was the 'leader of the plot', but this role appeared to fall to Grandi.[616] According to Castellano, Ciano knew of the contents even if he had not seen the draft's details.[617] It is generally understood that on 17 July Grandi and Ciano spent time with Bottai retouching the draft resolution, at which point Ciano agreed to the procedures, though he was uncertain that the Grand Council would be the best venue.[618]

When the meeting took place, in the Sala del Pappagallo,* many members took guns with them. Some, including Grandi, even carried hand grenades, and armed agents were secreted around the premises. Mussolini started with a two-hour speech, indicating that he was aware of the plot by pointing out that the Allies were at war against Italy the country, not with the fascists.[619] Ciano's speech was more an attack on the Germans than on Mussolini; it was cleverly constructed and presented in a 'quiet and measured' way.[620] Ciano stated that it was necessary to resist the Allies – failing, however, to state the obvious, that without the detested Germans the Italians would lose. Ciano emphasised that the Germans had violated the pact, they had betrayed the Duce, and had too frequently 'lit the fuse' ahead of time and without consulting Mussolini. The 'loyalty Italy had given Germany', Ciano said, was 'never returned'. Some observed Mussolini's anger

---

*   Parrot Room

when Ciano disclosed the German lack of trust in Mussolini as Italy's leader. Farinacci introduced a resolution which called for fidelity to the Axis and for the military power to be given to the king with Mussolini retaining the political role. Ciano supported this, saying it was not an admission of defeat to hand the powers to the king. Grandi's speech was full of compliments for Mussolini, almost fawning, but made the same point. Bastianini spoke of the schism developing between the party and the nation, but Mussolini suddenly intervened, stating that 'the origin of the fracture can perhaps be found in certain rapid enrichments of some personality', with Alfieri noting that he looked directly at his son-in-law as he blamed the rupture on senior fascist leaders.[621] Bottai made the last speech, in which he appealed to those who might have been wavering.

When it came to signatures, some suggested that because of familial relations Ciano need not sign, but he insisted on patriotic grounds, and the final vote was 19 for the resolution, 8 against it, and 1 abstention. Following the meeting, many of the delegates must have wondered what would happen next, and if there had been anxiety before the meeting it became nervous tension afterwards. Mussolini left with Scorza, undoubtedly with *et tu Brute* in his mind, and Ciano took Bottai in his car. This whole voting procedure could not have happened in Germany or Russia at that time, and 'it seems somewhat unfascist of the Council even to call a vote, and even more unfascist of Mussolini to take any note of its democratic will', which news he took to the king (whom he used to call 'the little sardine').[622]

The next day Anfuso was convinced that Ciano would be arrested too, and he offered him sanctuary in his own residence. Ciano decided against the offer until he realised his telephone lines had been cut, then swiftly accepted. On the way to Anfuso's house they called on Grandi and heard disconcerting news; the Duce had arrived in his Alfa Romeo expecting his usual chat with the king and heard comforting words from the monarch, but had then been arrested and driven away in an ambulance. Mussolini had had no idea about the monarchical-military plot, and it might be the case that the king was the key component by recognising the significance of two coups, the fascist and royal one.

According to some accounts Ciano was surprised, because his involvement had been in the Grand Council not the king's rooms. It has been suggested that even without the political decision the king would have arrested Mussolini; others argue that the arrest gave the monarch a constitutional opportunity. Although it can only be speculation, it cannot be denied that the political vote probably gave the king the necessary courage. It immediately dawned on Ciano that he might very soon be in the same position, because the king's action had become an attack on fascism. If Edda were correct in her memoirs, Ciano might have recalled Anfuso's warning that 'any motion hostile to Il Duce's policies would have grave consequences'.[623]

In the words of General Westphal 'fascism had been laid like a ghost within a few hours'. It would return in a temporary form, neo-fascism, but Westphal was basically correct.[624] This was somewhat echoed by Churchill in a speech to the House of Commons when he referred to Mussolini as a principal criminal whose downfall caused 'the keystone of the fascist arch to crumble ... and broke the spell which in Italy held these masses for so long ... the guilt and folly of Mussolini have cost the Italian people dear', but for the time being, he told the Commons, 'they [the Italians] must stew in their own juice'.[625]

When Himmler conveyed the news to Hitler he was in conference, and told those present he had 'always known Ciano as a charlatan', that as foreign minister he 'had run brothels', and that Edda was 'a slut', with SS officers being assigned 'for her maintenance'. He then instructed Himmler to find out whether Mussolini was still alive and where he 'was holed up'.[626] Many of those present claimed later that Hitler was in deep distress and virtually threw a tantrum.[627] He ordered two operations: Eiche, which concerned the rescue of Mussolini, and Student, for the restoration of fascism in Italy.[628]

THE FLIGHT

Much has been written, in varying and often contradictory accounts, on Ciano's final year, so I have made an effort to be brief, for two reasons: the first, to try and keep to the known facts, and the second, that although his final months took some bizarre twists and turns Ciano's relevance in terms of Italian history evaporates. As soon as the Badoglio government took charge martial law was imposed: some 81 people were shot, a further 320 were wounded, and some 850 arrested.[629] Badoglio's new government wanted peace, but had to tread with care to avoid a total German occupation, and so attempted to impose an iron grip on the Italian people.

Ciano soon realised that he had become an embarrassing liability to the new government, and he had helped oust Mussolini without having a safety line for himself. Grandi had been given a passport by the Badoglio administration to travel to Spain and then Lisbon; it was anticipated that with his diplomatic background he could seek peace feelers through Samuel Hoare. He knew better, however, and fled to Brazil, not returning to Italy until the 1960s. By the first week of August the Nazis knew the purpose behind Grandi's proposed visit to the Iberian peninsula, confirming Hitler's deep distrust of Badoglio.[630] Bottai, meanwhile, sought refuge in a Vatican monastery, and Muti, who had warned Ciano to leave Rome, was killed at his home. These events must have rung serious warning bells to Ciano.

It prompted him, too, to reflect on the safety of his family as he returned home at three in the morning. On the way he witnessed crowds of people celebrating the collapse of fascism. It must have crossed his mind that for years he had misread the popular mind, always thinking Mussolini was admired and himself loved. He had, however, helped light a fuse with results which, like others, had not been incorporated into his calculations.

In her memoirs Edda stated that Grandi had never been trusted, and that none of the conspirators realised they were betraying Mussolini.[631] Grandi was regarded as the elder statesman with his knowledge of foreign affairs, and it was the 'misfortunes of the Axis alliance' which had brought 'Ciano remorselessly into line with Grandi's own appreciation of Italy's external position', which eventuated in their co-conspiracy but no intimate friendship.[632] However, there is little doubt that although Ciano was part of the plot he failed to forecast the possible outcomes. Throughout her memoirs Edda held the belief that the dissidents had no intention of disposing of her father but merely of changing the emphasis in fascist rule, whitewashing her husband's role.[633] It turned out, however, that there could be no halfway measures, because after Mussolini's arrest the internal revolt opened the door for the destruction of fascism.

At the end of July Ciano resigned as ambassador to the Vatican. The king had initially suggested he stay on, and whether the king reneged or whether Ciano thought it better to resign is difficult to establish from the varied accounts. He was, in any case, promptly placed under house arrest. The Vatican even refused him and his family sanctuary, which was unusual, and it has been suggested that this was because of Badoglio's advice or possibly the demands of the Allies.[634] The latter was unlikely, though, because at this stage the Allies, preoccupied with military matters, knew little of these events and were probably not that interested. They were of course aware, as was Badoglio, that in the first week of August the Germans, without the permission of the Italian Supreme Command, had sent nine divisions into Italy.[635]

During August the press declared Ciano a public disgrace, because it was known he had opposed the war, had helped create the Greek disaster, and had enriched himself; this last point would become the principal focus of criticism. Ciano felt alienated from what he believed had been an adoring public, and he felt anger about the way he was being treated. He decided that that his family had to leave the country for Spain or Argentina. Edda, despite their colourful past, now became the devoted wife and turned against her father – but now that he had lost power, it dawned on her she too was vulnerable. No car came for her or the family, so she was obliged to take the train to Rome, when she and the children witnessed the public hatred towards the fascist regime and especially her father, and thereby Ciano. She was aware that the outcome was serious, and noted that even Ciano's father's memorials were being torn down.[636]

A Milan newspaper published a scathing article on Costanzo's wealth, accrued while he had been in authority. Ciano protested to Badoglio and received no reply. The silence indicated Ciano's isolation. In her memoirs Edda protested that Ciano had never made any money from his position of power, not even claiming expenses – all part of her whitewash effort.[637] But in fact, even when Ciano had been in office the Italian secret service had gathered a dossier on his accumulation of wealth.[638] He owned nearly 100 apartments in Rome, with properties elsewhere, and undeniably had plenty of valuables and money. The Badoglio government, out of self-justification, then demanded an inquiry into the way the leading fascists had enriched themselves.

Life was appearing hazardous to Ciano, and he, having decided to leave the country, pondered whether to ask for German assistance. This clearly indicates how he tended to lack judgement, based on his sense of self-importance, and many tried to dissuade him. Edda, with her well-known pro-German attitudes, believed she was admired in Germany and made contact with the SS Chief Dollmann, who met her but handed the arrangements on to his subordinate, Kappler.[639] Ciano knew that the Germans suspected him of being a traitor, but was still prepared to put himself 'right in the mouth of the German lion', hoping that the Germans liked Edda.[640]

By 11 August a meeting had been agreed and a Lieutenant-Colonel Wilhelm Höttl became involved.* On 27 August Edda and the children slipped away from under house arrest, and Ciano took another car; they were taken by truck to an awaiting aircraft. They believed that the destination was to have been Spain, and in her memoirs Edda said they became disturbed as they realised the plane was flying north and not west. The Germans later insisted that Munich had been agreed on, and the truth remains elusive. They were greeted at Munich by Dollmann, and Höttl took them to a store where they restocked their wardrobe, as they had brought only some valuables and money. They felt some comfort when photographs were taken for false passports; Ciano was shown with a moustache and glasses, and given the identity of an Argentinian of Italian birth. This was probably part of a German ruse arising from a possible suggestion by Ciano to Höttl that on arrival in Spain he would hand over his papers.[641]

Ciano never seems to have learnt; he confided in Höttl that his diaries would compromise Ribbentrop. His trust in his hitherto enemies defies belief, and unsurprisingly this information was passed on to Kaltenbrunner, then third chief of the Reich Security Main Office, and to Himmler, who wanted Ribbentrop's fall

---

* Höttl had been in Italy under Himmler's instructions from the time when Hitler, out of respect for Mussolini, did not want the SS there. It was Höttl who had been behind the reports on Italy's and Mussolini's decline, and the conspiracy group of Ciano, Grandi and Bottai.

and took an active interest in Ciano's diary. Edda was more aware, realising that Himmler would be in pursuit of the diaries.[642] Goebbels in his notes wrote that Ciano had put himself in danger by letting the Germans know of the diaries, and he would have to be kept in custody. As a direct consequence of this information Höttl brought in a female SS major, Hildegard Burkhardt Beetz, who was an excellent Italian speaker and whose husband was a pilot on the Russian front. She thought Ciano was 'vain and frivolous,' but she began to like him.[643] Ciano recognised her as a pretty female cunningly placed there to keep an eye on him, but the female–male connection eventually turned against the Germans.

During the end days of August Edda insisted on seeing Hitler as, knowing his penchant for beautiful women, she hoped to use her charm; although many tried to dissuade her, she was successful and became a guest in Hitler's railway carriage. Paul Schmidt wrote that Hitler 'remained obdurate on the question of Ciano and his wife going to Spain. "I fear you would only have unpleasantness there … you are better off with us in Germany".' This cost Ciano his life.'[644] Edda, however, lacked tact, challenging Hitler on his views that the war could be won and making him furious. Her brother Vittorio was present, and told Edda she was no diplomat. She then made a further blunder by asking if the 6 million lire they had brought with them could be exchanged for pesetas. (It was a *faux pas* because it assumed that they would go to Spain despite Hitler's objections to the idea, so for the Führer it was a demeaning request.) But then on 1 September Hitler gave her some orchids for her birthday, and she wrongly assumed that she and Ciano were safe, as Hitler's personal guests.

In the meantime, the worried Ribbentrop told Kaltenbrunner that Ciano would 'create a stink' if allowed abroad, which alone would have aroused Himmler's interest.[645] Edda had hoped her visit would release them or at least give them protection, but when Major Beetz saw Ciano in the first week of September she found a changed man; he was feeling down because it had dawned on him that he was a prisoner. Edda wrote in her memoirs that their treatment was poor, describing how a defrocked priest called Otto, who was now an SS guard, had killed Marzio's cat.[646]

On 12 September Ciano heard that Mussolini had been liberated – in the well-known daring rescue by Otto Skorzeny from where he had been held in the ski resort of Campo Imperatore in Gran Sasso, high in the Apennines – and that he was now in Germany. This occurred four days after the Allies attack on Salerno and the surrender of Italy. It has been claimed that when Hitler met Mussolini Hitler had suggested that the traitors, Ciano in particular, should be executed.[647] It has also been recorded that at this stage of events Mussolini defended Ciano against Hitler's views.[648] Edda demanded to see her father and eventually overcame

German resistance; according to various accounts they were both shocked at one another's appearance (which is not surprising, given their ordeals). A few days later Ciano was permitted to meet Mussolini at his temporary residence near Hirschberg, and apparently the meeting went well. Anfuso wrote that Mussolini never accused Ciano of betraying him, 'but he had put himself in the midst of people without scruples'.[649] Speculatively it was more likely that Mussolini, who was always fond of Edda, was keeping the family peace. Ciano told Mussolini that he was prepared to do anything, including returning to the air force, as they dined as a family under these bizarre circumstances. Goebbels in his diary reflected on the family relationships, wondering who wielded the influence; it was certainly a dysfunctional family.

By the end of September Ciano became anxious about his diaries, which he had entrusted to various family members and friends, and he persuaded Edda to collect them, which would be no easy task under the watchful eye of the Germans. Edda rose to the occasion, however, with some strength of character. She manipulated the procurement of an *Ausweis* (identity card for travel) in the name of Santos, which was difficult because the Germans kept all visitors under strict surveillance, and on 27 September took a train to Italy.[650] The day after she left, Kaltenbrunner arrived and moved the family to the castle of Waldbickel, but Mussolini himself was missing because the Germans had returned him to Italy to establish his puppet state. Ciano remained a prisoner in the Oberallmannshausen as a supposed government guest.

Edda's mission during October was not straightforward, and her accounts are dramatic, perhaps too much so. Her first port of call was her Uncle Gino's residence near Lucca, where Ciano's mother Carolina was staying. Gino had buried the documents – he had been seen doing so by a mystery person who dug them up – but following a bribe they were returned. The critical files, known as the German Files, as they related to Ribbentrop, were in Rome, where Edda then headed. Having succeeded in retrieving them she met her father Mussolini at Rocca della Caminate, where he was staying; he was immediately concerned that her nerves were at breaking point and arranged for her to enter a clinic at Ramiola, near Parma, run by the Melocchi brothers, under her false name. It was not that secret, however, because her ex-lover Lieutenant Emilio Pucci came looking for her as she recovered. In the meantime, Ciano had let Anfuso (now Mussolini's ambassador in Berlin, for what that was worth) know that he wanted to return to Italy.

PRISON

Höttl arrived on 17 October to inform Ciano that he was to be returned to

Happier days, in 1935; Pavolini leaning against a plane, with (probably) Ciano.
(Storia illustrate)

Italy, but Ciano knew that he was being returned as a prisoner, not a pilot. Höttl was somewhat embarrassed, as he was reneging on previous promises, but behind this move was the hand of Alessandro Pavolini, the secretary of the Fascist Republican Party; even Edda was aware of his intentions.[651] Pavolini had risen to his position because of his early friendship with Ciano, and he was later known for his ruthlessness in the deployment of the Black Brigades, which even the SS officer Dollmann condemned as too brutal. Ciano was permitted to bid farewell to his children and on 19 October was taken by military plane to Verona. The minute he stepped onto Italian soil he was arrested, and he must have understood his only hope was Mussolini, even though he was under German control and politically limited. Mussolini had become the epitome of the puppet, reacting to the string-pullers who were the German overseers, with a few strings tugged by the extreme fascist elements who now dominated proceedings. Italy was now known as the Republic of Saló, a mere reflection of Mussolini's earlier dreams, but the Germans had basically imprisoned him in their own fiefdom, where he was guarded and monitored. Hassell, deep in Germany, heard that Mussolini was powerless, and was even 'prevailed upon to have himself photographed at chess, a game he did not play, in the act of checkmating the opponent'.[652] Mussolini seemed to descend into a state of listlessness and would 'rouse himself from a lethargic somnolence only for his mistress' living just up the road.[653]

Ciano was taken to the Scalzi prison, an ex-Carmelite monastery in Verona, and given the prison number of 11902. He was deprived of his money and valuables but allowed to keep a religious icon with a family photograph. Major Beetz saw Edda and informed her of what had happened. On 21 October Edda went to the Villa Feltrinelli, by Lake Garda, to see her father. He assured her that although Ciano's trial would take place he would arrange the outcome – but times had changed; as it turned out there was no substance in this offer. The German official who had let Edda in was reprimanded; clearly, Mussolini was a prisoner in a luxurious cell.

The persuasive Edda gained access to the Verona prison, telling the provincial chief that she had Mussolini's permission to visit Ciano. When she pretended to kiss him goodbye she managed to whisper in his ear that the diaries had been safely recovered. She then gathered that such future visits would be banned, while Mussolini instructed his son Vittorio to keep an eye on his sister. Vittorio was technically Mussolini's liaison officer with Hitler, and this gave him some access to higher officials. Whether Vittorio suggested he retrieve Ciano's children or Edda asked him to do so varies in the different accounts, but he went to Berlin while it was being bombed, and failed. Edda remonstrated with him, and he became more astute on his next visit. He travelled to Munich, claiming that Mussolini wanted his family with him in Italy, and this time proved successful.

In late October Major Beetz went to Scalzi prison and gained access to Ciano, as she claimed, probably correctly, that she had been ordered to discover the whereabouts of the diaries. From various accounts it seems that Ciano and Beetz became good friends, playing cards and chess, and reading together. Apart from this friendship Ciano was tightly monitored most of the time, though it was claimed he could buy better meals from outside the prison, which may have been possible with some bribery from access to his confiscated money.

Edda concluded that the Germans seemed to know everything she said to her father, but whether he was confiding in his German overseers or his rooms were bugged is difficult to establish. She realised this when she once told Mussolini that it would be easy to help Ciano escape, and the next day Ciano was suddenly put into solitary confinement with two permanent SS guards, and was no longer allowed to exercise in the yard. Some of the other Grand Council dissidents – Giovanni Marinelli, Tullio Cianetti, Luciano Gottardie and Carlo Pareschi – who had voted against Mussolini were then moved Scalzi, indicating that the trial was being prepared, but most realised that Ciano was the major target. Most of the others who had voted had fled; as Edda observed out of the 19 members of the Council who had supported Grandi's motion only 6 had been arrested.[654]

On 9 November Goebbels wrote in his diary that 'those in the know are certain Mussolini will not allow Ciano to be killed', but it is more likely that Mussolini was resigned to the fact, knowing he could not control the Germans, or indeed the extreme fascists.[655] Ciano, suffering from the cold in the prison cell, probably had no idea how unpopular he was; at a Fascist Party conference in Verona on 14 November, those attending chanted for his death. His case was not helped when the newspaper *Corriere della Sera* published an article implying that he had associated with a shipowner – which indeed he had, over newspaper finances. He denied this in an article in response.[656]

Life in the prison was, hardly surprisingly, unpleasant. Ciano heard that a lifelong friend of his had been incarcerated there as well, because he had once passed on a message for Ciano, but he had not attended the Grand Council meetings. Major Beetz arranged a secret meeting for the two of them in the toilets. Edda managed a visit on 27 November, then complained to her father that whenever she met with her husband, they were attended by a Reich member, a Fascist Party member, and a prison representative.

Having met her father on the first day of December, it dawned on her there was nothing she could do, because he was controlled by the Germans, or he had decided he was not going to tarnish his name further, given the reaction of the anti-Ciano sentiments at the Verona meeting. She and Pucci decided that under the circumstances the children should escape to Switzerland, which was not an easy task.[657] In the clinic they warned the children of possible adventures, but avoided the details in case the rooms were bugged. The children's Christian names were changed to Spanish, with the surname Santos, matching Edda's. To bribe the Alpine guides Edda sacrificed some of her priceless jewellery, including the wedding brooch given her by the royal family in happier times, and Pucci led the children north to the border, where Swiss police were expecting members of the Aosta family. The plan worked, and Pucci was able to report back on 12 December that the children were safe.

Two days later the Examining Magistrate Vincenzo Cersosimo met Ciano and presented the charges of treachery against the State.* Ciano was furious at the accusation and made his objections abundantly obvious. He asked why Major Beetz was there, which given their friendship must have seemed a strange request; it has been suggested, however, probably correctly, that Ciano raised this issue to undermine the gossip that they were lovers.[658] (After the war Major Beetz would deny this rumour, claiming she loved her Luftwaffe husband, but nevertheless admitting she had grown to like Ciano; she was in fact an unlikely SS officer, as she exhibited compassion towards Ciano and took many personal risks on his behalf.) Ciano also protested to Cersosimo that he had spent most of his time in his Livorno home and was not involved in any plotting, and he had had no

---

* Cersosimo was arrested post war, but benefited from the Togliatti Amnesty and in 1949 published a memoir on the Verona trial.

idea that supporting Grandi would lead to Mussolini's downfall. Throughout her post-war memoirs Edda persistently made the same point. His defence, however, whether true or not and whether flawed or not, would never stand in a court which was clearly politically motivated, especially in view of the reputation he had gained over the past few years.

On 17 December Edda wrote to Ciano explaining that she was having considerable difficulty in persuading the authorities to give permission for her visits. The next day she confronted her father in a turbulent meeting during which she attacked him on many issues. As in her meeting with Hitler, she lacked tact and achieved nothing. When she stormed out, Mussolini ordered that she had to be watched, and reinforced his order that Ciano had to be kept segregated.[659] Mussolini was now totally subservient to the Germans, who, Edda recalled, had convinced Mussolini that they would win the war, having shown him the production of the V1 and V2 rockets.[660]

On 23 December she made another effort, bringing Christmas presents, but was refused entry. At least her gifts were passed on to Ciano, as he wrote and thanked her. It was clear that despite the years of their open marriage they had managed to stay affectionate, and Edda would stand by him to the end. On Christmas Eve, it was claimed that three drunken armed German officers accompanied by three prostitutes stormed into his cell to ridicule him and when discovered they were instantly demoted.[661] The prison chaplain, Don Giuseppe Chiot, insisted he hold a mass on Christmas day, but unlike with the other prisoners was not permitted to visit Ciano; he was only allowed to officiate from the corridor with the cell doors open.

Ciano wrote letters to the Italian king and Churchill, adding an introduction to his diary (in the English editions it is a final note) which had one theme throughout, namely that he was not responsible for the war. It can only be speculated that these letters were entrusted to Major Beetz, who secreted them to Edda. It is believed that Edda sent them to her brother-in-law Massimo Magistrati (by then the Italian minister in Bern), who managed to organise their transmission or postage.[662] Churchill introduced Ciano's letter into his post-war history with the telling words 'my account of this Italian tragedy may fittingly be closed here by the letter which the unlucky Ciano wrote me shortly before his execution at the orders of his father-in-law'.[663] In his own style Churchill summarised the situation from his perspective.

Meanwhile, there was another subplot during these tumultuous weeks, which has proved difficult to detail accurately because of the secrecy and the differing accounts. It was a curious operation, which the military historian Richard Lamb described as 'so melodramatic as to be worthy of Hollywood'.[664] On 27 December

Edda and Pucci planned to flee to Switzerland; before their departure Edda wrote letters to SS officer Harster,* Hitler and her father.† Edda and Pucci left for Como, but paused in Verona to meet the trusted Major Beetz, who surprised them by suggesting they delay escaping because she had plans to save Ciano's life. She had warned her superior, Harster, of the dangers if Ciano's diaries fell into Allied hands. No Germans knew where the diaries were – some thought the Vatican, others that Serrano Suñer held them – and Beetz played a risky game by letting Kaltenbrunner think they were in Switzerland. There followed, according to many accounts, a barter consisting of an exchange of the documents in return for Ciano's life, and Himmler and Kaltenbrunner established Operation Conte to take possession of Ciano's papers – significantly, and suspiciously bravely of Himmler, behind Hitler's back. The plan was for the papers to be given to the Germans and Ciano's escape made to look like an Italian effort. Harster, through Beetz, managed to obtain Ciano's agreement to the plan, but they needed proof of Ciano's goodwill by being given access to some of the documents first.

The Conte operation was set out in four stages: the first demanded that Ciano reveal the whereabouts of his papers; secondly he would be sprung from his cell; thirdly, when he was safe in Switzerland he would hand over the diaries to Beetz; and finally she would give them to Harster.[665] This was all planned around Ciano's springing from prison on 7 January – his trial had been set for the next day – and his two SS guards, Krutsch and Guck, would be told to appear as if they had been overcome.

It might seem difficult to fathom why Ciano should have trusted the Germans, as it must have been obvious to him that once they had got the documents they could easily have him shot. However, the arrangement provided at least a chance for him; he knew he was otherwise facing a death sentence for sure, and no doubt hoped that once in Switzerland he could disappear.

Edda, who according to many authorities was on the edge of nervous collapse, was instructed to collect and hand over the file entitled Conversation Files (mere Italian meetings) but the crucially important German Files had to find their way into Allied hands. She fell ill, and Pucci went in her place, accompanied by Germans, through a snowstorm. He took the Conversation Files, somehow managing to hide the German Files in his uniform, and on 6 January Beetz gave the Conversation Files to Harster.

Despite her nerves Beetz then set off to meet Ciano at the appointed spot after his escape from Scalzi, but when no car turned up as anticipated she was

---

* Harster had been a senior SS officer in the Netherlands seeking out Jews, and had arrived in Verona under orders to establish a headquarters there.

† These letters are reproduced in Smyth, Howard McGaw, *Secrets of the Fascist Era* (Illinois: Southern Illinois University Press, 1975) pp.44–45

obliged to hide in a freezing ditch. She managed to find her way back to Verona and met Harster, who explained that the operation had been called off. What happened next remains somewhat obscure. It has been suggested that Ribbentrop had heard of the plot and told Hitler, who phoned Harster directly; Hitler then dressed Himmler and Kaltenbrunner down. However, Höttl later suggested that the more likely reason was that Himmler suddenly got cold feet. Despite the varying evidence it seems reasonably certain that Hitler was aware of Conte and phoned Harster.[666]

The Germans had mysteriously asked for a delay in the trial, but Pavolini, wondering why, told Mussolini. He, however, said that the trial must go ahead for 'public reasons'. Hence the subtitle of this book.

Mussolini's secretary, Giovanni Dolfin, when he heard of the consequent inevitability of Ciano's trial, wrote 'no intervention can now halt the course of events. Ciano is already dead ... whoever voted for Grandi's order of the day will be condemned'.[667]

In the meantime, Pucci warned Edda that they had to escape while they had time. Edda wrote an interesting account, as far as it can be trusted, of the escape; she eventually made it into Switzerland despite Kaltenbrunner's order that she had to be closely watched during her residence in the clinic.

If Pucci had thought about the situation more realistically he would have escaped with her; later he was arrested and badly tortured, suffering a fractured skull. The Germans then abruptly stopped the torture, possibly because of Beetz's suggestion that if Pucci were permitted to cross into Switzerland he could persuade Edda not to go public with the diaries, or perhaps because they realised that Pucci was worthless if dead. He was smuggled north across the border and Beetz followed, under the guise of being technically attached to some German mission.

The Germans were, of course, not the only ones interested in the diaries. Mussolini was concerned that they should not fall into German hands, which would cause him embarrassment. He was aware that his own documents might already be in Hitler's hands, and when it was discovered that Edda had escaped from Italy Mussolini sent Vittorio in (fruitless, as it turned out) pursuit of her. After some months had passed the Swiss would virtually make Edda a prisoner as she was something of an embarrassment to them, first because of who she was, and later because of her behaviour.

The whole story, especially the part written by Edda, sounds overly dramatic, but this account has only dwelt on the known facts, which hopefully reflect the reality. There is a degree of irony that Emilio Pucci, Edda's one-time long-term lover, now a friend of the family, nearly died in his efforts to help Ciano and Edda with their family, and it took a friendly female SS officer to enable the family's escape to happen.*

TRIAL AND EXECUTION

The trial was eventually set for 11 January 1944 in the ancient Veronese fortress of Castelvecchio, and Mussolini demanded that Justice Piero Pisenti examine the prosecution case against Ciano. Pisenti reported that there was no substance to the charge of treason, which angered Mussolini, who retorted that judicial matters were of less importance than political demands, thereby denying the priority of jurisprudential principles; everyone knew it was a political trial. The Germans informed Mussolini that it was an Italian affair; although many histories refer to a German trial, this is only because of the Germans' vested interests. The trial was basically conducted by the extreme fascists who now ruled the roost and probably wanted to please Hitler. The German Ambassador Rahn said that he would have preferred the trial not to take place because he felt that it would unsettle Italian life based on family loyalty, but Hitler insisted it was 'exclusively Italian'.[668]

It was the word 'treason' which infuriated Ciano, making him prone to outbursts of anger, and prompting Cianetti to threaten him because his aggressive attitude put them all in danger. The trial was technically open to the public, but the court was filled with Italian fascist blackshirts often shouting 'death to the traitors', and some curious Germans. A huge fascist emblem with a crucifix formed the backdrop to the proceedings. The defendants were seated on broken chairs to accentuate their degraded position, but Ciano as always, appeared dressed as if attending an important social occasion; his appearance was a matter of personal pride. He had asked for a leading lawyer, Luigi Perego, to represent him, but he claimed health issues to avoid the embarrassment of refusing, as did some others, and Ciano had to accept the court's nomination of Paolo Tommasini, who was generally agreed to be mediocre and from the legal point of view made frequent blunders.

The day before the trial Marshal Emilio De Bono, by then aged 77, and who had been with Mussolini from the beginning, was called as the first defendant. He set the tone for the defendants, arguing that in supporting Grandi's proposal he had had no intention of eliminating Mussolini but hoped to unite Italians under the crown to fight the enemy. All the other defendants followed this line of defence. As the prime culprit, Ciano was the last to be cross-examined, in the late afternoon. He was clearly angry both at the accusation and at having to defend himself in court. He explained that had Mussolini sought his advice he would

---

* Emilio Pucci stayed in Switzerland until after the war; in the latter half of the 20th century he meddled in politics. He died in Florence in 1992.

have suggested not holding a Grand Council in the first place, as the concept lacked prudence, and he only wanted to 'engage the crown'. The prosecutor asked why he had failed to contact Mussolini, to which Ciano replied that since he had ceased being foreign minister he no longer had any serious contact with the Duce. Judge Franz Pagliani (in the Italian system there were nine judges, who could fire questions at the defendant) asked Ciano why he had not tried to help Mussolini, to which Ciano responded that he had been under house arrest with his telephone line cut. It is generally agreed that the prosecution was weak and it had no witnesses – but as this was a political trial legal principles were irrelevant. The main arguments focused on Mussolini, who had warned the dissidents that they would create a crisis but they had still gone ahead and voted. The prosecution then asked why if they had been so innocent 13 of the 19 voters had fled, and finally why did Cianetti repent and write an apology to the Duce.[669]

Judge Enrico Vezzalini posed two more questions to the defendants: the first as to why they had turned towards what he referred to as the disinterested monarchy in the first place; and second, why the holders of the Collar of the Annunciation, namely Ciano and De Bono, had not intervened with the monarchy after the arrest.[*] Ciano replied that the appeal to the monarchy was an effort to bring the king 'down from his cloud', and that even as a holder of the collar he had had no contacts with the monarchy. The main case for the prosecution claimed that the moral order of the country had been shattered and that the defendants, in destroying the Duce, had only been interested in themselves. Judge Vecchini raised some judicial questions which on the surface gave the defendants a sense of hope (false, as it turned out) that they might evade conviction. Vecchini was evidently being Machiavellian, because he was one of the judges who was adamant for the death penalty, and as the defendants left the court room they heard from the guards that the execution squad was already assembled. There was also the ominous rumour that if the accused were acquitted the lawyers for the defence would be in danger.

It transpired that not all the judges agreed that all the defendants should be executed: a Judge Montagne had some support in this proposal, and the last judge, Giovanni Riggio, was undecided. When Montagne continued to argue for not executing everyone, Vezzalini stated that the only decision they had to make was who was shot in the back and who in the face,[†] and he accused the doubters of betraying fascism. In the end only Cianetti was spared, though many of the votes were on a five-to-four decision margin. But Ciano's death penalty was voted

---

[*] The collar made the nominee a cousin to the king, supposedly giving unlimited access to the royal palace.
[†] The Italian tradition was that traitors were shot in the back.

unanimously. Vecchini read out the judgments, pausing at Ciano's to accuse him of being more interested in saving himself than Mussolini.

Mussolini heard the news that afternoon, but before he had been returned to Italy he had already divided the dissidents into three groups: the traitors, the accomplices and the ignorant.[670] It would appear from different accounts that it was a fluid list, because at one moment Ciano appeared safe, being promised a return to the air force, and the next Mussolini was claiming that he had documentary evidence that Ciano was a traitor. Ciano had often criticised Mussolini for vacillating, and now this insight was proving deeply personal.

Back in the prison Ciano tried to give some comfort to Benini, who was in a state of collapse. Ciano wrote farewell letters to his mother and to Edda, which Beetz made sure were delivered, and she stayed with him to the end. The prison commander came around with forms to apply for a pardon. Ciano refused to sign, but Cianetti persuaded him otherwise on the grounds that his refusal might endanger the others. Ciano from his cell told the passing prison Chaplain Don Chiot that he wanted to 'die a Catholic', but his two SS guards, Guck and Krutsch, would not permit him to leave his cell for a mass. Beetz went above their heads to gain permission.

Ciano informed the surprised Benini he had no intention of being shot because he had some cyanide, but Benini begged him not to kill himself because the pardons might be granted. Ciano agreed but then went ahead with the potion; but it did not work. As with Göring later in Nuremberg, no one is entirely sure as to how the poison found its way into the prison. Edda in her memoirs claimed she managed this, as did Beetz, or perhaps it was a joint arrangement; either way it failed.[671] When Benini heard of the failure he reproached Ciano for going against his word. Ciano was happier, as at Don Chiot's final service he gathered that Edda was safe in Switzerland – news probably leaked by Dr Olas, the prison governor. They then heard that there was a cabinet meeting taking place, and their spirits rose as they hoped their pardons were being discussed; but Ciano must have realised that even if pardons were being considered he was an unlikely candidate for one.

Outside the prison the question as to who should sign a pardon was being debated; no one wanted the responsibility, and it was decided not to ask Mussolini. Pavolini, Ciano's erstwhile friend, was against any pardon, and won the day. He managed to browbeat Vianini, the lowly local commander of the Fascist Militia, into signing the rejection slip.[672]

In the meantime, according to one historian, Mussolini had phoned SS General Karl Wolff asking what the Führer was thinking, and also asking whether a 'failure to execute could harm me in the consideration of the Führer', to which Wolff had replied, 'Yes, very much so.'[673] This conversation was apparently recorded by the secret service, and if it is a true account it underlines Mussolini's acceptance of Hitler's total dominance. Mussolini had given way 'to his own overwhelming desire for revenge, or to ingratiate himself with Hitler', and even with the benefit of hindsight it is impossible to know the final reasons for his actions.[674]

As the condemned Ciano and his colleagues started to leave their cells Ciano was angry, but Don Chiot managed to calm him, Ciano then responding 'I die without rancour'.[675] They were taken to the firing range at the Forte San Procolo and seated on old wooden chairs with their backs to the firing squad. Ciano refused a blindfold, remained calm, and was caught on a camera turning at the last moment to stare at the squad. Bosworth, Mussolini's biographer, wrote 'as a camera whirred to record the deaths for a gratified public, Ciano swivelled to face his executioners more worthy in this last gesture than he had been in most of his life's actions.'[676] There are many speculations as to his final act; whether it was to demonstrate he was not a traitor, or a show of defiance, or an act of contempt are all questions which can never be answered. It may well be that it was a mixture of all these possibilities. The shooting was not an effective procedure, and although Ciano was hit by five bullets he still needed two pistol shots to end his agony; it was an execution carried out with 'horrible inefficiency'. He died on 11 January 1944, aged 40.[677]

When Mussolini, asking about Ciano's demeanour, was told that Ciano had met death in the face, he apparently found this difficult to believe. From many accounts he was unhappy, concerned that he had not been approached about the pardon, and warned Pavolini and Vianini that they would answer to him. Edda later wrote that 'I believe it was done without my father having been informed of the hour of execution'.[678] The veracity of her claim will never be known, but the facts and timings indicate that Mussolini had put his hands in his pockets and waited for the inevitable result from his own regime, over which he had limited control. It would make Goebbels think again, because as his diaries record, he had thought it would never happen. Edda was informed of Ciano's death on 14 January, and in April his coffin was laid alongside those of his father and sister, as requested.

Concluding remarks

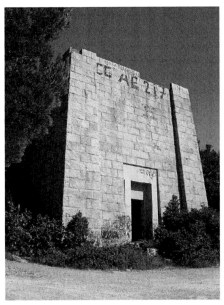

Livorno: the Ciano family mausoleum, left unfinished. (Etienni Li)

After Ciano's death Edda remained in Switzerland, still being watched carefully by the authorities, with the Germans wondering how they could confiscate the feared diaries, which Edda had offered to the British only to find they 'were completely negative' in response to her offer.[679] The Americans, however, discovered the implications of the diaries and following long negotiations with Dulles obtained Edda's copies. Although that in itself is an interesting saga it does not form part of this study.

Edda was unsettled and had to receive treatment for the symptoms of a nervous breakdown. Post war, she became an even greater embarrassment to the Swiss, who sent her back to Italy for a trial. She was sentenced to two years on the island of Lipari, where Mussolini had exiled political opponents. Rachele and her children were also exiled for a brief time, on the island of Ischia. Edda moved around the world and died on 11 April 1995.

Sadly, the Ciano family had all the hallmarks of being dysfunctional (Marzio died from excessive drinking in 1974), and there is no need for further detail. In sum, the family came from horrendous circumstances, rose to social importance, then descended to hopeless prisoners: a father who was executed as a traitor, and a grandfather who had ordered this to happen and who was himself humiliated and killed by fellow Italians. It would be a classic case for a modern social psychologist.

As for Ciano, there are no memorials to him, and from historians there are mixed messages. He was 'perceived to be a nepotistic parvenu. Ciano's attachment to the dictator was familial rather than political, or rather the familial became political. Aspiring to be the man who succeeded Mussolini'.[680] He has also been described as 'the resolutely cynical Count Galeazzo Ciano'.[681] Bottai socialised with Ciano during the war years, and wrote that 'he came to like him although he was well aware not only of Ciano's slick intelligence, but also of his superficiality and love of attention and the perks which came with high office, that deadly mix of laziness and ambition blighting Ciano as a man and politician'.[682] Ciano was indiscreet and an intriguer, and knew the latest political gossip; he adopted his father's habit of accumulating personal wealth and funds. He 'was vain and giddy, utterly charmed with himself, his own importance and success'.[683] His American biographer described him as having 'political amorality coupled with vaulting ambition', but later added that 'beneath the swagger and the pomposity there was a decent human being struggling to come out'.[684] Ciano was a mass of contradictions in both his lifestyle and his professional life.

From his privileged position Ciano has provided historians with considerable insight into these important historical years, not least because he was there in person, meeting the major players as decisions were made. He was close to Mussolini, and although this book is not a biography of Mussolini, Ciano's diaries provided many incisive insights into the Duce's mind and the events of the day. Often overlooked in the literature is the curious relationship between Mussolini and Hitler, which Ciano had so carefully noted. Hitler had initially admired Mussolini, yet within a few short years their relative positions reversed within the blink of an eye, Hitler becoming the dominant partner and Mussolini his puppet. Ciano's diary and papers outline why Mussolini fell from power: in them he appeared as a person obsessed with a sense of self-importance, seeking glory for Italy and himself as the great warrior chief. He was not as barbaric or evil as

Hitler, but he sought imperial glory and a place on the world stage in his futile pursuit of power. To achieve this end, he pandered to the developing military power of Germany. He soon, however, regretted this as he came to fear Nazi power; but he nevertheless persisted, against advice, to remain loyal to the Nazi tyranny even though he knew the Nazis distrusted the Italians (mere 'macaroni') at all levels. In searching for glory, he had made himself commander-in-chief of the armed forces, but with no military experience at this level his leadership was disastrous: he was unable to find competent commanders, he knew that Italy lacked the critical resources for a major war, and he failed to comprehend the potential power of the Allies. Furthermore, he had no control over Italy's failing economy. This picture clearly emerges from Ciano's writings, as he bitterly (and correctly) described Mussolini's 'see-sawing' state of mind, his unsettled domestic life with its consequent pressures, and his fatal weaknesses.

Ciano, who had had some initial affection for his father-in-law, became his critic, realising late in the day that Mussolini was becoming unpopular yet without realising that he was himself in the same situation. Ciano believed himself astute, but on the home front he lacked the necessary ability to survive the turbulent Italian politics of the day. In his early days he may have played with the idea he was Mussolini's natural successor, but later he failed to realise that Mussolini's decline was taking him towards the same abyss.

Many critics enjoy painting a popular picture of Ciano's personal lack of moral standards, his widely known sexual exploits, his dubious accumulation of wealth, his love of gossip, his showing off, his imitation of the Duce, and his often haughty disposition. Such issues are almost unavoidable, and they prompt the famous adage 'let him who is without sin cast the first stone'. Ciano was a man of his Italian times, and he had, as an inexperienced youth, been placed in a position of considerable influence on the international stage. His marriage, like that of many others, was far removed from the ideal, but to the very end he and his wife remained together despite their myriads of lovers. Ciano's love of golf and the reports of his vibrant lifestyle at a social level raises a question as to whether any of us might have enjoyed his company. Nevertheless, he remains a somewhat enigmatic if not perplexing character. Despite his personal moral behaviour, and despite Mussolini's atheistic views on the Church, it is apparent that Ciano retained some residual Christian faith – even if it did, like that of so many Christians, appear somewhat hypocritical. His anti-Semitic views appeared to have been related more to social snobbery of the English golf club than to the racially biological evil of the Nazi regime. For Ciano, and probably for Mussolini too, the Jewish question was more of a political matter than what turned out to be the attempted liquidation of a race.

This is not an apologia for Ciano but rather a matter of historical perspective. In diplomatic discussion he confessed in his diary that he was condescending and arrogant towards less significant people, while with the more important, especially the British and Americans, he was more congenial; although there were times when he could stand up to Hitler he could also be intimidated by the Führer. These observations could be categorised as all too human, but because of his position in life he is more open to criticism.

Ciano did grow up, possibly somewhat late, and was prone to go with the tide, 'see-sawing' himself as the circumstances changed. However, from the time of the German invasion of Poland, his earlier distaste for Germans was transformed into a deep distrust. He stood up to Ribbentrop, despised Himmler and Göring, and painted pictures of these men which were close to the truth. In his final diary note a few days before his execution he wrote: 'During the period of Italian neutrality and during the war, the policy of Berlin toward Italy was nothing but a web of lies, intrigue, and deceit. We were never treated like partners, but always as slaves. Every move took place without our knowledge; even the most fundamental decisions were communicated to us after they had been carried out. Only Mussolini in his supreme cowardice could, without reaction, tolerate this and pretend not to see it'.[685]

He was of course hypocritical insofar as he had promoted the invasion of Albania and encouraged the war against Greece without notifying the Germans beforehand, but back in 1939 he had had the foresight to understand that the German conflict in Poland would not be a localised affair. He had also realised that Italy could not win the war, and that Germany would eventually lose it, too. He perceived this, as did Franco eventually, whereas Mussolini, who had been told about the 'wonder-weapons' in Germany, persisted, against all the odds, in believing in a Nazi victory. Ciano, having recognised that Italy could not win the war, sent out peace feelers behind Mussolini's back; he, like others such as Grandi, realised that Mussolini would not seek a peaceful solution and hoped that the British might negotiate with them, representing as they did a milder form of fascism than Mussolini's.

He was wrong in his evaluations, but at least he recognised Italy's impossible situation. He had hoped for the best but his perceptions, hence his manipulations, were all flawed, and none of his hopes were realised. He was realistic enough to reflect that 'victory had a hundred fathers', later adding 'defeat is an orphan'.[686] It was indeed Ciano who coined this famous expression, though it is often accredited to President John F Kennedy.

As with most human beings, there are no easy conclusions about Ciano, and it is tempting to recall Shakespeare's Macbeth that 'life's but a walking shadow, a poor player that struts and frets his hour upon the stage and then is heard no more. It is a tale told by an idiot, full of sound and fury, signifying nothing'. Ciano as a politician, a diplomat, a person, achieved little; but he did leave a significant record of the years 1934–1944 in Italy – albeit one, like himself, flawed.

APPENDICES

HISTORIOGRAPHY

An Italian historian once told me that in his opinion Italian historiography, when seen in the clearer light of hindsight, will always betray that the writers were influenced by the politics of their day. And of course every country tries to interpret its own past in the best possible light, be it the victor, the defeated, the oppressor, the victim, the belligerent or the neutral. In this sense many histories have a nationalistic blend, but the best history is that which attempts to be as objective as possible, which may be regarded by the more cynical as impossible because historians are human.

I asked an Italian historian with whom I work as to how far Italian histories have been affected by the politics of the day. He replied, 'Italian historiography is much more politicised than others because in most cases, academic and related careers depend upon political support.' The frequent Italian political swings have often reflected the interpretations of the Italian past. There have been serious debates over Mussolini's partnership with Hitler, war crimes, colonialism, whether fascism was the same as Nazism, the partisan war, and so on. These interpretations of the past have had long-term ramifications.

Over a long period one of Italy's best-known historians, Renzo De Felice, produced many volumes on Mussolini and fascism which, depending on his readers' political positions, were either praised or treated with scepticism. His major work was a gigantic series of volumes, at times inconsistent, on Mussolini, published between 1965 and 1997. The initial volumes were less contentious because they dealt with Mussolini's early years, but the later volumes sparked a historical debate. De Felice set the cat among the pigeons when he argued that fascism's central support was the growing middle class, portraying Mussolini as creating a new Italy by presenting an alternative to communism and capitalism. De Felice argued that it was this which brought Mussolini success from a receptive population.

The common criticism was that De Felice's shone a favourable light onto Mussolini. Many historians had regarded the years prior to the Ethiopian conquest as the best of the fascist period, but De Felice took it further, claiming that under Mussolini there was a genuine consensus of fascism among Italians. In the post-war era these arguments were deeply controversial, not least because it was maintained that during these years there had been considerable hostility towards the fascists, especially after the Ethiopian War and the Race Legislation.

Every time De Felice produced a new history there were considerable debates as he appeared to touch sensitive political nerves; as Bosworth has pointed out, an anti-fascist consensus had prevailed in Italian political life since the end of the World War II.[687] In the mid-1970s there were prolific arguments over De Felice's work, but it was generally conceded that fascism had established some form of consensus. This was a contentious area, comparable to the work of German historian Bartov when he exposed the Wehrmacht's participation in massacres. France under de Gaulle rewrote its account of these fraught years, like all countries justifying their past, but Italy's fascist system, aligning with Nazi Germany, had led to defeat and civil war and so has remained a sensitive issue.

At the historical level De Felice was often criticised for painting Mussolini as an original thinker, which most people could not accept. De Felice was also accused, along with many biographers, of over-favouring his subject and giving him the benefit of too many doubts. De Felice's work was key to the historical debate, challenging the nature of Mussolini, whether he was a modernising politician with new revolutionary ideas for a better Italy, or a Machiavellian seeking the best way forward to avoid confrontations: the great mediator or a 'Sawdust Caesar'.*

The argument, sharpened by the post-war Italian politics, was whether the national identity should be based on anti-fascist readings of the past, and this debate continues. The complicity with Nazism has supported the anti-fascist position, especially during the period when the communists were influential in Italy, but the well-known neo-conservative Silvio Berlusconi has claimed that this attitude destructively changed the Italian regard of their past and alienated them from republican principles.

During the 1930s the anti-fascist elements across Europe and elsewhere were hostile to Mussolini, referring to him as a gangster, a clown, a tyrant and a Sawdust Caesar. Some, such as Chamberlain and even Churchill, had hoped at

---

*   It was a 1936 book by American journalist George Seldes which put the epithet 'Sawdust Caesar' into circulation.

one point that they could work with him, but the irruption of Hitler on the scene swiftly toned down these sympathetic circles. The 'dominant image of Mussolini as an international statesman partook of the broader discourse of derision', and opinion remained divided and changing.[688] Many regarded Mussolini as a man whose actions were controlled by events, some proposing that it was the fear of Germany which had motivated the Pact of Steel; but even this explanation still makes Mussolini something of a lightweight.

Mussolini's reputation found support from the far right wing, including Luigi Viallari (1876–1959), a historian, journalist, and diplomat. He built Mussolini up as a staunch anti-communist, and pointed out that the greatest barbarities came from the communist partisans and the invaders. Viallari argued that Mussolini had simply tried to correct and change the misdeeds of the Versailles Treaty, and it had been the British and French failure to be constructive with Italy that had unleashed Hitler. As the historian Finney noted, Viallari's main argument was that once war broke out Mussolini had struggled manfully in the cause of peace, but his hand was ultimately forced 'because Italy was being strangled economically by the unneutral economic actions of Britain' – the same British who had been responsible for 'tricking Italy's ally Hitler, into war in September 1939'.[689]

Many major historians made derogatory remarks about Mussolini; for example, A J P Taylor stated in 1961 that 'everything about fascism was a fraud', and Mussolini was 'a vain blundering boaster without either ideas or aims'.[690] Alan Cassels regarded fascism as a betrayal of many of Italy's glorious traditions, and the general feeling was that Mussolini was indeed a mere Sawdust Caesar.

However, as the 1960s progressed these views were regarded as oversimplified, and a more nuanced and sophisticated approach was demanded. A serious study exploring collective memory started to be drawn up, and a new focus examined the shifting ideological landscapes; but anti-fascism remained at the centre of the debate. The anti-fascist historians exposed the murderous aspects of the regime, but there were others who, while not trying to exonerate fascism, argued that Mussolini's time was not just a black hole. Some acknowledged that he had often wanted action and was always restless; others, such as Giorgio Rumi, posited that Mussolini had definite goals, including revisionist views and the overturn of some established orders.

With De Felice and other historians normalising Mussolini and setting him in an acceptable background, there came a vigorous counterblow from the historian Denis Mack Smith, who specialised in Italian history of this period. He made a study of many its aspects, including a biography of Mussolini, portraying him as a 'serial bungler' who steered Italy towards imperialism and wars.[691] This did not sit well with De Felice's Mussolini, but it is curious that in 1996 Mack Smith was named 'Grand Official of the Order of Merit of the Italian Republic'. De Felice in the 1970s tended to be the focal point of acceptance and Mack Smith was regarded as offering more sarcasm than serious analysis.

By the mid-1990s, with the fiftieth anniversaries of liberation and resistance, Italy's fascist past became more evident. De Felice had turned the communist resistance upside down from previous versions, treating it as a group of ideologically driven individuals. He died in 1996, but his legacy of the 'anti-anti-Fascism' approach remains, thereby giving to the study of Italian history two distinct schools of thought; neither have been renounced. Berlusconi decided to commemorate victims of atrocity, and instituted a national 'Day of Memory on 10 February 2005 – solemnly intoning that in this instance we cannot and should not forget [that] the victims concerned were (non-Jewish) Italians, killed by communist partisans around Trieste'.[692] It was seemingly impossible for non-Italian historians not to become entangled in a world of a thousand bits and pieces of contrary evidence. Richard Overy regarded political realism as Mussolini's driving force, and Richard Lamb attacked British politicians for not taking Mussolini seriously enough in his attempt to restore diplomatic normality after the Ethiopian war. One of Mussolini's biographers, Nicholas Farrell, opined that Mussolini was a great man who failed and was not evil, and in that opinion seemed to follow De Felice's line of thinking.[693] Some believe that Farrell was trying to normalise Mussolini and fascism, as with De Felice's work.

On the other hand, the American historian MacGregor Knox in 1982 drew the opposite picture, where fascism meant war and where Mussolini utilised force both internally and abroad.[694] It was a study welcomed by those from the left wing. Anglo-American history tended to side with Knox (not comprehensively) focusing on the co-belligerency with Hitler, which had always been Mussolini's choice. During the 20th century Italian history has a huge ambit of interpretation, but it is often believed that De Felice and Knox came to be associated with the two ends of the spectrum. There are those who waver, and some who, like Bosworth, actively seek a midway form of scholarship.

Jan Ifversen wrote that 'historians were certainly active in the post-war debate on Europe … some chose the nostalgic path of saving an inheritance from the ruins … others criticised the revival of past unity and inheritance. They opted, rather, for a new European history, which would recognize the new conditions after 1945'.[695] This issue has befuddled Italy.

Every country involved in the last global war has created its own explanations by drawing on common myths, reinterpreting evidence, looking back either for justification or in sorrow and pain or humiliation or with a sense of exaggerated victory – but always with the principal purpose of building a portrait to assist its current-day politics. Most countries still endure this process, but it strikes me that it is more contentious in Italy than most other countries. As Patrick Finney wrote, 'the issue of whether Fascism should be an object of unceasing critical meditation, a component of a positive national heritage or merely a fading element in an anodyne past remains of urgent relevance', not just because of the past, but because of the ramifications for the future.[696]

CIANO'S DIARY AT NUREMBERG

In January 1944 American diplomats in Switzerland became aware of Ciano's diary when they heard of Edda's entry into that country. Edda had 'strapped five volumes of Ciano's diary about her body when she escaped from Italy', and Dulles personally negotiated for their possession, recognising they would be valuable in the forthcoming prosecution of Ribbentrop, and ensured they made their way to the US chief prosecutor, Justice Robert Jackson.[697]

There were of course immediate suspicions as to the authenticity of the diaries, but they were generally accepted as providing some genuine insights into the enemy mind, especially when supported by other sources, and were utilised by the prosecution against Ribbentrop, who was using the defence of forgetfulness (which Ciano would have relished).

Ribbentrop challenged the diaries as forgeries, but 'he might have noticed in all the months he sat in court that any document submitted had to be accompanied by a certificate of its source and authenticity'.[698] Later, a few historians who had a degree of sympathy for the Nazi regime claimed they were forgeries, especially the infamous David Irving who quoted Dollmann, who on being interviewed said he believed that some of the diary writings had been revised. However, Dollmann in his own memoirs occasionally quoted the diaries, admitting they provided some accurate insights.[699]

'The diaries provided direct support for the prosecution's claim that this defendant [Ribbentrop] had been actively involved at the diplomatic level in knowingly preparing the grounds for waging aggressive war.'[700] 'Maxwell-Fyfe referred to the somewhat pessimistic statement by Count Ciano as portraying Ribbentrop's actions and orientation in a far more realistic, if less positive, light than appears from the official record in rebutting Ribbentrop's claims that he thought it possible to end the conflict.'[701] In a court case Ciano's more graphic way of expressing his thoughts and insights would certainly have been more persuasive than the mundane minutes of meetings.

Ciano's diary was used to rebut Ribbentrop's claim that he was not responsible for Nazi foreign policy and was only obeying Hitler's orders. 'The judges shared Ciano's view that Ribbentrop's actions demonstrated that he must have known perfectly well that Hitler's view of diplomacy was a prelude to and instrument for war, and that he had been appointed specifically to implement the aggressive nature of Hitler's actions.'[702]

Undoubtedly Ribbentrop was guilty, and Ciano's diary outlined his character and intentions, but although Ciano could have been indicted on a similar claim of causing a breakdown in European stability and peace, the case would not have been so clear-cut as that of Ribbentrop.

ANTISEMITISM IN ITALY

The Italian stereotype once claimed that 'the Italians were good people, the Germans, bad. Simple, straightforward, and complete nonsense, if what makes the Italians good is that they only burnt to the ground 500 Greek villages compared to the German total of 1,000'.[703] The belief that Italians were good people especially when compared with Germans has become a major identifying myth which is passionately defended through institutions and in the cinema.

When Mussolini published the Race Laws it was often depicted as a political move to pander to the Nazi regime; generally it was not acted on fully, it died a natural death, and it was not deemed to be part of the Italian historical landscape. The general impression is that for Mussolini it was not a biological but a political matter. The Italians in the post-war era made much of this when individuals showed that Jews were safer in Italian areas. Nevertheless, while it is generally accepted that the Italian form of anti-Semitism did not lead to dedicated extermination camps, it was rife and it was dangerous, and Mussolini's laws gave it unwelcome encouragement. The historian Patrick Bernhard wrote that 'Such sentiments led Italian authorities to pursue increasingly repressive policies against the Jews in North Africa. In order to prevent Jewish property speculation, the Italian governor general of Libya issued a decree prohibiting the transfer of land between Libyan Jews and *citizens of the Aryan race*, as Italians were officially called after racial laws were introduced'.[704]

Part of the Italian post-war recovery attempted to demonstrate that despite the anti-Semitic legislation most Italians played no part in supporting it, but would actually protect Jews. In the 1960s Hannah Arendt mentioned the humanity of an ancient, civilised people who rejected fascist anti-Semitic laws.[705] She intended to make a distinction between Italian fascism and German Nazism as two different ideologies, to demonstrate the singularity of Nazism, which had led to the extermination of so many Jews. Most Italian historians kept silent for a long time on issues concerning anti-Semitism and the occupied territories; other scholars led new research on this topic.[706]

Although there was a difference, as noted above, between Nazi anti-Semitism and the Italian version, the latter did develop, and 'it can hardly be described as aimless'.[707] When Mussolini passed the laws before the outbreak of World War II the text was composed entirely by Italians with an incoherent 'mixture of biological and scientific ideas … the objective of Italian racism was never the extermination of the Jews … it was intended to exclude Jews from the job market, to abolish their civic and political rights and to … eliminate them from national life'.[708] Many in the leading ranks of the Italian military regarded Jews as inferior, but unlike in Nazi Germany adverse public reactions to the legislation were more likely. In early 1943 Bismarck told Pietromarchi that all European Jews were to be exterminated, and later Ribbentrop raised the same issue with Mussolini. On the surface Mussolini appeared to accept deportation, but quietly informed General Mario Robotti not to hand over a single Jew. When in February 1943 the Germans in Greece informed the Italians that they would be deporting all Jews and suggested a similar policy in the Italian areas, Ciano wrote to Pellegrino Ghigi, the Italian plenipotentiary in Athens, asking him to arrange for 'Jewish elements' with Greek nationality in Italian-occupied territory to be sent to a concentration camp in the Ionian Islands – better than being deported to Nazi-held territory further north.

The belief that the Italians rescued Jews proliferated, in the hope of demonstrating that they (the Italians) were not German robots, but were humane. It was part of the effort to rebuild the country in the post-war years. However, there were serious crimes against humanity by the Italians in the occupied areas, especially in Ethiopia, while in the Balkans anti-Semitism was rife, which puts the post-war Italian myth to the test. However, there were differences between Italian fascism and Hitler's Nazi regime. The Germans had of course been indoctrinated to accept dictatorship, and as the German General von Senger und Etterlin wrote: 'in all its history this unfortunate German people had never been given the opportunity to appreciate democratic processes, or to act according to them', later in his memoirs noting his view that the Italians were more politically astute. Senger argued that the Italians had the monarchy and the Church, and 'morally fascism was not as tainted as the Nazi regime'.[709]

There are many views on this dichotomy of Nazism and Italian fascism, but although Italian anti-Semitism was morally corrupt, it never went to the extremes of Nazism – and, more to the point, individual Italians were still able to make their own on-the-spot decisions. Many were anti-Semitic and carried out barbarous acts, but there were more exceptions than in Nazi Germany. It was the exceptions which provided post-war Italy with the myth that the Jews were safe (which they were not; but they were safer than those under Nazi control).

BIBLIOGRAPHY

PRIMARY SOURCES

Ciano's Diary, Muggeridge M (Ed), *Ciano's Diary 1939–1943* (London: William Heinemann, 1947)

Ciano's Diary, (Ed) De Felice, Renzo, *Ciano's Diary 1937–1943* London: Phoenix Press, 2002)

Ciano Papers, (Ed) Muggeridge, *Ciano's Diplomatic Papers* (London: Odhams Press, 1948)

Daily Telegraph, 25 July 1935

Fuehrer Conferences on Naval Affairs 1939–1945 (London: Chatham Publishing, 1990)

German Collection, The German Foreign Office Archives, Mackensen telegrams

Hansard, HC Debate 31 January 1939, Vol 343 cc36–41

Kew National Archives, FO 954/13A/51

Kew National Archives, FO 954/13A/216

Kew National Archives, FO 954/13A/222

The Times, 1935 16 December

US Army Historical Division, *Mediterranean War Part V, Campaign in Italy Part II*, MS C-064, Generalfeldmarschall Albert Kesselring 1 May 1949 - 007732 ref: 007718

DIARIES AND MEMOIRS

Anfuso, Filippo, *Da Palazzo Venezia al lago di Garda* (Bologna, Cappelli, 1957)

Bottai, Giuseppe, (Ed) *Giordano Bruno Guerru, Diario 1935–1944* (Milan: Rizzoli, 1982)

Caviglia, Erio, *Diario* (Rome: Gherardo Casini, 1952)

Ciano, Edda, *My Truth* (New York: William Morrow, 1977)

Ciano, Fabrizio, *Quando il Nonno Fece Fucilare Papa* (Italy: Milan)

Colville, *The Fringes of Power* (London: Hodder and Stoughton, 1985)

De Felice, Renzo, *Storia degli ebrei italiani sotto il fascismo* (Turin: Franco Angeli, 1978)

Dollmann E, *The Interpreter* (London: Hutchinson, 1967)

Eden, A, The Rt. Hon. The Earl of Avon, *The Eden Memoirs, Facing the Dictators* (London: Cassell, 1962)

Goebbels, Josef, (Ed, Fred Taylor) *The Goebbels Diaries, 1939–1941* (London: Hamish

Hamilton, 1982)

Hassell, von Ulrich, *The Ulrich von Hassell Diaries, 1938–1944* (London: Frontline Books, 2011)

Kesselring, Albert, *The Memoirs of Field-Marshal Kesselring* (London: William Kimber, 1953)

Mussolini, Rachele, *La mia vita con Benito* (Milan: Arnoldo Mondadori, 1948)

Orwell, George, *Diaries* (London: Penguin, 2009)

Schellenberg, *Schellenberg* (London: Mayflower, 1965)

Schmidt, Paul, *Hitler's Interpreter* (Cheltenham: The History Press, 2016)

Senger, General Frido von Senger und Etterlin, *Neither Fear nor Hope* (London: Macdonald,1963)

Vassiltchikov, Marie, *Berlin Diaries, 1940–45* (London: Pimlico, 1999)

Westphal, General Siegfried, *The German Army in the West* (London: Cassell and Company, 1951)

Wiezsäcker, Ernst von, *Memoirs* (London: Gollancz, 1951)

Secondary sources

Arendt, Hannah, *Eichmann in Jerusalem. A Report on the Banality of Evil* (New York: Penguin, 1963)

Barbar, John, in Suny Ronald, *The Structure of Soviet History, Essays and Documents* (Oxford: OUP, 2014)

Bastianini, Giuseppe, *Uomini, cose fatti* (Milan: Vitagliano, 1959)

Beevor, Anthony, *The Second World War* (London: Weidenfeld & Nicolson, 2012)

Bernhard, Patrick, Behind the Battle Lines: Italian Atrocities and the Persecution of Arabs, Berbers, and Jews in North Africa during World War II, in *Holocaust and Genocide Studies* 26, No. 3 (Winter 2012): (425–446)

Bosworth, R J B, *Mussolini* (London: Hodder Arnold, 2002)

Bosworth, R J B, Italian Foreign Policy and Its Historiography in *Altro Polo: Intellectuals and Their Ideas in Contemporary Italy*, Richard Bosworth, and Gino Rizo, (eds) (Sydney,1983)

Brown, Anthony, *Bodyguard of Lies* (London: Allen, 1976)

Burgio, Alberto, *Nel nome della razza: Il razzismo nella storia d'Italia 1870–1945* (Bologna 1999)

Burleigh, Michael, *Moral Combat* (London: Harper Press, 2010)

Cassels, Alan, *Mussolini's Early Diplomacy* (Princeton: Princeton University Press, 1970)

Cervi, Mario, *The Hollow Legions* (London: Chatto and Windus, 1972)

Churchill, W S, *The Second World War* Vol. 2 (London: Cassell, 1949)

Davies, Norman, *No Simple Victory* (London: Viking, 2006)

Deakin, FW, *The Brutal Friendship: Mussolini, Hitler, and the Fall of Fascism* (London: Penguin Books, 1966)

Delzell, C (ed.), *Mediterranean Fascism, 1919–1945* (London, Macmillan, 1971)

Delzell, C, Benito Mussolini: a guide to the biographical literature, *Journal of Modern History*, vol. 35, no. 4, 1963

D'Este, Carlos, *Fatal Decision* (London: Fontana, 1992)

Di Rienzo, Eugenio, *Ciano* (Italy: Salerno Publishing, 2018)

Dolfin, Giovanni, *Con Mussolini nella tragedia* (Milan: Grazanti, 1949)

Eade, C, (compiler) *Onwards to Victory, Churchill's 1943 War Speeches* (London: Cassell & Company, 1944)

Eberle & Uhl, (Eds) *The Hitler Book* (London: John Murray, 2005)

Farrell, Nicholas, *Mussolini: A New Life* (London: Sharpe Books, 2018)

Finney, Patrick, *Remembering the Road to World War Two* (London: Routledge, 2011)

Fonds, Davide Rodogno, Italiani brava gente? Fascist Italy's Policy Toward the Jews in the Balkans, April 1941–July 1943 in *European History Quarterly Copyright* (Vol 35(2), 213–240.)

Forcardi, Filippo and Klinkhammer, Lutz, The question of Fascist Italy's war crimes: the construction of a self-acquitting myth (1943–1948), in *Journal of Modern Italian Studies*, (September 2004, pp.330–348)

Guerri, Giordano Bruno, *Galeazzo Ciano* (Milan: Bompiani, 1979)

Gun, Nerin, *Hitler's Mistress* (London: Frewin, 1968)

Höttl, Wilhelm, *The Secret Front* (London: Weidenfeld & Nicolson, 1953)

Ifversen, Jan, in (Spiering, Menno and Wintle, Michael, Eds) *European Identity and the Second World War* (London: Palgrave Macmillan, 2011)

Jackson, Julian, *France: The Dark Years 1940–44* (Oxford: OUP, 2003)

Judt, Tony, The Past is Another Country: Myth and Memory in Post-War Europe, in *Memory & Power in Post-War Europe. Studies in the Presence of the Past*, (Ed: Jan-Werner Müller) (Cambridge: CUP, 2002), pp. 157–183

Kirkpatrick, I, *Mussolini: Study of a Demagogue* (London, Odhams, 1964)

Knox, MacGregor, *Mussolini Unleashed, 1939–1941* (Cambridge: CUP, 2008)

Lamb, Richard, *War in Italy, 1943–1945* (London: Murray, 1993)

Liddell Hart, B H (Ed), *The Rommel Papers* (New York: De Capo Press, 1953)

Mack Smith, Denis, *Mussolini's Roman Empire* (London, Longman, 1976)

Mack Smith, Denis, *Mussolini* (London, Granada, 1983)

Malaparte, Curzio, *Kaputt* (Milan: Daria Guarnati, 1948)

Michel, Henri, (translated by D Parmée) *The Second World War* (London: Andre Deutsch, 1975)

Moradiellos, Enrique, *Franco: Anatomy of a Dictator* (London: I B Tauris, 2018)

Morgan, Philip, *The Fall of Mussolini* (Oxford: OUP, 2008)

Moseley, R, *Mussolini's Shadow, The Double Life of Count Galeazzo Ciano* (London: Yale University Press, 1999)

Overy, Richard, *The Road to War* (London, Macmillan, 1989)

Overy, Richard, *Goering* (New York: Barnes & Noble, 2003)

Packard, Reynolds and Eleanor, *Balcony Empire* (New York: Chatto and Windus, 1943)

Page, Giorgio Nelson, *L'americano di Roma* (Milan: Longanesi, 1950)

Paxton, Robert, *Vichy France* (New York: Columbia UP, 1972)

Picknett, Prince, Prior, Brydon, *War of the Windsors* (London: Mainstream, 2002)

Porch, Douglas, *Hitler's Mediterranean Gamble* (London: Cassell, 2005)

Preston, Paul, *Franco* (London: Fontana Press, 1995)

Rees, Laurence, *The Dark Charisma of Adolf Hitler* (London: Ebury Press, 2012)

Roberts, Andrew, *The Storm of War* (London: Allen Lane, 2009)

Salter, Michael, *Nazi War Crimes, US Intelligence & Selective Prosecution at Nuremberg* (Oxford: Routledge-Cavendish, 2007)

Salter, Michael and Charlesworth, Lorie, Ribbentrop and the Ciano Diaries at the Nuremberg Trial, in *Journal of International Justice* (Oxford: OUP, 2006)

Sangster, A and Battistelli P-P, *Myths, Amnesia and Reality in Military Conflicts, 1935–1945* (Newcastle: Cambridge Scholars, 2016)

Sangster, Andrew, *Probing the Enigma of Franco* (Newcastle: Cambridge Scholars, 2018)

Shirer, William, *The Third Reich* (London: Mandarin,1960)

Smyth, Howard McGaw, *Secrets of the Fascist Era* (Illinois: Southern Illinois University Press, 1975)

Susmel, Duilio, *La "vita sbagliata" di Galeazzo Ciano* (Milan: Aldo Palazzi, 1962)

Taylor, A J P, *The Origins of the Second World War* (London, Penguin, 1964,)

Toland, John, *Adolf Hitler* (Ware: Wandsworth Editions, 1997)

Tusa, Ann and John, *The Nuremberg Trial* (London: BBC Books, 1995)

Vergani, Orio, *Ciano, una lunga confessione* (Milan: Longanesi, 1974)

Villari, L, *The Liberation of Italy, 1943–1947* (Appleton, WI, Nelson, 1959)

Warner, Geoffrey, *Pierre Laval and the Eclipse of France* (London: Eyre & Spottiswoode, 1968)

Webster, Paul, *Pétain's Crime* (London: Pan Books, 2001)

Welles, Sumner, *The Time of Decision* (New York: Harper, 1944)

Weinberg, Gerhard, *A World at Arms* (Cambridge: CUP, 1994)

Werth, Alexander, *France 1940–1955* (London: Hale, 1956)

Zeiler, W Thomas, *Annihilation, A Global Military History of World War II* (Oxford: OUP, 2011)

OTHER SOURCES

WEBSITES

(A) For Ciano's visit to Warsaw see visual filming on: https://www.britishpathe.com/video/VLVADVLXSHCITFU35KN2U3SB9NW9S-POLAND-COUNT-CIANO-IN-WARSAW/query/Ciano

(B) For the king picking up rumours about Ciano and the Americans see: https://forum.termometropolitico.it/804808-giorgio-nelson-page-1906-1982-un-americano-nella-roma-fascista.html

(C) CIA-related: https://www.cia.gov/library/center-for-the-study-of-intelligence/kent-csi/vol13no2/pdf/v13i2a16p.pdf

BROADCASTING

BBC Radio Four Broadcast, *Great Lives*, 4.30 p.m. 4 August 2020

Endnotes

Preface

1   Farrell Nicholas, *Mussolini: A New Life* (London: Sharpe Books, 2018) p.322.

Introduction

2   Churchill W S, *The Second World War Vol. 2* (London: Cassell, 1949) p.548.

3   See Ciano's Diary, Muggeridge M (Ed), *Ciano's Diary 1939–1943* (London: William Heinemann,1947) p.viii.

4   See Ibid., p.xiv.

5   Ciano's Diary, Muggeridge, p.xii.

6   Ciano Fabrizio, *Quando il Nonno Fece Fucilare Papa* (Italy: Milan) pp.36–7.

7   Schmidt Paul, *Hitler's Interpreter* Cheltenham: The History Press, 2016) p.257.

8   Bosworth R J B, *Mussolini* (London: Hodder Arnold, 2002) pp.8–9.

9   Ciano Edda, *My Truth* (New York: William Morrow, 1977) p.51.

10   Goebbels Josef, (Ed, Fred Taylor) *The Goebbels Diaries, 1939–1941* (London: Hamish Hamilton, 1982) p.290.

11   BBC Radio Four Broadcast, *Great Lives*, 4.30 p.m. 4 August 2020.

12   Bosworth, *Mussolini*, p.208.

13   Ibid., p.321.

14   Mussolini Rachele, *La mia vita con Benito* (Milan: Arnoldo Mondadori, 1948) p.31.

15   Ciano Edda, *My Truth*, p.48.

16   Ibid., p.37.

17   Bosworth, *Mussolini*, p.264

18   Kesselring Albert, *The Memoirs of Field-Marshal Kesselring* (London: William Kimber, 1953) p.107.

19   Smyth, Howard McGaw, *Secrets of the Fascist Era* (Illinois: Southern Illinois University Press, 1975) p.24.

20   Bosworth, *Mussolini*, p.312.

21   Smyth, *Secrets*, p.19.

22   Ibid., pp.21–2.

Chapter 1

23   Deakin FW, *The Brutal Friendship, Mussolini, Hitler, and the Fall of Fascism* (London: Penguin Books, 1966) p.61.
24   Ciano Edda, *My Truth*, p.52.
25   Ibid., p.53.
26   Smyth, *Secrets*, p.20.
27   Moseley R, *Mussolini's Shadow, The Double Life of Count Galeazzo Ciano* (London: Yale University Press, 1999) p.9.
28   Picknett, Prince, Prior, Brydon, *War of the Windsors* (London: Mainstream, 2002) pp.96–7.
29   Ciano Edda, *My Truth*, p.53.
30   Moseley, *Mussolini's*. p.1.
31   Ciano Edda, *My Truth*, pp.62–3.
32   Moseley, *Mussolini's*, p.4.
33   Ciano Edda, *My Truth*, p.80.
34   Ibid., p.103.
35   Ibid.
36   Bosworth, *Mussolini*, p.152.
37   Ciano Edda, *My Truth*.
38   Bosworth, *Mussolini*, p.305.
39   See Farrell, *Mussolini*, p.324.
40   Bosworth, *Mussolini*, p.320.
41   Ibid., p.309.
42   Eden, A, The Rt. Hon. The Earl of Avon, *The Eden Memoirs, Facing the Dictators* (London: Cassell, 1962) pp.214–5.

Chapter 2

43   Bosworth, *Mussolini*, p.312.
44   Ciano Edda, *My Truth*, p.23.
45   Ibid., p.24.
46   Ciano Papers, (Ed) Muggeridge, *Ciano's Diplomatic Papers* (London: Odhams Press, 1948) p.9.
47   See Farrell, *Mussolini*, p.324.
48   Ciano Papers, p.4.
49   Bosworth, *Mussolini*, p.317.
50   See Eden, A, *The Eden*, pp.403–4.
51   Ibid., p.431.
52   See Ciano Edda, *My Truth*, p.119.
53   Ibid., p.125 and p.143.
54   Ciano Papers, p.47.
55   Burleigh Michael, *Moral Combat* (London: Harper Press, 2010) p.31.
56   Bosworth, *Mussolini*, p.326.

57   Ciano Papers, p.60.
58   Ibid., p.66.
59   Kew National Archives Ref: FO 954/13A/51.
60   Ibid.
61   See Moseley, *Mussolini's*, p.32.

CHAPTER 3

62   Kirkpatrick I, Mussolini, *Study of a Demagogue* (London, Odhams, 1964), p.318
63   Schmidt, *Hitler's*, p.75
64   Ciano Papers, p.93.
65   Ibid., p.103.
66   Ibid., p.123.
67   Sangster A and Battistelli P-P, *Myths, Amnesia and Reality in Military Conflicts, 1935–1945* (Newcastle: Cambridge Scholars, 2016) p.60.
68   Bosworth, *Mussolini*, p.318
69   Ciano's Diary, De Felice, p.1
70   Ibid.
71   Eden, *The Eden*, p.462.
72   Ciano's Diary, De Felice, p.5.
73   Ibid., p.6.
74   Ibid., p.10.
75   Finney Patrick, *Remembering the Road to World War Two* (London; Routledge, 2011) p.110.
76   See for example Delzell C (ed.), *Mediterranean Fascism, 1919–1945* (London, Macmillan, 1971) pp.202–5.
77   Ciano's Diary, De Felice, p.9.
78   Eden, *The Eden*, p.458.
79   Ciano Papers, p.137.
80   Ciano's Diary, De Felice, p.16.
81   Ibid., p.12.
82   See Eden, *The Eden*, p.474.
83   Ciano's Diary, De Felice, p.20.
84   Burleigh, *Moral*, p.11.
85   Ciano Papers, p.143.
86   Ciano's Diary, De Felice, p.23.
87   Ibid., p.22.
88   Ibid., p.33.
89   Eden, *The Eden*, p.449.
90   Moseley, *Mussolini's*, p.40.

CHAPTER 4

91   See Bosworth, *Mussolini*, p.299.
92   Ciano Papers, p.158.
93   Eden, *The Eden*, p.559 and see p.579 and p.573.

94   Kew National Archives, FO 954/13A/216.

95   Eden, *The Eden* p.598.

96   Wiezsäcker, Ernst von, *Memoirs* (London: Gollancz, 1951).

97   Ciano's Diary, De Felice, p.61.

98   Ibid., p.49.

99   Ibid., p.51.

100   Ibid., p.57.

101   Ciano Papers, p.171.

102   Ibid., p.183.

103   Ibid., p.184.

104   See Toland John, *Adolf Hitler* (Ware: Wandsworth Editions, 1997) p.453.

105   Ciano's Diary, De Felice, p.67.

106   Ciano Papers, p.197.

107   Ciano's Diary, De Felice, p.74.

108   Eden, *The Eden*, p.589.

109   Ciano Papers, p.202.

110   Ciano's Diary, De Felice, p.80.

111   Ibid., p.78.

112   Ibid., p.85

113   See Toland, *Adolf*, pp.460–62.

114   Ibid., p.461.

115   Ciano's Diary, De Felice, p.88.

116   See Schmidt, *Hitler's* p.93.

117   Toland, *Adolf*, p.462.

118   Schmidt, *Hitler's* p.94.

119   Ciano's Diary, De Felice, p.89.

120   Ibid., p.91.

121   Ibid., p.93.

122   Salter Michael, *Nazi War Crimes, US Intelligence & Selective Prosecution at Nuremberg* (Oxford: Routledge-Cavendish, 2007) pp.181–2.

123   Ciano's Diary, De Felice, p.104.

124   Ibid., p.100.

125   Ciano Papers, p.223.

126   Ibid., p.224.

127   Ciano's Diary, De Felice, p.113.

128   Ibid., p.107.

129   Bosworth, *Mussolini*, p.147.

130   Ibid., p.343.

131   Ciano's Diary, De Felice, p.125.

132   Bosworth R J B, *Mussolini*, p.344.

133   Ciano's Diary, De Felice, p.153.

134   Ciano Papers, p.230.

135   *The Times*, (7 September 1938) Leading Article.

136   Ciano's Diary, De Felice, p.122.

137   Moseley, *Mussolini's*, p.44.
138   Schmidt, *Hitler's*, p.122.
139   Ciano's Diary, De Felice, p.145.
140   See Ciano Papers, p.238.
141   Ibid., p.243.
142   Ciano's Diary, De Felice, p.157.
143   Ibid., p.166.
144   Ibid., p.166.
145   Ibid., p.163.
146   Ibid., p.168.

Chapter 5

147   See Ciano Papers, pp.258–9.
148   Ciano's Diary, De Felice, p.172.
149   Ibid., p.175.
150   See Ciano Papers, pp.259–66.
151   Ciano Papers, pp.267–272.
152   Ciano's Diary, De Felice, p.181.
153   Hassell, von Ulrich, *The Ulrich von Hassell Diaries, 1938–1944* (London: Frontline Books, 2011) p.27 and p.106.
154   Ciano's Diary, De Felice, p.191.
155   Ciano Papers, p.273.
156   See Website (A) in bibliography.
157   Susmel Duilio, *Vita shagliata di Galeazzo Ciano* (Milan: Aldo Palazzi, 1962) p.87.
158   Ciano's Diary, De Felice, p.198.
159   Bosworth, *Mussolini*, p.350.
160   Ciano's Diary, De Felice, p.200.
161   See Ciano Papers, pp.276–278.
162   Ibid., p.278.
163   Ciano's Diary, De Felice, p.204.
164   Ibid., p.206.
165   Ibid., p.209.
166   Finney, *Remembering*, p.111.
167   Ciano's Diary, De Felice, p.213.
168   See Moseley, *Mussolini's*, p.54.
169   Ciano Papers, pp.280–81.
170   Ciano's Diary, De Felice, p.218.
171   Guerri, Giordano Bruno, *Galeazzo Ciano* (Milan: Bompiani, 1979) p.389.
172   Moseley, *Mussolini's*, p.58.
173   Ciano Edda, *My Truth*, p.90.
174   Ibid., p.92 and p.86.
175   Schellenberg, *Schellenberg* (London: Mayflower, 1965) p16.
176   See Moseley, *Mussolini's*, p.60.
177   Ciano's Diary, De Felice, p.223.

178   Bosworth, *Mussolini*, p.351.
179   Ciano Papers, p.283.
180   Ibid., p.286.
181   Eden, *The Eden*, p.579.
182   Ciano's Diary, De Felice, p.228.
183   Ibid., p.226.
184   Ibid., p.234.
185   Colville, *The Fringes of Power* (London: Hodder and Stoughton, 1985) p.49.
186   Ibid., p.142.
187   Ciano Papers, p.287.
188   Ciano's Diary, De Felice, p.238.
189   Ibid., p.239.
190   Goebbels, p.373.
191   Ciano's Diary, De Felice, p.245.
192   Ciano Papers, p.287.
193   Moseley, *Mussolini's*, p.70.
194   Ciano's Diary, De Felice, p.250.
195   Ibid., p.250.
196   Ciano Papers, p.291.
197   Ibid., p.294.
198   Sangster Andrew, *Probing the Enigma of Franco* (Newcastle: Cambridge Scholars, 2018) p.181.
199   Ibid., p.250.
200   Quoted in Moseley, *Mussolini's*, p.69.
201   See Moseley, *Mussolini's*, p.70.
202   Ciano's Diary, De Felice, p.255.
203   Bosworth, *Mussolini*, p.354.
204   Ciano Papers, p.297.
205   Ciano's Diary, De Felice, p.257.
206   See Moseley, *Mussolini's*, p.74.
207   Toland, *Adolf*, p.538.
208   Bottai *Diario 1935–1944.*
209   Toland, *Adolf*, p.538.
210   Caviglia, Erio, *Diario* (Rome: Gherardo Casini, 1952) p.225.
211   Schmidt, *Hitler's*, p.136.
212   Ibid., p.137.
213   Ciano's Diary, De Felice, p.258.
214   Gun, Nerin, *Hitler's Mistress* (London: Frewin, 1968) pp.158–9.
215   Ciano's Diary, De Felice, p.258.
216   Susmel, *Vita*, pp.164–5.
217   Bosworth, *Mussolini*, p.354.
218   Ciano's Diary, De Felice, p.261.
219   Ibid., p.262.
220   Moseley, *Mussolini's*, p.86.

221   See Bottai, *Diario*, pp.154–6.
222   Ciano's Diary, De Felice, p.274.
223   Ibid., p.274.
224   See Bosworth, *Mussolini*, p.360.
225   Ciano's Diary, De Felice, p.280.
226   Ibid., p.284.
227   Schmidt, *Hitler's*, p.166.
228   Ibid., pp.166–7.
229   Susmel, *Vita*, p.182.
230   Ciano's Diary, De Felice, p.285.
231   Ibid., p.286.
232   See Bosworth, *Mussolini*, p.360.
233   Ciano's Diary, De Felice, p.290.
234   Goebbels, p.26.
235   Ibid., p.54.
236   Bosworth, *Mussolini*, p.14.
237   Ciano's Diary, De Felice, p.294.
238   Ibid., p.297.
239   Ibid., p.298.
240   Ibid., p.302.
241   Goebbels, p.66 and p.68.
242   Ciano's Diary, De Felice, p.303.
243   Ibid., p.305.
244   Ibid., p.307.
245   Colville, *The Fringes*, p.61.

CHAPTER 6

246   Ciano's Diary, De Felice, p.308.
247   Ibid., p.309.
248   Goebbels, p.88.
249   Ciano's Diary, De Felice, p.314.
250   Ibid., p.317.
251   Ciano's Diary, Muggeridge, p.ix.
252   Moseley, *Mussolini's*, p.91.
253   Ciano's Diary, De Felice, p.318.
254   Ibid., p.319.
255   Bosworth, *Mussolini*, p.364.
256   Ciano's Diary, De Felice, p.323.
257   Ciano's Diary, Muggeridge, p.viii.
258   Ibid., p.ix.
259   Ciano's Diary, De Felice, p.324.
260   See Moseley, *Mussolini's*, p.92.
261   Ciano Papers, p.340.
262   Ciano's Diary, De Felice, p.327.

263   See Bosworth, *Mussolini*, p.366.

264   Ciano Papers, p.343.

265   Ibid., p.346.

266   See Ibid., pp.339–359.

267   Westphal, General Siegfried, *The German Army in the West* (London: Cassell and Company,1951) p.102.

268   Ciano's Diary, De Felice, p.330.

269   Welles, Sumner, *The Time of Decision* (New York: Harper, 1944) pp.135–6.

270   See Ciano Papers, p.365.

271   Bosworth, *Mussolini*, p.365.

272   Ciano's Diary, De Felice, p.336.

273   Guerri, *Galeazzo*, p.456.

274   Ciano's Diary, De Felice, p.337.

275   Ibid., p.340.

276   Ibid., p.341.

277   See Susmel, *Vita*, p.202.

278   Ciano's Diary, De Felice, p.344.

279   Ibid., p.345.

280   Ibid., pp.345–6.

281   Ibid., p.346.

282   Overy, Richard, *Goering* (New York: Barnes & Noble, 2003) p.233.

283   Ciano's Diary, De Felice, p.349.

284   Ibid., p.350.

285   Michel Henri, (translated by D Parmée) *The Second World War* (London: Andre Deutsch, 1975) p.19.

286   Ciano's Diary, De Felice, p.351.

287   Ibid., p.352.

288   Ibid., p.353.

289   Quoted in Overy Richard, *The Road to War* (London, Macmillan, 1989) p.143.

290   Ciano's Diary, De Felice, p.354.

291   Bosworth, *Mussolini*, p.368.

292   Ciano's Diary, De Felice, p.356.

293   See Brown Anthony, *Bodyguard of Lies* (London: Allen, 1976) p.198 and Moseley, *Mussolini's*, p.99.

294   Fuehrer Conferences on Naval Affairs 1939–1945 (London: Chatham Publishing, 1990) p.79.

295   Zeiler W Thomas, *Annihilation, A Global Military History of World War II* (Oxford: OUP, 2011) p.88.

296   Shirer William, *The Third Reich* (London: Mandarin,1960) pp.741/2.

297   Ciano's Diary, Muggeridge, p.258.

298   Ciano's Diary, De Felice, p.358.

299   Ciano's Diary, Muggeridge, p.261.

300   Ciano's Diary, De Felice, p.361.

301   Bosworth, *Mussolini*, p.369.

302   Colville, *The Fringes*, p.176 and Orwell George, *Diaries* (London: Penguin, 2009) p.265.

303 See Moseley, *Mussolini's*, p.109.

304 Ciano's Diary, Muggeridge, p.263.

305 Beevor Anthony, *The Second World War* (London: Weidenfeld & Nicolson, 2012) p.147.

306 Ciano Papers, Muggeridge, p.373.

307 Schmidt, *Hitler's*, p.183.

308 Ciano's Diary, Muggeridge, p.267.

309 Ciano's Diary, De Felice, p.366.

310 See Moseley, *Mussolini's*, p.108.

311 See Bosworth, *Mussolini*, pp.370–1.

312 Ciano's Diary, De Felice, p.368.

313 Weinberg Gerhard, *A World at Arms* (Cambridge: CUP, 1994) p.145.

314 Bastianini, Giuseppe, *Uomini, cose fatti* (Milan: Vitagliano, 1959) pp:149–50.

315 Ciano's Diary, De Felice, p.369.

316 Vassiltchikov, Marie, *Berlin Diaries, 1940–45* (London: Pimlico, 1999) p.22.

317 Ciano Papers, p.376.

318 Ibid., p.377.

319 Ciano's Diary, De Felice, p.370.

320 Bosworth, *Mussolini*, p.372.

321 Ciano's Diary, De Felice, p.371.

322 Bottai, *Diario*, p.210.

323 Ciano's Diary, De Felice, p.372.

324 Ibid., p.374.

325 Ciano Papers, p.384.

326 Bosworth, *Mussolini*, p.373.

327 Hassell, *The Ulrich*, p.96.

328 Ciano's Diary, De Felice, p.376.

329 Ciano's Diary, Muggeridge, p.282.

330 See Ciano Papers, p.385.

331 Ibid., p.386.

332 Ciano's Diary, De Felice, p.378.

333 Ciano's Diary, Muggeridge, p.287.

334 Ibid., p.288.

335 Ciano's Diary, De Felice, p.384.

336 Ciano's Diary, Muggeridge, p.289.

337 Ibid., p.291.

338 Ciano's Diary, De Felice, p.383.

339 Ciano Papers, p.392.

340 Ibid., p.391.

341 Ciano's Diary, Muggeridge, p.292.

342 Ciano's Diary, De Felice, p.385.

343 Weinberg, *A World*, p.180.

344 Ciano's Diary, Muggeridge, p.295.

345 See Ciano Papers, p.395.

346 Ibid., p.398.

347   Ciano's Diary, Muggeridge, p.296.

348   Ibid., p.297.

349   Porch Douglas, *Hitler's Mediterranean Gamble* (London: Cassell, 2005) p.73.

350   Ciano's Diary, Muggeridge, p.300.

351   Roberts Andrew, *The Storm of War* (London: Allen Lane, 2009) p.113.

352   Moseley, *Mussolini's*, p.116.

353   Ibid., p.116.

354   Bastianini, *Uomini*, pp.257–8.

355   Farrell, *Mussolini*, pp.440–1.

356   Michel, *The Second*, p.186.

357   Ciano's Diary, Muggeridge, p.302.

358   Ciano Papers, p.405.

359   Ciano's Diary, Muggeridge, p.303.

360   Bottai, *Diario*, pp.229–30.

361   Ciano's Diary, De Felice, p.396.

362   Goebbels, p.173.

363   See Roberts, *The Storm*, p.124.

364   Ciano Papers, p.408.

365   Ibid., p.410.

366   Ciano's Diary, De Felice, p.397.

367   Ciano's Diary, Muggeridge, p.308.

368   Ibid., p.312.

369   Weinberg, *A World*, p.212.

370   Moseley, *Mussolini's*, p.119.

371   Ibid., p.120.

372   See Moseley, *Mussolini's*, p.62.

373   Bosworth, *Mussolini*, p.375.

374   Ciano's Diary, De Felice, p.401.

375   Ciano's Diary, Muggeridge, p.316.

376   See Roberts, *The Storm*, p.120.

377   Ibid., p.122.

378   Goebbels, pp.196, 198, & 200.

379   Ibid., pp.205 & 208.

380   Ciano's Diary, Muggeridge, p.316.

381   Ciano's Diary, De Felice, p.406.

382   Ciano's Diary, Muggeridge, p.317.

383   Ciano Papers, p.412.

384   Ciano Edda, *My Truth*, p.95.

385   Warner Geoffrey, *Pierre Laval and the Eclipse of France* (London: Eyre & Spottiswoode, 1968) p.213.

386   Ciano Papers, pp.411–412.

387   Bosworth, *Mussolini*, p.377.

388   Ibid., p.378.

389   Farrell, *Mussolini*, p.480.

CHAPTER 7

390 Ciano's Diary, De Felice, p.410.
391 Ibid., p.411.
392 Ibid., p.414.
393 Ibid., p.413.
394 Ciano Papers, p.419.
395 Ibid., p.417.
396 Malaparte, Curzio, *Kaputt* (Milan: Daria Guarnati, 1948) p.360.
397 Goebbels, p.231.
398 Ibid., p.233.
399 See Ciano Papers, p.410.
400 Ciano's Diary, De Felice, p.416.
401 Susmel, *Vita*, p.237.
402 Anfuso, Filippo, *Da Palazzo Venezia al lago di Garda* (Bologna, Cappelli, 1957) p.153.
403 See Moseley, *Mussolini's*, p.124.
404 Ciano Papers, p.422.
405 Ibid., p.421.
406 Ciano Edda, *My Truth*, p.69.
407 Quoted in Moseley, *Mussolini's*, p.125.
408 Ciano Papers, p.432.
409 Ibid., p.438.
410 Cervi, Mario, *The Hollow Legions* (London: Chatto and Windus, 1972) pp.303–5.
411 Ciano's Diary, De Felice, p.418.
412 Ciano Papers, p.439.
413 See Moseley, *Mussolini's*, p.127.
414 Ciano's Diary, De Felice, p.430.
415 Ibid., p.425.
416 Ibid., p.433.
417 Ibid., p.421.
418 Ibid., p.425.
419 Ibid., p.425.
420 See Ibid., p.424.
421 Ibid., p.424.
422 Ibid., p.429.
423 Ibid., p.430
424 See Moseley, *Mussolini's*, p.128 and Page, Giorgio Nelson, *L'americano di Roma* (Milan: Longanesi, 1950) pp.626–30.
425 Ciano's Diary, De Felice, pp.432–3.
426 Ciano Papers, p.446.
427 Barbar John in Suny Ronald, *The Structure of Soviet History, Essays and Documents* (Oxford: OUP, 2014) p.292.
428 Ciano's Diary, De Felice, p.438.
429 Ibid., p.439.
430 Bosworth, *Mussolini*, p.380.

431 Goebbels, p.422.
432 See Bottai, *Diario*, p.274.
433 Kew National Archives, FO 954/13A/222, September 20th 1941.
434 Ciano's Diary, De Felice, p.440.
435 Ibid., p.441.
436 Ibid., p.442.
437 Ibid., p.441.
438 Ibid., p.446.
439 Ibid., p.446.
440 Susmel, *Vita*, pp.243–4.
441 See Website (B) in bibliography.
442 Ciano's Diary, De Felice, p.444.
443 See Ciano Papers, pp.487–452.
444 Ciano's Diary, De Felice, p.447.
445 See Bottai, *Diario*, p.21 and Moseley, *Mussolini's*, p.133.
446 Ciano's Diary, De Felice, p.448.
447 Ibid., p.450.
448 Ciano Papers, p.453.
449 Farrell, *Mussolini*, p.469.
450 Ciano's Diary, De Felice, p.451.
451 Ibid., p.453.
452 Ibid., p.451.
453 Ibid., p.454.
454 Vergani Orio, *Ciano, una lunga confessione* (Milan: Longanesi, 1974) p.126 and quoted in Moseley, *Mussolini's*, p.134.
455 Ciano's Diary, De Felice, p.454.
456 Ibid., p.456.
457 Ibid., p.456.
458 Ibid., p.458.
459 Ibid., p.459.
460 See Moseley, *Mussolini's*, p.134.
461 Ciano Papers, p.454.
462 Moseley, *Mussolini's*, p.136.
463 Ciano Papers, p.459.
464 Ibid., p.456.
465 Ibid., p.457.
466 Ibid., p.459.
467 Ciano's Diary, De Felice, p.460.
468 Ibid., p.463.
469 Ibid., p.464.
470 Ibid., p.467.
471 Ibid., p.465.
472 Moseley, *Mussolini's*, p.139.
473 Ciano Papers, p.461.

474   Ibid., p.462.

475   Ibid., p.464.

476   Ciano's Diary, De Felice, p.472.

477   Ibid., p.477.

478   Ciano Papers, p.466.

479   Moseley, *Mussolini's*, p.138.

480   Ciano's Diary, De Felice, p.470.

481   Ibid., p.472.

482   See Paxton Robert, *Vichy France* (New York: Columbia UP, 1972) p.108.

483   Werth Alexander, *France 1940–1955* (London: Hale, 1956) p.79.

484   Jackson Julian, *France The Dark Years 1940–44* (Oxford: OUP, 2003) p.178.

485   Ciano Papers, p.469.

486   Ibid., p.471.

487   Moseley, *Mussolini's*, p.138.

488   Ciano's Diary, De Felice, p.473.

489   Packard, Reynolds and Eleanor, *Balcony Empire* (New York: Chatto and Windus, 1943) p.320.

490   Ciano's Diary, De Felice, p.473.

491   Ciano Papers, p.471.

492   Ciano's Diary, De Felice, p.480.

493   Ibid., p.474.

494   Ibid., p.490.

495   Ibid., p.393.

CHAPTER 8

496   Ciano's Diary, De Felice, p.481.

497   Bosworth, *Mussolini*, p.383.

498   Quoted in Bosworth, *Mussolini*, p.385.

499   Ciano's Diary, De Felice, p.483.

500   Ciano Papers, pp.477–8.

501   Ciano's Diary, De Felice, p.484.

502   Ibid., p.486.

503   Ibid., p.486.

504   Ibid., p.486.

505   See Bosworth, *Mussolini*, pp.387–8.

506   Ciano's Diary, De Felice, p.489.

507   Ibid., p.490.

508   Ibid.

509   Ibid., p.491.

510   Ciano Papers, February 17, p.480.

511   Ciano's Diary, De Felice, p.494.

512   Ibid., p.494.

513   Ibid., p.496.

514   Ibid., p.497.

515 Ibid.
516 Ibid., p.501.
517 Ibid., p.503.
518 Ibid., p.504.
519 See Moseley, *Mussolini's*, p.142.
520 See Susmel, *Vita*, p.254.
521 Ciano's Diary, De Felice, p.503.
522 Deakin, *The Brutal*, p.287.
523 Ciano's Diary, De Felice, p.507.
524 Ibid., p.510.
525 Ibid., p.511.
526 Ibid., p.514.
527 Ibid., p.512.
528 US Army Historical Division, *Mediterranean War Part V, campaign in Italy Part II*, MS C-064, Generalfeldmarschall Albert Kesselring 1 May 1949 -007732 ref: 007718.
529 Liddell Hart B H (Ed), *The Rommel Papers* (New York: De Capo Press, 1953 p.120.
530 Ciano's Diary, De Felice, p.515.
531 See Ciano Papers, p.481.
532 Ibid., p.483.
533 Ibid., p.484.
534 Moseley, *Mussolini's*, p.144.
535 Ciano's Diary, De Felice, p.515.
536 Goebbels' diary quoted in Moseley, *Mussolini's*, p.142.
537 See Moseley, *Mussolini's*, p.144.
538 Ciano's Diary, De Felice, p.518.
539 Ibid., p.519.
540 Ibid., p.521.
541 Ibid., p.523.
542 Ibid., p.531
543 Moseley, *Mussolini's*, p.145.
544 Ciano Edda, *My Truth*, p.183.
545 Susmel, *Vita*, p.26.
546 Ciano's Diary, De Felice, p.526.
547 Ibid., p.526.
548 Ibid., p.531.
549 Ibid., p.528.
550 Ibid., p.533.
551 Fuehrer Conferences, p.345.
552 Kesselring, *Memoirs*, p.107.
553 Senger, General Frido von Senger und Etterlin, *Neither Fear nor Hope* (London: Macdonald,1963) p.152.
554 Ciano's Diary, De Felice, p.540.
555 Ibid., p.541.
556 Quoted in Moseley, *Mussolini's*, p.147.

557 Ciano's Diary, De Felice, p.542.
558 Ibid., p.538.
559 See Moseley, *Mussolini's*, p.147.
560 Ciano's Diary, De Felice, p.546.
561 Beevor, *The Second*, p.375.
562 Ciano's Diary, De Felice, p.548.
563 Ibid., p.550.
564 Deakin, *The Brutal*, p.75.
565 Ciano's Diary, De Felice, p.554.
566 Deakin, *The Brutal*, p.59.
567 Ciano's Diary, De Felice, p.558.
568 Ibid., p.559.
569 Paxton, *Vichy* p.306.
570 Ciano's Diary, De Felice, p.565.
571 Ibid., p.567.
572 Moseley, *Mussolini's*, p.149.
573 Vergani, *Ciano*, p.192.
574 Ciano's Diary, De Felice, p.568.
575 See Deakin, *The Brutal*, p.122.
576 Ciano's Diary, De Felice, p.569.
577 Vergani, *Ciano*, p.228.
578 Michel, *The Second*, pp.512–3.
579 Hassell, *The Ulrich*, p.200.
580 Farrell, *Mussolini*, p.492.
581 Deakin, *The Brutal*, p.112.
582 Moseley, *Mussolini's*, p.151
583 Ibid.
584 See Deakin *The Brutal*, p.123.
585 Ibid., p.163.
586 De Felice, Renzo, *Storia degli ebrei italiani sotto il fascismo* (Turin: Franco Angeli, 1978) p.400.
587 Jackson, *France*, p.377.
588 Webster Paul, *Pétain's Crime*, (London: Pan Books, 2001) p.228.
589 Guerri, *Galeazzo*, p.325.
590 Moseley, *Mussolini's*, p.140.

CHAPTER 9

591 Farrell, *Mussolini*, p.485.
592 Ciano's Diary, De Felice, p.578.
593 Deakin, *The Brutal*, p.167.
594 Ciano's Diary, De Felice, p.587.
595 Westphal, *The German*, p.140.
596 Ibid., p.141.
597 Ciano Edda, *My Truth*, p.213.

598 Quoted in Moseley, *Mussolini's*, p.160.

599 German Collection, *Mackensen telegrams*, quoted in Deakin, *The Brutal*, p.172.

600 Porch, *Hitler's*, p.414.

601 German Collection, *Mackensen telegrams*, quoted in Deakin FW, *The Brutal,* p.396.

602 Ciano Edda, *My Truth*, p.184.

603 Moseley, *Mussolini's*, p.162.

604 Hassell, *The Ulrich*, p.186.

605 Burleigh, *Moral Combat*, p.533.

606 Anfuso, *Da Palazzo*, p.278.

607 Porch, *Hitler's*, p.492.

608 Smyth, *Secrets*, p.25.

609 Moseley, *Mussolini's*, p.164.

610 Found in Italian Archives and quoted by Moseley, *Mussolini's*, p.162.

611 Dollmann E, *The Interpreter* (London: Hutchinson, 1967) p.220.

612 Moseley, *Mussolini*, p.167.

613 Ciano Edda, *My Truth*, p.187.

614 Eade C, (compiler) *Onwards to Victory, Churchill's 1943 War Speeches* (London: Cassell & Company, 1944) pp.137–8.

615 Moseley, *Mussolini's*, p.170.

616 D'Este Carlos, *Fatal Decision* (London: Fontana, 1992) p.31.

617 Deakin, *The Brutal*, p.262.

618 Ibid., p.471.

619 Farrell, *Mussolini*, p.515.

620 Deakin, *The Brutal*, p.488.

621 Bastianini, *Uomini*, p.128.

622 Roberts, *The Storm*, p.376.

623 Ciano Edda, *My Truth*, p.194.

624 Westphal, *The German*, p.145.

625 Eade, *Onwards*, pp.142–5.

626 Eberle & Uhl, (Eds) *The Hitler Book* (London: John Murray, 2005) p.124.

627 Farrell, *Mussolini*, p.532.

628 Fuehrer Conferences, p.346.

629 Farrell, *Mussolini*, p.533.

630 Fuehrer Conferences, p.356.

631 Ciano Edda, *My Truth*, p.189.

632 Deakin, *The Brutal*, p.141.

633 Ciano Edda, *My Truth*, p.25.

634 See Moseley, *Mussolini's*, p.178.

635 Farrell, *Mussolini,* p.542.

636 Ciano Edda, *My Truth*, p.191.

637 Ibid., p.75.

638 Moseley, *Mussolini's*, p.181.

639 Ciano Edda, *My Truth*, p.195.

640 Michel, *The Second*, p.520.

641 Smyth, *Secrets*, p.28.

642 Ciano Edda, *My Truth*, p.29.

643 See Moseley, *Mussolini's*, pp.184–5.

644 Schmidt, *Hitler's*, p.258.

645 Höttl Wilhelm, *The Secret Front* (London: Weidenfeld & Nicolson, 1953) p.281.

646 Ciano Edda, *My Truth*, p.200.

647 Guerri, *Galeazzo*, p.619.

648 Smyth, *Secrets*, p.28.

649 Anfuso, *Da Palazzo*, p.333.

650 Ciano Edda, *My Truth*, p.201.

651 Ibid., p.19

652 Hassell, *The Ulrich*, p.288.

653 Weinberg, *A World*, p.486.

654 Ciano Edda, *My Truth*, p.237.

655 Quoted in Moseley, *Mussolini's*, p.199.

656 See Ibid., p.200.

657 Ciano Edda, *My Truth*, p.215.

658 Moseley, *Mussolini's*, p.205.

659 Ibid., p.207.

660 Ciano Edda, *My Truth*, p.179.

661 Guerri, *Galeazzo*, p.646.

662 Smyth, *Secrets*, p.34.

663 Churchill, *The Second*, p.179.

664 Lamb Richard, *War in Italy, 1943–1945* (London: Murray, 1993) p.83.

665 Smyth, *Secrets*, p.30.

666 Ibid., p.40.

667 Dolfin Giovanni, *Con Mussolini nella tragedia* (Milan: Grazanti, 1949) pp.188–9.

668 Moseley, *Mussolini's*, p.224.

669 See Farrell, *Mussolini*, p.577.

670 Ibid., p.536.

671 Ciano Edda, *My Truth*, p.245.

672 Farrell, *Mussolini*, p.578.

673 Susmel, *Vita*, pp.352–3.

674 Lamb, *War*, p.85.

675 Moseley, *Mussolini's*, p.234.

676 Bosworth, *Mussolini*, p.13.

677 Lamb, *War*, p.84.

678 Ciano Edda, *My Truth*, p.19.

CONCLUDING REMARKS

679 Smyth, *Secrets*, p.53.

680 Morgan Philip, *The Fall of Mussolini* (Oxford: OUP, 2008) p.18.

681 Rees Laurence, *The Dark Charisma of Adolf Hitler* (London: Ebury Press, 2012) p.359.

682 Morgan, *The Fall*, p.20.

683 Bosworth, *Mussolini*, p.312.

684 Moseley, *Mussolini's*, p.239 and p.240.

685 Ciano's Diary, De Felice, p.590.

686 Davies Norman, *No Simple Victory* (London: Viking, 2006) p.384.

APPENDICES

687 See Bosworth R J B, 'Italian Foreign Policy and its Historiography' in Altro Polo: *Intellectuals and Their Ideas in Contemporary Italy*, Richard Bosworth, and Gino Rizo, (eds) (Sydney, 1983), 65–68.

688 Delzell C, *Benito Mussolini: a guide to the biographical literature*, Journal of Modern History, vol. 35, no. 4, 1963, pp.339–53.

689 Villari L, *The Liberation of Italy, 1943-1947* (Appleton, WI, Nelson, 1959) quotes at pp.246, x, viii, xvii, 60–61.

690 Taylor A J P, *The Origins of the Second World War* (London, Penguin, 1964,) p.85.

691 See Mack Smith Denis, *Mussolini's Roman Empire* (London, Longman, 1976) and Mack Smith Denis, *Mussolini* (London, Granada, 1983).

692 Morgan, *The Fall*, p.231.

693 See Farrell, *Mussolini: A New Life* (London: Sharpe Books, 2018).

694 See Knox MacGregor, *Mussolini Unleashed, 1939–1941*, (Cambridge: CUP, 2008).

695 Ifversen Jan, in (Spiering Menno and Wintle Michael, Editors) *European Identity and the Second World War* (London: Palgrave Macmillan, 2011) p.88.

696 Finney, *Remembering*, p.141.

697 Salter, *Nazi*, p.348.

698 Tusa Ann and John, *The Nuremberg Trial* (London: BBC Books, 1995) p.249.

699 See Dollmann, *The Interpreter*, p.137 .

700 Salter M and Charlesworth L, *Ribbentrop and the Ciano Diaries at the Nuremberg Trial*, in Journal of International Justice (Oxford: OUP, 2006) p.105.

701 Ibid., p.107.

702 Ibid., p.111.

703 Forcardi Filippo and Klinkhammer Lutz, *The question of Fascist Italy's war crimes: The construction of a self-acquitting myth (1943–1948)*, in Journal of Modern Italian Studies, (September 2004, pp.330–348) p.330.

704 Bernhard Patrick, *Behind the Battle Lines: Italian Atrocities and the Persecution of Arabs, Berbers, and Jews in North Africa during World War II*, in Holocaust and Genocide Studies 26, No. 3 (Winter 2012): (425– 446).

705 See Arendt Hannah, *Eichmann in Jerusalem. A Report on the Banality of Evil* (New York: Penguin, 1963).

706 See Fonds Davide Rodogno, *Italiani brava gente? Fascist Italy's Policy Toward the Jews in the Balkans, April 1941–July 1943* in European History Quarterly Copyright, (Vol 35(2), 213–240.).

707 See Burgio Alberto, *Nel nome della razza. Il razzismo nella storia d'Italia 1870-1945* (Bologna 1999).

708 Fonds, *Italiani*, pp.214–5

709 Senger. *Neither*, p.47.